A Bike Ride

A Bike Ride

12,000 miles around the world

ANNE MUSTOE

This edition first published in Great Britain in 1992 by
Virgin Books
an imprint of Virgin Publishing Ltd
338 Ladbroke Grove
London W10 5AH

A catalogue record for this book is available from the British Library

ISBN 0 86369 650 3

Designed by Geoff Green
Maps drawn by Carole Vincer

Typeset by Phoenix Photosetting, Chatham, Kent
Printed and bound in Great Britain by
Cox & Wyman Ltd, Reading, Berkshire

Contents

To my father, who wanted to travel

Illustrations

Maps

Acknowledgements

My grateful thanks are due to Sir Steven Runciman for his advice on the roads of Anatolia; to the following writers, publishers and agents for permission to quote: e. e. cummings (*Complete Works 1913–62*, HarperCollins), T. S. Eliot (*Coriolan*, *Triumphal March*, reprinted by permission of Faber and Faber Ltd from *Collected Poems 1909–62* by T. S. Eliot), Christopher Fry (*The Lady's Not For Burning*, Oxford University Press), Kenneth Grahame (*The Wind in the Willows*, Methuen Children's Books), Dorothy L. Sayers (*Five Red Herrings*, David Higham Associates), Edward Thomas (*Roads*, Miss Myfanwy Thomas and Faber and Faber Ltd); to my agent, John Pawsey, for his support and encouragement; and to my editor, Gill Gibbins, for her unfailing enthusiasm and her patience with a struggling novice.

A. M.

I

Breaking Loose

WHY are you doing it? Why did you do it? Everyone asks the same question and I give a different answer every time – adventure, travel, time for reflection, solitude, challenge, curiosity, historical research, freedom, fun . . . all are true and adequate reasons. But why go round the world? And why on a bicycle?

In January 1983 I was a headmistress taking a holiday in India to recover from the rigours of the long Autumn Term. Somewhere in Rajasthan I looked out of the bus window and saw a cyclist, a solitary European man, pedalling across the flat immensity of the Great Thar Desert. I was seized with sudden envy. I wanted to be out there myself on that road on a bicycle, alone and free, feeling the reality of India, not gazing at it through a pane of glass.

I was not athletic. I was not young. I had never been a keen cyclist. I had no idea how to mend a puncture. I hated camping, picnics and discomfort. In fact, my qualifications for an arduous cycle-ride were minimal. Yet it was the bicycle which had immediate appeal.

I had always loved travelling and, given plenty of time, the bicycle seemed to be the perfect vehicle. It would be faster than walking yet it would allow me much more leisure for reflection and detailed observation than a car. There would be no parking problems; I could pedal straight into city centres and chain my bicycle outside the cathedral or the grand mosque. If I travelled alone I could set my own pace, cycle comfortable distances and stop when I felt tired. I had never repaired my own car and had no intention of turning mechanic for a bicycle, but the machine was so simple and so universal that I was sure to be able to get it repaired anywhere in the world. Above all, the bicycle was classless. In remoter areas, it would put me into the hands of the local people and enable me to meet even the world's poorest on a level of mutual trust. And as cyclists are generally considered to be penniless, I was unlikely to be set upon by thieves or pestered by carpet-sellers.

In Jaisalmer that January three of us hired bicycles for the day, heavy, black Indian machines, sturdy enough to deal with the stones and potholes. Feeling very daring and slightly nervous, we pedalled out of the city gates to visit a desert temple. Already, for me, it was more than a holiday jaunt: I was testing the water. The day passed pleasantly, without incident, and by the time we got back to Jaisalmer my mind was made up. I would definitely cycle across India – but, never one for half-measures, I would do it as part of a journey round the world.

The choice of vehicle had been an instant certainty, but my route took more than two years to evolve. The first major decision concerned my direction: I would travel from West to East, so that I could gain confidence in familiar and much-loved countries like France and Italy before moving on into unfamiliar and daunting terrain. That satisfied common sense, but I wanted something more than a sensible reason for my route. History is an abiding interest of mine, and gazing for inspiration at the map of Europe I realised my eyes were tracking back along the paths on which Western civilisation had travelled eastwards. There I found my answer. With my Classical background, I should enjoy following the Roman road network across Europe, and joining Alexander the Great on his march from Greece to the Indus. Then I could follow the Moghuls into India, and the British Raj into India, Burma, Malaysia and Singapore. I would have to cross the USA in the wrong direction, from the West Coast to the East, but I could journey in spirit with the European pioneers. Finally, I could fly from New York to Dublin, take the ferry across to Holyhead and pick up Roman Watling Street at its northern end, near Chester. So the journey which would begin on Watling Street, between London Bridge and Dover, would end on Watling Street, with a ride down the Edgware Road to Marble Arch. I should have 'put a girdle round about the earth' and tied it very neatly.

By 1985 I was sufficiently committed to my journey to buy a notebook and label it 'Round the World'. I spent winter holidays in libraries doing historical research and summer holidays on reconnaissance. Roads, forests, mountains and the pageant of history unrolled before my eyes, but I nursed my project in secret. The whole world, or at least the northern hemisphere, was mine – and I had only to resign to grasp it. Extricating myself took time. Not only was I headmistress of St Felix, a large girls' boarding school in Suffolk, but I was also President of the Girls' Schools Association, a Suffolk magistrate and the chairman or member of at least a dozen other committees. I began to free myself quietly, little by little, from all those commitments. Nothing is more damaging to a school than uncertainty, so I made my arrangements stealthily and gave in my notice at the last possible moment, taking everyone by surprise.

I was untroubled by doubt. I was a widow. My step-sons were grown up. I had worked hard for most of my life and felt I had done my bit for society. I was not of pensionable age, but the rent from my London flat and the money I had saved would be enough to keep me going if I lived modestly abroad. In any case, I wanted so little: I had gone through the 'possessions phase' of my life. One of the attractions of cycling was its very simplicity – everything I needed would be on my bicycle in two small panniers. I should be breaking free, not only from my responsibilities but from my life's clutter.

Preparation for that ideal state was intensive if necessarily sporadic and owed a lot to various friends, in particular to Monty Young of Condor Cycles in the Gray's Inn Road in London.

My bicycle was a leaving present from the staff and girls of St Felix, specially designed and built for me by Monty. He was so enthusiastic about my project that he put in all the work for nothing, charging only the cost of the parts.

A tourer in gleaming sea-green enamel (Verde di Lago), it
has randonneur handlebars to give a variety of cycling positions, a real leather saddle for comfort, handbuilt wheels with
special alpine stainless steel spokes for extra strength, and
puncture-resistant lined tyres. Specifications:

Frame	Reynolds 531 twin-tube (mixte)
Wheels	Wolber rims, Shimano hubs, DT Alpina spokes
Gears	Shimano
Brakes	Shimano
Bars and stem	SR alloy touring randonneur
Saddle	Brooks
Block	14–34
Headset	Shimano
Seatpin	Shimano
Chain	Sedisport
Pedals	Shimano ATB
Chainset	TA touring with gear ratios 36–48
Tyres and tubes	Specialised Kevlar tyres
Rack	Vetta alloy
Guards	Esge

I took:
 1 spare tyre and 2 inner tubes (a second spare tyre was
brought out to me in Bangkok); 1 spanner; 1 screwdriver; 1
set of Allen keys; 6 spokes, 1 gear cable, 1 brake cable;
puncture repair kit; and bicycle oil.

I set out in:
Cotton T-shirt, long-sleeved shirt, pure wool jersey, mittens,
luminous belt, corduroy knickerbockers, ankle socks, leg-
warmers, trainers. Waterproofs (cagoule, leggings and
sou'wester) were tied to the rear rack, ready to hand. Light
clothing, which can be worn in layers, is the most satisfactory.
When the weather turned hot, I threw away the knickerbockers and wore black cotton trousers, which I cut off below
the knee. They were short enough to be clear of the chain, but
long enough to be acceptable in churches and mosques.

My luggage consisted of:

Handlebar pannier (Freewheel, 2 lbs) containing leather handbag (for money, travel documents and current notebooks), camera, map, torch/magnifier, compass, Swiss Army knife, sunglasses, sun cream, lipsalve, whistle.

Two rear panniers (Carradice Super C, 30 lbs equally divided) containing 1 long-sleeved shirt, 1 cotton T-shirt, 3 short-sleeved blouses; black cotton trousers and white cotton trousers; silk suit with silk T-shirt, black high-heeled sandals and tights (for smart parties); flat white sandals, doubling as slippers; nightdress, underwear, socks; bathing costume, large multicoloured cotton square for use as dressing gown/ sarong/sheet/pillowcase/bath towel/laundry bag; 4 slide films; maps of Europe and Asia; Greek and Turkish pocket dictionaries; Horace's *Odes*, stacks of *Times* crosswords, sewing kit, universal plug; writing pad and envelopes, photographs for visas and newspapers, cosmetics, suncream and medicaments, tools and spare parts

Rear rack: light down sleeping-bag in nylon rucksack (the rucksack was used to carry my luggage when I travelled without the bicycle), sleeping-mat, bivvy bag, waterproofs.

I carried few changes of clothing, replacing worn and faded articles en route. I could have managed with less. I disposed of the bivvy bag in Greece and acquired an enamel mug and a small padlock. I saved weight by cutting away my maps, leaving only the strips showing my road and the 100 miles or so either side of it. I acquired maps of the USA in Los Angeles. Guide books I picked up in each country as I passed through and either sent them home after use or discarded them.

I had a complete check-up at the BUPA Medical Centre, paid a visit to the dentist and was vaccinated against tetanus, polio, rabies, and meningococcal meningitis. (As cholera and hepatitis B vaccinations give only a six-month immunity, I had my cholera injection in Ankara and my gamma globulin in Islamabad.) I carried with me: Nivaquine and Proguanil (antimalaria tablets); two courses of Amoxil (wide spectrum antibiotics); 40 Loperomide (diarrhoea); 100 Senokot and 6 glycerine suppositories (constipation); Jungle Formula (insect repellant); antihistamine cream; Savlon antiseptic cream; plasters; 50 Veganin tablets; Rennies (indigestion); Strepsils (throat pastilles); thermometer; three boxes of 48 Puritabs (water purifiers).

I tried to work to a budget for food and accommodation of £15 a day, with £20 a week in reserve for emergencies. Total: £125 a week. In Northern Europe and America it was difficult to keep within this, but over-spending there was balanced out by under-spending in the East. My average over the whole trip worked out at £82.98 a week (excluding the cost of holidays I took with friends, when we treated ourselves rather well).

I started out with £200 sterling, £100 in French francs and £900 in sterling traveller's cheques. In Europe, right to the south-east corner of Turkey, I was able to use a combination of credit cards and Eurocheques, but was careful to keep a supply of the local currency for use in villages and small towns. In Pakistan, where I experienced the greatest difficulties in changing money, I cashed traveller's cheques in major cities. In India, accounts at tourist hotels have to be settled in foreign currency, so that credit and charge cards are readily accepted. I changed traveller's cheques and sterling notes to obtain rupees for non-tourist hotels and general expenditure on the road. Thailand, Malaysia and Singapore are very sophisticated financially: plastic money, traveller's cheques and sterling are all acceptable in cities. I asked the friends who came out to see me in India and Thailand to bring me fresh supplies of sterling notes. It was prudent to have them, but I could in fact have managed without. In the USA I wrote Eurocheques to buy American Express Dollar Traveller's Cheques, which are treated as cash. This is a service for Amex card-holders.

I took out a year's travel insurance through the Cyclists' Touring Club (1 September 1987 to 31 August 1988) and it was a great comfort to know I had sufficient medical cover for a flight home in case of dire emergency. I economised on the first three months, as I was eligible for medical treatment in Western Europe under Britain's reciprocal arrangements. I carried Form E111 from the DHSS. I had no insurance for my bicycle, as I could replace it with a perfectly adequate machine for less than the premium quoted.

Working out that I would cover an average distance of 50 miles a day, five days a week, I could plan my overnight stops and rest days for periods of two or three months at a time. These schedules gave me the dates for visiting friends and making arrangements for collecting mail well in advance. They provided a comforting framework and were not over-ambitious: I could dawdle in beautiful places or spend a rainy day over a book and then catch up without difficulty. I never booked accommodation, but aimed to stop for the night in places large enough to have a hotel or guest house. Camping out is not a good idea for a lone woman.

Not to record my journey was unthinkable. What I called my 'basics book' took diary form and contained date, time of departure, the day's route, distance covered, cumulative distance, climatic conditions, time changes, altitudes of passes, health problems, a record of letters and postcards sent, name of hotel, cost of meals and accommodation. At the end of each week I noted total expenditure and mileage. Even if I was exhausted or my room had no electricity, I could always manage to put down these basic facts. At the back of this notebook I kept my cycling schedule and a note of all the photographs I took. Fuller, more descriptive writing was done in a succession of small notebooks. The early evening was my best time for writing, but I sometimes stopped during the day to jot down ideas or describe particularly interesting scenes. I kept my basics books with me throughout, but entrusted notebooks to friends who were returning to London. I never risked posting them.

As I am not a skilful photographer, I took an Olympus AF-1 automatic with built-in flash. It served me well, though I came to regret not having a telephoto lens for village scenes, where people are shy of the camera. I had the slides developed and mounted as I went along, posting them home from Europe and sending them back with friends from India and Thailand. I exercised restraint and shot only 29 films of 36 slides.

Letters were sent out to me care of friends in Italy, Ankara, Karachi and California. I used the Poste Restante successfully in Brindisi and Thessaloniki, but changed to

American Express for Lahore, Delhi, Calcutta, Bangkok and Kuala Lumpur, as I had been told that it was a more reliable service out East than the Post Office. Crossing the USA, I used American Express.

My arrangements made, I set out on 31 May 1987. I was 54, overweight, out of condition and I wobbled slightly on my unfamiliar bicycle. But my spirits were high. I knew I was going to have a wonderful trip – and if things became too difficult, there was always plastic money to pay my air-fare home. After years of work and duty, I was setting out unashamedly to please myself. Even this book has been fun to write. Retracing my route in the comfort of my hotel in Southern Turkey, I sometimes marvelled at the hardships I endured, but more often I looked back with longing at those vibrant, carefree days.

2

Watling Street

> I travel light; as light,
> That is, as a man can travel who will
> Still carry his body around because
> Of its sentimental value.
>
> *(Christopher Fry)*

I lay in my warm bed in London and listened to the rain drumming on the skylight. Everything was ready. After endless packing and repacking, I had managed to squeeze all my luggage into two rear panniers. There was even a rational system: current needs in the left-hand pannier; spare clothing, cycle parts and maps in the right. Everyday items at the top; and the things I hoped I should never need at the bottom. My finances were in order and Monty had given my bicycle its final check-up. The day I had imagined for so long was finally dawning – and suddenly, in the cowardly small hours, I had my first fit of nerves. I had been so brave and unfaltering in the daylight. Now, in the darkness and the pouring rain, I thought not only of the dangers but of uncomfortable beds, inadequate plumbing, disagreeable food and bad weather. When I valued my comfort so highly, why had I committed myself to the vagabond life?

But, as usually happens, my spirits rose with the sun and I hit on the cunning piece of self-deception which was to keep me going through many crises and spells of despondency. I told myself that I was just going to cycle to Dover and if I didn't like

it I could come straight back on the train. The world is too big
to encompass, even in the imagination. Better to take it a few
miles at a time.

I got up early and dressed in my carefully layered cycling
outfit: pink T-shirt, red-and-white check long-sleeved shirt,
black wool jersey, burgundy corduroy knickerbockers, trainers,
ankle socks and brightly striped legwarmers. I added cycling
mittens and a luminous yellow Sam Browne belt when I set out
and bundled my waterproofs on the rear carrier, ready to hand.
Fortunately it had stopped raining by the time breakfast was
over, and I arrived at St Paul's Cathedral in bright sunshine.

My colleagues in the Girls' Schools Association and the
Independent Schools Information Service had arranged a
splendid champagne send-off for me in the small garden behind
the cathedral, the last of the farewell parties, dinners and
general celebrations which had sent my weight soaring to an
unathletic 10 st 11 lb. Family and friends together, we toasted
the enterprise liberally and just before one o'clock on Sunday,
31 May 1987, I cycled off alone to begin my adventure.

The southern branch of the Roman road called Watling Street
runs from Dover (Dubris) to London (Londinium), crossing
the Stour at Canterbury (Duroverum) and the Medway at
Rochester (Durobrivae). A glance at the map of south-east
England will show exactly where it lies. From Dover, it follows
the valley of the River Dour via Temple Ewell, then makes good
use of high ground to cut a straight path across the open Downs to
Canterbury. From Canterbury's West Gate to Rochester's East,
the country is easy and the road runs straight, with only minor
changes of alignment from the modest hilltops. Then an alignment from Swanscombe leads directly to the old ford at
Westminster, deviating through Deptford and New Cross to
avoid the curve of the Thames at Greenwich and the marshy
ground. The Romans later directed the road to London Bridge,
merging it at Borough High Street with their road from Chi-
chester, Stane Street. On all but the most detailed maps, the
main sections of the road can be seen to run straight as arrows; the
alignment to Westminster ford can be tested with a ruler.

I knew the route well. Down the small Watling Street behind
St Paul's, past the office in Cannon Street where I had once

worked for the engineering group GKN, then over London Bridge to Southwark, the starting-point of other, more famous pilgrimages. It takes a lot of imagination to see the Pilgrims' Way in the dingy streets of south London, especially on an empty Sunday afternoon. A chapel to St Thomas à Becket once stood in the middle of London Bridge. Southwark Cathedral was part of the great monastic house of St Mary Overie, whose hospital merged with the nearby leper hospital after the Fire of Southwark in 1213 to form the original St Thomas's. Then there was Chaucer's Tabard Inn and scores of others like it, whose landlords acted as couriers to bands of pilgrims. Kings, princes and footsore penitents had passed along this way in droves. I cycled through silent streets, past empty offices and closed shops, congratulating myself on my choice of a traffic-free day to get clear of central London.

I followed the A2 signs down the Old Kent Road, through New Cross to Blackheath; then I took the straight line of the Roman road, the present A207. On Shooter's Hill I sat on a garden wall in the sun and ate a bag of cherries. For the first time, I had leisure to reflect that this was really it. I was on my way. My spirits soared as I bowled along Welling High Street, Bexley Heath Broadway, Crayford Road and Dartford High Street. When Watling Street rejoined the A2, roadworks offered me a safe path behind a palisade of bollards. The towers of Cobham Hall, another former work-place, winked at me through the trees and reminded me of my new-found freedom and leisure.

I had chosen the bicycle as my means of transport chiefly because I wanted to travel slowly and talk to people. I knew I had made the right choice as soon as I stopped for a cup of tea. Not wishing to leave my bicycle with all my belongings out of sight near a motorway café, I pulled up at a refreshments caravan in a lay-by.

Two hefty truck-drivers, mugs in hand, strolled over to inspect my bicycle.

'You going a long way with all that gear?'

'I'm going round the world.'

'Blimey! On your own? You be careful, darlin'.'

One was an international truckie, who knew the problems.

'How you getting across the Middle East then?'

'I don't know yet. I didn't manage to get visas in London, so I'm going to try again in Rome or Ankara.'

'Well, you watch out on that bike. And look after your money, darlin'. Split it up and hide it in lots of different places. Don't carry much on you.'

The stall-holder joined in:

'Here's your tea, love. You'd be amazed what interesting people stop at this stall. You on your bike. And last week a great big car drew up and it was the Mayor of Greenwich!'

I had been embraced into the camaraderie of the road. As the banter was exchanged and the well-meant advice given, I remembered a winter's day in Norfolk. I had pulled up at a similar stall in my Alfa Romeo and smart executive suit, to be cold-shouldered and treated to glances as frosty as the morning. Now, my bicycle had unlocked the first of many doors around the world and I was delighted to find myself so readily and warmly accepted.

As we were discussing routes, a young woman with two little boys drew up in a battered car piled to the roof with boxes, cases and bedding. She looked thin and tired, her straggly blonde hair falling untidily over the collar of her worn blouse, but her plans made my own pale to insignificance. She was divorced and unemployed, her two sons aged ten and eight. Three years ago, in happier times, when they were on a family holiday in Spain, she had been offered a job in a bar. Now, deciding that she had nothing to lose, she had left her home in Doncaster, sold everything to buy a second-hand car and was setting out with her two little boys to start a new life in Spain. She hoped the job would still be available. They were all three quite cheerful and excited in their undemonstrative, Northern way, tucking into tea and hot dogs and speculating about Spanish wages and schools. It was a monumental risk to take but somehow I felt that the girl had the enterprise and determination to succeed. I have often wondered how she fared.

Rochester was a surprise. A Dickens Festival had packed the streets with David Copperfields, Sarah Gamps and Little Dorrits. It had also packed the hotels with Mr Pickwicks, morris dancers and a glee club from Texas. Disappointed of the good hotel and celebratory dinner I had promised myself, I toiled up Chatham Hill beside some jogging Gurkhas and found modest accommodation and Turkish kebabs on the outskirts of Gillingham. My photograph appeared in *The Daily Telegraph* next morning. As I cycled through Sittingbourne, a young woman wound down her car window and shouted, 'Good luck! I saw you in the *Telegraph*.' After Sittingbourne came the apple orchards and hop fields, green and fresh after Sunday's rain, and the smell of cedars in front gardens. Then through Ospringe and Faversham to Upper Hambledown, where the penitent Henry II dismounted to go on foot into Canterbury. My progress was swifter. I swept down the hill, crossed the Stour and entered the city by the West Gate to St Peter's Street and the cathedral.

The mediaeval pilgrims would have recognised Canterbury, with its milling crowds and its stalls selling badges, brooches and tourist souvenirs. I too was recognised by more *Daily Telegraph* readers, as I sat in the cathedral precincts eating a bun. 'Have a good trip!' 'Bon voyage!'

The A2 from Canterbury led me across open fields and downs where sheep were grazing, the stretches of busy dual-carriageway redeemed by Kent's impeccably clean hard shoulders, perfect for the cyclist. I was twice thrown off balance and tossed onto the grass verge by strong winds and the blasts in the wake of lorries, but gradually I gained better control of my machine. By the time I reached the outskirts of Dover, the rain, which was to be my constant companion for the next month, had forced me to stop and put on my cagoule, sou'wester and waterproof leggings. I freewheeled in the wind and rain down the precipitous road to the East Docks, where the gulls were wheeling and crying over a grey sea. I had finished the first leg of my journey and I had no wish to go home.

3

Across France to the Mountains

BOULOGNE — MONTREUIL-SUR-MER — ARRAS —
ST QUENTIN — LAON — CHÂLONS-SUR-MARNE — VITRY
LE FRANÇOIS — JOINVILLE — CHAUMONT — LANGRES —
GRAY — MARNAY — BESANÇON

> I struck the board and cried, 'No more;
> I will abroad.'
>
> *(George Herbert)*

THE morning started badly with the cancellation of the 9.30 crossing to Boulogne. Boulogne had to be my port of entry because that was the Romans' Bononia, their main channel port. Adjusting to the new tempo of my life, I quelled my irritation and took a gentle stroll up to Dover Castle, a sight I had, as usual, rushed by on my way to the ferry. The slopes were thick with beech, maple, oak and ash, all very English trees, and the views in every direction from the battlements were a general's delight. There was even a Roman lighthouse within the walls. I sailed at 12.30.

One of my most regular daydreams over the previous two years had been the image of myself in summer clothes cycling beside the canal out of Boulogne towards the N1. In this dream, the brightly coloured plasticated shells of the factories gleamed in the sunlight and the prevailing north-westerly wind from the Channel gave wings to my wheels. In reality, I landed in drizzle which soon developed into a downpour, and a stiff wind from the south-west made the going very tough. By the time I reached Montreuil I was a drowned rat, stiff-backed and weary from the roller-coaster hills.

I should like to draw a veil over my crossing of France. What I had intended as a June holiday, a pleasant trip to break me in for more rigorous cycling ahead, turned out to be misery from start to finish. It rained and rained and rained. The heavy panniers grew heavier as the rain soaked into the canvas (fortunately, it never got right through) and I took a constant sideways buffeting from the wind which swept across the open countryside from the Atlantic and often slowed me to a snail's pace. My waterproofs dripped and flapped. I was overweight and still very tired from the rush of preparation and departure.

Leaving a resident post is a nightmare, as it involves moving house just at the very time you need to give all your attention to the smooth hand-over of the job. In my case, things had been as bad as they possibly could be. My official residence had been huge and my possessions had inevitably grown to fill it over the nine years I had lived there. By contrast, my London flat was minute, so deciding what to store for my eventual return there, what to give away and what to sell had caused me months of anguish. I had always liked to think that I could live happily anywhere and be content with very little, but I had in fact become accustomed to plenty. The strength of my attachment to my house and my accumulated possessions took me by surprise and the wrench of parting with so much intensified the exhaustion of packing the remainder. There had been little time for brooding in the final flurry of visa applications, insurance arrangements, injections and farewells but now, alone in rain-soaked France, I had unlimited leisure for reflection. My family and friends would still be there when I got home, but my house, my lovely curtains, my furniture, my piano and most of my books were gone for ever. The sense of loss overwhelmed me. I realised then that I still had a long way to travel before I gained possession of myself and found the contentment I was seeking.

The sheer physical hardship of cycling did nothing to raise my spirits. So much for my carefully calculated daily distances. I had had no time to train and steep hills were quite beyond me. Even on flat stretches, the wind was so exhausting that I had to get off from time to time and lean against a tree to catch my breath. I lived in a watery world, with rain in my face and rivers running beside me.

France is a country most blessed in its waterways. The major rivers never run dry; they are free of ice all the year round; and

the watershed between the Atlantic and the Mediterranean is
neither particularly high nor very steep. From earliest times,
the ancient Gauls took advantage of this splendid network of
navigable rivers, linked together by convenient portages, or
gap-routes. They also had a good natural road system along
river valleys and over intermediate uplands with gentle gradients, where their wheeled transport could bowl along without
difficulty. When Caesar arrived, he found ideal conditions for
his army. The prodigious marching feats in which he took such
pride would have been impossible without the well-worn Gallic
tracks. All that rushing up and down Gaul in his various
campaigns suddenly makes sense when you realise that the
contestants were usually rushing to gain control of a river.

Gaul was a rich prize for the Romans. There was iron ore,
gold, tin and potter's clay in abundance; and as the Romans
improved the agriculture, there was an almost embarrassing
surplus of grain and wine from the fertile soil. The EEC wine
lake is by no means a recent phenomenon. Once Gaul was
occupied, the Romans had the perfect corridor through to
Britain from the Alps or the Mediterranean. Heavy goods could
be transported by river and all they needed to do was to metal
existing main roads and portages. In Claudius' reign they even
considered canals, but abandoned the idea as being too expensive. The modern Canal de l'Est, which links the Saône with
the Moselle by means of 150 locks and tunnels, began life as an
ambitious scheme on a Roman drawing-board.

Travellers from Britain to Rome normally crossed over to
Boulogne, as Calais had undrained marshes behind the port,
and made straight across the dry Artois plain to Arras (Nemeta-
cum). Arras was the capital of the Atrebates, whose King
Commius was sent ahead by Caesar to demand submission and
hostages of the Britons in 55 BC. The next important stop was
either St Quentin, where a modern canal now links the Somme
and the Oise with the L'Escaut, or Amiens on the Somme itself.
Then Soissons, the River Aisne and its tributaries to Rheims
(Durocortorum), the capital of the Remi and a major road
centre; then along the Marne from Châlons to Langres.
Finally, the traveller would follow the Saône from Gray to
Lyon (Lugdunum), the hub of the Roman road network in

France, where he had a choice between following the Rhône upstream into the Alps or downstream to Marseilles (Massilia).

This route is so natural, so obvious, that it is still the most direct way to Italy, used by thousands of holiday-makers each year. I had often sped that way in my car, anxious to reach Venice in three days. Now, on my bicycle, with a target of 50 miles a day, five days a week, I found that I covered roughly the same distance in a day as I had covered in an hour by car. But, despite the rain, I saw France as I had never seen it before.

Depressed by the weather and my inability to cycle up hills, I tricked myself again with limited objectives. The first was to reach St Quentin by Thursday evening. Years ago, I had promised my friends Marcelle and Michel that no matter where I was in the world or what I happened to be doing at the time, I would join them in Bordeaux for their thirtieth wedding anniversary on Saturday, 6 June 1987. St Quentin had a good train service to Paris and I planned to leave my bicycle in a hotel, pack my party clothes in my small rucksack and set out by train on Friday for a festive weekend in the warmth of southern France. That prospect kept me going.

Along the Canche valley from Montreuil to Arras I started to pass the cemeteries. There were four British and Commonwealth War Cemeteries along the short 33 mile road from Hesdin to Arras: Arras itself, which withstood constant bombardment in two world wars and rose again from the rubble, was a standing monument to the folly and waste of war. Between Arras and St Quentin I lost count of the graveyards, the seas of neat, white crosses. They were so sad in the rain that I tried to concentrate on the Romans, my lunch, Bordeaux – anything to keep my mind off the carnage. But at cycling speed, each cross came into sharp focus and there was no blurring of the horror. Every cross was a young life. As I passed from the Pas de Calais into the Somme district, I came to the greatest desolation of all. There was a hill at Rancourt, overlooking the gently flowing Somme. Its quiet slopes held four huge cemeteries, one each for the French, English, German and South African troops who had died in their bid to take that lonely hill. I stood in the pouring rain and wept.

Bordeaux was a much-needed restorer of the spirits. On

Saturday there was a family lunch for eighteen and in the
evening a buffet supper for 80. The party flowed out into the
garden under the warm sky and my rusty French was oiled into
action by the excellent claret. The celebrations were crowned
by the candle-lit entry of a miraculous French *pièce montée*, a
three-foot-high pyramid of meringue, cake, cream, toffee, nou-
gat and sugared almonds. The family party continued throughout a musical weekend; we all played instruments and sang. I
was given a pretty pink, blue and white Swatch so that I should
think of my friends whenever I checked the time. On Monday
evening I was back in St Quentin and the rain.

My next limited objective was to get myself to Besançon by
Sunday, 14 June, as my friend Priscilla, who is keen on mountains, was meeting me there to ride with me over the Jura and
the Alps.

I had chosen the St Quentin route rather than Amiens/
Soissons because I wanted to visit Laon, 'La Cité Couronnée'.
As I pedalled across the River Oise and through the beeches and
limes of the Forêt de St Gobain, the sun miraculously broke
through and showed up Laon in all its splendour, dominating
the plain from its huge fortress hill. As Laudunum it had been
an important city in Roman times and its strategic position
between the Aisne, the Oise and the Meuse had made it the
Carolingian capital of France from the eighth to the tenth
century. I had always sped past it along the highway. Now I
huffed and puffed, struggling to push my heavily laden bicycle
up to the ramparts. The great cathedral of Notre Dame, with
inquisitive stone bulls peeping out from the four corners of its
towers (an allusion to the miraculous bull which helped in its
construction), stood in a maze of narrow streets. It was much
restored but uncluttered inside, so that its clean, early Gothic
lines could be appreciated. Yet even in the tranquillity of its
nave there was no escape from the carnage: I read a memorial
plaque to the million troops of the British Empire who gave
their lives in the 1914–18 war and now rest in France.

That evening in the village of Festieux, just off the main road
from Laon to Rheims, I had my first real taste of provincial
France. Time had stood still in its tiny Grande Rue, where the
Cidrerie de Festieux and the Garage Automobiles with their

peeling paint stood beside two antique school buildings, the École des Garçons and the École des Filles. I wonder if they are still segregated? Further along the street was the Mairie. The windows were open to the still June evening and I could see Monsieur le Maire himself, at his desk in his shirt-sleeves, addressing a public meeting. He was obviously explaining something of great local importance, for his audience of twenty or so were listening with rapt attention. Looking at the buildings in the Grande Rue, I realised that I was moving south. The materials of the Pas de Calais, the dark bricks with strongly contrasting pointing and the black slate roofs, were beginning to yield to a warmer stone, with or without stucco, and fired red tiles. The town's one hotel was shabby, with cracked brown linoleum over the uneven, creaking floorboards, and rickety furniture and faded cottons, but it was clean and cheap, and the dinner of good local produce was perfect in its simplicity. So was the *pichet* of local wine.

The Champagne Country kept its vineyards well hidden. The big champagne houses had impressive offices in Rheims but their vines were nowhere to be seen. Far more visible were the huge cement works which dominated the valleys like cathedrals. At a crossroads I found a memorial to General Estienne, quaintly described as 'Le Père des Chars'. Surrounded by tanks, armoured cars, a tricolour and a cross, it stood on the spot where French tanks were first deployed on 16 April 1917, finally breaking the stalemate of years of trench warfare.

Rheims Cathedral, another victim of the 1914–18 war, was not at its best under the grey sky but the remnants of its mediaeval glass still managed a quiet glow. I contemplated the spectacular Gothic west front over bread, cheese and beer, then paid my respects to a third-century Roman arch, L'Arc de Mars, which with good French chauvinism was labelled 'Gallo-Romain'.

Châlons-sur-Marne, Sogny-aux-Moulins, Mairy-sur-Marne, Togny-aux-Boeufs. Beautiful, bucolic names. The Place d'Armes in the centre of Vitry le François must be the most perfect small-town square in the whole of France, but that day the rain had washed away its colour and vitality. Even the

burning salamander of François Ier seemed to be drowning in
the downpour. As the day progressed, the songs which I hum-
med in time with my pedalling became slower and more lugubrious, descending the scale of misery from Schubert's
'Winterreise' to Duparc's settings of Baudelaire.

At 1.20 precisely I stopped under a tree once more to hitch up
my flapping waterproof trousers and wipe the rain from the
back of my neck. Water poured off me in rivulets, soaking my
trainers and socks, and a wild gust of wind sent my bicycle
flying, strewing the contents of my handlebar bag across the
flooded gutter. As I scrabbled in the roadside mud I asked
myself, not for the first time, 'Why on earth am I doing this?'
Then I asked myself what I should be doing at that particular
moment had I not embarked on the trip. 'At 1.20 on a
Thursday, I should be taking lunch in Fawcett.' I pictured the
House dining-room, the school lunch and the anxious fourth-
formers, doing their best to make suitable high-table conversation with their headmistress. Perhaps, on balance, the wind and
rain were less demanding.

Cycling is a popular sport in France and I often had company
on the roads. A rain-soaked cyclist would draw up beside me,
cast a fanatical eye over the mechanism of my bicycle and start
to interrogate me about my gear-ratios. We would cycle along
together, he braking and freewheeling to get down to my speed
and I toiling and straining to get up to his, until he despaired of
getting the technical information he wanted and sped off with a
jaunty wave. The cyclists were always male and never carried
any luggage. They were just out on their mean machines to
break their speed record.

One afternoon a swift young cyclist appeared from a side
road, resplendent in shiny black knickers and team racing vest,
the peak of his cycling cap pointing backwards. He kept me
company for five minutes, chatting of this and that. Then he
hesitated for a moment:

'May I ask you a question?'

'Yes. Of course.'

'You promise you won't be angry?'

'I don't know till I hear the question. Try me.'

I waited, confidently expecting the usual technical enquiries or perhaps a rather more presumptuous question about the cost of such a bicycle in England.

'Will you go to bed with me?'

'No.'

'Oh dear! Now you *are* angry with me,' he said, in great confusion. 'I'm so sorry. I've offended you.'

'No. I'm not angry, or offended. I just don't want to go to bed with you. That's all.'

We smiled weakly at each other and he sped off on his own, disappearing rapidly into the distance – only to swoop out at me again an hour later from another side road to ask if I had by any chance changed my mind.

On Friday, 12 June, I spotted the newspaper headline: 'Elle a gagné.' It was the result of the British General Election and Mrs Thatcher was clearly so famous in France that only the pronoun was necessary. 'Super Maggie', as another newspaper called her – the politician the French loved to hate – made all the headlines even in small provincial towns. That Friday was a red letter day for me too; the sun shone for a few hours during the afternoon and I was able to take off my legwarmers for the first time. There were wooded hills in the Haute Marne and rich pastures where startled little calves peered at me through clouds of wild lupins, mustard and buttercups. I might even have heard the chirp of an uncertain cicada. Between Joinville and Chaumont I passed General de Gaulle's village of Colombey Les Deux Eglises, nestling in beautiful countryside. Then on to Langres, another natural fortress rising high above the valley, with a second-century Roman gate and the main square dedicated to the city's most famous son, Diderot.

By the time I reached Langres, the strain of keeping to my schedule of 50 miles a day even in wind and rain was beginning to tell. I climbed up to the ramparts at the end of the day with a racing pulse and wobbly knees, scarcely able to summon the strength to find a hotel. Even parking and unloading my bicycle was an ordeal. Once in my hotel room, I collapsed fully clothed and unwashed onto the bed and slept like a log for two hours. Physically, that was the low point of my whole trip. I never felt quite so exhausted again.

The next morning I started to climb in earnest, up from the

Marne valley, through oaks, beeches, limes and horse chestnuts to a plateau where cornflowers, poppies and buttercups grew in profusion. Occasionally I really did hear cicadas, but over the roll of distant thunder. Between showers I sat outside a café and gazed at the elegant, symmetrical façade of the Château de Champlitte. It was a sad, almost autumnal scene. Gusts of wind tore the leaves from the trees and overturned the plastic tables and chairs. I was the only customer.

The Sâone which, according to Caesar, flows with great gentleness, was full and turbulent at Gray. The town was crowded with French weekenders and posters announced an evening of dancing and fireworks. I guessed the hotels would be booked up for the fête so, as the sun was shining and it was only four o'clock, I decided to press on. The main Roman route to the Alps would have taken me down the Sâone to Lyon, then up the Rhône to Geneva. Having motored round Lyon on one occasion and been frightened out of my wits by the traffic, I decided not to commit suicide by cycling there. The alternative Roman route across the Doubs at Besançon (Vesantio), then over the Jura to Lausanne, promised to be much more peaceful and would also be more direct, so I left the Sâone at Gray and climbed up to the plateau dividing it from the Doubs. Thunder, lightning, torrential rain and finally hail pursued me. I raced along, terrified by the fury of the storm and feeling far too vulnerable on my metal bicycle on such high, exposed ground. I made Marnay in record time and was relieved to find that my panniers had stood the test. Even though I was soaked to the skin, I had dry clothes to wear at dinner.

My bicycle stood in the tiled corridor just outside my room. As I was draping my dripping cycling gear over the furniture and the cold radiators, I heard two pairs of feet and a good Midlands voice exclaiming, 'Ooh look, a cyclist!' I emerged from my room and greeted them with, 'Yes. A *wet* cyclist.' Then I heard *their* tale of woe. The couple were keen travellers by camper. They loved the scenery and the climate abroad but spoke nothing except English and were suspicious of foreign food. So when they travelled, they liked to be as self-contained as possible, stocking up their camper for the whole journey, even down to wrapped bread and tins of home-made cake. In that way they could insulate themselves from the strange ways of the locals: they liked them, but preferred to peer out at them from the security of their camper.

They were currently in a state of shock. As they were driving near Marnay on their way to enjoy the scenery of Switzerland, a tyre had burst and their camper had careered into a ditch. They themselves had escaped with minor bruises but the camper was a write-off. Suddenly, their safe little goldfish bowl was shattered and they had been forced to come out among the French. They had been astonished to find that many of those in authority spoke English and had dealt efficiently and sympathetically with their emergency. Their insurers had offered to provide them with a hired car, so that they could complete their holiday, and they were awaiting its arrival at the hotel. Sorties to the wrecked camper had retrieved some of their English food, but much of it had been ruined in the crash. Encouraged by my presence, they braved the hotel dining room at dinner-time, where their worst suspicions were probably confirmed by the first course, a salade niçoise. The main course fortunately turned out to be nothing more outlandish than steak and chips, so they took courage and set off next morning with burgeoning confidence to spend a motoring holiday among the Swiss.

I arrived at Besançon on schedule the next day, achieving my third limited objective. I spent the afternoon in bed with a magazine and a bar of chocolate, while my cycling clothes dried off and the rain beat against the window. Priscilla arrived, uncharacteristically flustered, on the 22.20 train from Paris. She had been robbed in the Gare du Nord but, miraculously, the police had been following that particular thief and they had caught him red-handed. Priscilla had found her handbag with her money and her passport waiting for her in the office of the station police.

BESANÇON — PONTARLIER — COL DE JOUGNES —
LAUSANNE — BLONAY — MONTREUX — MARTIGNY —
ORSIÈRES — BOURG ST PIERRE — GREAT ST BERNARD
— AOSTA — VERCELLI — NOVARA — MILAN

The prospect of cycling over the Great St Bernard, the highest motor pass in Europe, filled us with a mixture of excitement and anxiety. Admittedly, we had the Jura to practise on before we got there but the Alps would still be a major challenge to two inexperienced cyclists well past the first flush of youth. We waited a day in Besançon, hoping for a break in the weather, but Tuesday dawned as rainy as ever. As we were due to spend Thursday night with friends in Switzerland, we had no choice but to don the waterproofs and set out.

Vaubon's masterpiece of a citadel towered above us as we climbed steeply out of Besançon; below, on the Doubs, we could see the river traffic bound for the Rhine-Rhône Canal. We cycled up the Loue valley through Ornans, where a Roman column stood in the square, and found a wonderful gorge of beech trees near the river's source. Then up and up. We struggled all day, often on foot, to cover the 38 miles to Pontarlier.

My struggles were always greater than Priscilla's, as she was by far the fitter. Since giving up the City grind for the comparative freedom of financial consultancy, she had been taking her fitness seriously, strenuously climbing hills, cycling, downhill-skiing and even charging off relentlessly for 8 a.m. swims, while I had been lying snug in my bed. Admittedly my baggage was heavier than her ten-day pack and my 486-mile crawl from London had done little to build up my stamina, but Priscilla's small, neat form and whirling feet were always way ahead of me, and hill-tops found her sitting peacefully on a fence, admiring the view as she waited for me to finish the gruelling climb.

We reached Pontarlier in the evening in the most violent hail storm, but that was the least of our problems. The good hotel I knew in the town was full and so were all the others in the centre. Dripping wet and thoroughly dejected, we decided that our last hope was the railway station. Failing a hotel nearby, we could at least spend the night under cover in the waiting-room. But we were in luck. The hotel opposite the goods yard was so seedy we were probably the only guests it had received in years. But it had ample room – and it was a port in the storm.

I have never in Europe stayed in such a shabby hotel. The bedroom furniture was so decrepit and the general ambience so gloomy that we took flash photographs of each other standing on the bare boards beside the marble wash-stands and the ancient iron bedsteads to act as proof. *Monsieur le patron*, whose tight brown jersey showed off his ample form to perfection, was very fond of notices. The lavatory stood on a dais in a large, dingy room where tattered, yellowing signs covered the walls: 'Fermer [sic] la porte, s.v.p. Merci.' 'Non pas ouvrir la fenêtre, s.v.p. Merci.' And downstairs in the chocolate-painted bar, the local bus timetable bore the notice: 'Mettez vos lunettes pour regarder l'horaire, s.v.p. Merci.'

Surprisingly, breakfast was excellent. The coffee was superb and the croissants and bread crisp and hot from the oven. By eight o'clock the bar was crowded, the dripping donkey jackets of railway workers steaming gently in the heat of an ancient iron stove. Two gendarmes on their bar stools lit up cheroots and took a cognac with their coffee, *Monsieur le patron* perched like a benign buddha behind his bar and the room filled with a warm, comfortable fug. Priscilla and I sat at our zinc-topped café table enjoying the conviviality. Our host pressed us to second and third helpings of the delicious new bread with a philosophical 'Tant pis pour la ligne!' (Too bad for the figure!) As he let us out of his garage with our bicycles he startled us with the information, solemnly conveyed, that he too was 'sportif'.

The River Doubs makes an enormous loop, halfway to the Rhine and back again. Having left it at Besançon, we met it again at Pontarlier and followed it for a few miles out of town. We soon reached the Col de Jougny, at 3,363 ft our highest point in the Jura, and decided to call it a day. We had set out from Pontarlier in damp clothing and the rain at our present altitude was icy cold. Chilled to the marrow, we stumbled into a comfortable hotel in Jougny, soaked ourselves in hot baths and

spent the afternoon reading in bed. Tomorrow would be all
downhill.

It was with a great sense of achievement that I pedalled along to
the Swiss Customs at Vallorbe, 539 miles from St Paul's. It
should have been a beautiful ride down to Lausanne, but once
again the weather was unkind. Dark clouds sat heavily on the
mountains and Lake Geneva was hidden behind a curtain of
mist and rain. Lausanne was difficult to negotiate. The tram-
lines lay near to the kerb and the narrow space between was full
of puddles and potholes. Motorists were short-tempered in the
driving rain, out of patience with cyclists, and the road was
solid with cars all the way along the lakeside to Vevey. With
enormous relief we boarded the little mountain train bound for
Blonay and a warm, dry home.

Jill and David had invited us to stay for one night but in fact
we were marooned with them for four: the incessant rain was
falling as snow above 5,250 ft, closing the Great St Bernard
Pass. We heard that the Rhône had risen high above the dam
which normally prevents logs from entering Lake Geneva, so
that shipping was at risk from floating debris. Altogether, the
season had started very badly for the Swiss. We finally took
advantage of a break in the weather and swooped down the
mountain from Blonay to Montreux on Monday morning.

When the Romans began to cross the Alps, they probably laid
their first paved road over the comparatively low and sheltered
Col du Mont Genèvre (6,100 ft). After Caesar's conquest of
Central and Northern Gaul, the more direct routes over the
Little St Bernard (7,178 ft) and the Great St Bernard
(8,100 ft) were metalled by Augustus and Claudius
respectively. Despite its daunting height, the Great St Bernard
Pass was their most favoured route, as it offered easy
approaches. Their paved road there must have been very
carefully sited and maintained, for Vitellius' general, Caecina,
was able to lead his army over the top in early spring. The pass
was known as Mons Jovis until the eleventh century, when St
Bernard founded his hospice at the summit to offer food and
shelter to pilgrims and clerics bound for Rome. It is recorded
that no fewer than twenty mediaeval emperors made their way

through the pass, including Frederick I Barbarossa in 1162. The last great army to pass that way was Napoleon's force of 40,000 on their way to victory over the Austrians at Marengo in 1800. Each regiment had to make three night halts: at Bourg St Pierre, St Rhémy or Étroubles and at Aosta. In its wealth of historical association, there is no Alpine pass to compare with the Great St Bernard. It was my obvious route into Italy.

The approach road to the pass led us up the Rhône to Martigny, a magnificent ride with the Dents du Midi gleaming on our right. At St Maurice (Agaunum) the river thundered through a spectacular gorge, where powerful fortifications attested the strategic importance of the site: whoever controlled St Maurice would control that stretch of the Rhône. We took our lunch in the neat little Swiss square, where every window had its box of geraniums, and explored the fourth-century abbey, the oldest Christian foundation in the Alps.

The next stretch of road followed the River Drance up to Sembrancher, then took its southern fork through the Entremont valley. Orsières had a fine Romanesque campanile and Bourg St Pierre a Roman column embedded in the wall of its simply carved Romanesque tower. Between Orsières and Bourg St Pierre the deciduous trees gradually thinned out and we began to cycle among conifers. Cicadas sang in the forget-me-nots and pink campions. We spent the night at Bourg St Pierre and dined Au Bivouac de Napoléon.

We had already climbed to an altitude of 5,360 ft and were beginning to get short of breath even when walking. We had walked for considerable stretches, struggling to push our heavily laden bicycles up the steep gradients and round the hairpin bends: the last twelve miles had taken us six hours. Ahead, between Bourg St Pierre and the summit, lay a climb of 2,740 ft over another eight miles, with nowhere to stop for the night should we fall short. It was then that we saw the bus bound for Aosta and had our brainwave. To catch the bus ourselves would be cheating, but a little help with the baggage would be well within the rules. With a little persuasion, the driver agreed to take our panniers in his luggage compartment. There was no proper bus station in Aosta, but he promised to leave them at the Ca'Rossa, where he usually had his lunch. So with light hearts and light bicycles we set off to conquer the summit.

For the first four miles, as far as the entrance to the motor tunnel (6,233 ft), the gradient proved surprisingly comfortable and even I was able to cycle most of the way. Stretches of the road were covered over as protection against avalanches. We felt very vulnerable cycling along those gloomy corridors, with the solid rock to our left and a row of pillars to our right to let in light and air. Cars and lorries roared by and we hoped that their lights would pick out our luminous yellow belts. It was a great relief to reach the point where the lonely road up to the Col branched off to the right, leaving the traffic to thunder on through the tunnel. The day had dawned grey, but now the sun came out and lit up the Grand Combin. The air was crisp after the fumes of the corridor and the recent snow was sparkling white. We could not have had a lovelier day. Pushing our bicycles cheerfully up through the Marengo Gorge, we found ourselves slowing down to a resolute, gasping plod as we mounted ever higher up the steep zig-zag road. I noted with quiet satisfaction that for once I was able to forge on ahead of Priscilla – but only because my legs were longer. There was no traffic, no living creature, no vegetation to stir in the empty landscape. We had the top of Europe to ourselves. When we finally reached the summit we basked in the admiration of a group of Italian motorists, had a celebratory beer and sandwich, visited the Hospice Church and museum, then pedalled across to the Italian frontier, 642 miles from St Paul's.

The descent from the pass was one of life's great experiences – 22½ miles of heady freewheeling: between the summit and Aosta, we never once turned our pedals. The road was very steep at first, with vertiginous drops down to a bleak plateau. The rush of the icy wind in our faces made us gasp for breath and we had to stop occasionally to recover our breathing and allow our brakes to cool. But the southern face of the Alps is gentle and we soon reached the gentians and yellow anemones, lingering in sweet-smelling pine woods, pausing to shed layers of clothing among the poplars, ash and limes. Within an hour of the summit, we were relaxing in the warmth of the Italian summer. We took rooms at the Ca'Rossa, where our panniers awaited, and I threw my worn corduroy knickerbockers and leg-warmers into the wastepaper basket. I had left the North behind. Later we learned that we had only just got over the pass in time. An avalanche the next day had blocked the road on the Italian side and swept two cars over a precipice. Fortunately, the occupants had just got out to take photographs and so escaped unharmed.

Aosta (Augusta Praetoriana) was founded by the Emperor Augustus in 24 BC to guard the Dora Baltea valley and the approaches to the two St Bernard passes. Roman remains, the beautiful Romanesque Church and Cloister of Sant'Orso, the elegant eighteenth- and nineteenth-century stucco façades and the bustle of the modern city all testify to its continuing importance. It was here that St Anselm was born, in the days when the Church was truly universal. After a spell in France as Abbot of the great Monastery of Bec-Helouin, he became Archbishop of Canterbury in 1093 and spent sixteen years quarrelling with William II and Henry I over the papal right to appoint bishops.

We spent Priscilla's last day sightseeing in Aosta and attempting to cycle down beside the Dora Baltea river. A terrific wind from the east sprang up in the afternoon, funnelling down the narrow valley with such force that even Priscilla could make no headway against it. We gave up at the fashionable spa of St Vincent, where she prepared to go home by train the next day. We treated ourselves to a special farewell dinner.

I had looked forward to wheeling down the Valle d'Aosta to Ivrea, enjoying the sunshine, the scenery and the gentle descent, but once again I was disappointed. Mont Blanc, the Matterhorn and Monte Rosa were hidden in cloud and the light was so bad that my camera's automatic flash came on at midday when I stopped to photograph a stretch of the original Roman road. There was a chill wind and I shivered in my black cotton trousers, regretting the haste with which I had abandoned my warm corduroys. But the Valle was magnificent, even in the gloom. The modern motorway tunnelled and hacked its brutal path along the west bank of the Dora Baltea while the old Statale, which I was riding, jostled for space with the railway

line along the east bank. There were narrow gorges, where the
road clung to the cliff edge and fortresses guarded the route.
The colossal Forte di Bard, built in the eleventh century,
probably on Roman foundations, to command the upper Dora
Baltea from its narrowest point, almost changed the course of
European history by halting Napoleon's march in 1800. It was
taken after a long siege, destroyed on Napoleon's orders but
rebuilt in 1825. The railway when it came had to go under the
fortress, though the road crept round on a narrow ledge under
the beetling battlements.

All the signs from the Italian border had been in French first,
Italian second. By the time I reached Pont St Martin, named
for its Roman bridge, the order had changed and I began to feel
that I was really in Italy. A beautiful little sculpture caught my
eye: a simple plinth with doves ascending, dedicated to blood
donors. It is the only tribute I have ever seen to the millions
throughout the world who perform this vital, unsung service.

In Ivrea the Dora Baltea was broad and impressive, but still a
white water course, marked out for a kayak slalom. The roads in
the city centre were cobbled, as is generally the case in Italy,
and my teeth would certainly have been jolted out of my head
had I not joined the local slalom cyclists on the pavement,
weaving in and out of the unconcerned pedestrians along the
river promenade. I saw my first oleanders.

As I cycled across Piedmont, the scenery changed. Straight
roads, canals and lines of poplars cut the land into neat squares
of wheat, barley and rice. Although the day happened to be
chilly and the afternoon had more than its fair share of rain, the
climate had clearly changed, for the wheat and barley were
almost ripe in late June. I braved the cobbles of Santhià town-
centre to cash a Eurocheque and met a very old man who told
me he had cycled all the way across Russia in his youth. We
stood outside the bank in the pouring rain while he recounted
his adventures. We were joined by a carabiniere, also a keen
cyclist, and the inevitable conversation about gear-ratios and
tyre-pressures ensued. My odometer, which showed the day's
mileage as well as the total distance covered, was particularly
admired.

The weather held one more surprise for me – thick fog. It

delayed my departure next morning from Vercelli. The fog-bound motorists in the hotel bar fulminated over their espresso coffees. Never had they known such a rainy summer! And now fog! I left the rain behind me at Vercelli after four weeks when my cagoule and waterproof leggings had almost become a second skin. But the bad weather continued in the Alps. On 18 July, after weeks of incessant rain, the River Adda burst its banks with such force that it swept away the entire village of Tartano and created a major new lake, changing the map of that entire region near the Swiss border.

Between Vercelli and Novara the last wisps of mist cleared, the sun came out and the snow-covered Alps gleamed on my left. The road was flat, the surface good, there was a moderate following wind and I bowled along at 12 mph. The extrovert Italians tooted their horns and waved at me, shouting 'Forza!' and 'Avanti, Coppi!' (Coppi is their legendary cycle-racing champion.) It was my first taste of the joyous, carefree cycling I had dreamed of. Feeling elated and rather frivolous, I decided to visit Magenta, for no profounder reason than that magenta is one of my favourite colours. I miscalculated my gear-change on a hump-backed level-crossing and fell off; then I was almost laid low twice, first by a car door and then by a youth speeding out of an archway on a moped. These three near-misses sobered me and it was a more cautious cyclist who shopped for cherries and cooled off under a tree in Magenta's square. In 1859 the French under Napoleon III and Cavour's Sardinians had defeated the Austrians here, just two years before Victor Emmanuel II was proclaimed King of a united Italy. Magenta's Via Garibaldi, Via Mazzini, Piazza della Liberazione and Caffé della Libertà were potent reminders of the struggle.

I had arranged my schedule so as to cross Milan on Saturday afternoon: major cities are safer for cyclists at weekends. Having no parking problems, I cycled straight up to the cathedral and chained my bicycle to a convenient railing at the corner of the west front. Although I have seen this white marble miracle on many occasions, its forest of Gothic pinnacles, gables, buttresses, spires, towers, gargoyles and statues, crowned by its treasured Madonnina, never ceases to astonish.

Yet inside, its lines are clear, austerity tempered only by the light from the enormous stained glass windows. I mingled with the fashionable Milanese, drinking coffee in the Galleria and gazing at the exquisite silks and leather goods in the glittering shops. Milan is extravagantly, ostentatiously rich. As Mediolanum, it grew in importance during Roman times until it eventually became the capital of the Western Empire. Now it is the banking capital and silk market at the hub of the northern road and canal system, drawing its wealth from the industry and fertile soil of Lombardy and still guarding the approaches to the Alps.

The city centre was full of bicycles. They were all yellow, of identical make and size, and all carrying advertisements for IBM. They seemed to be there for the taking by anyone who needed to make a short journey – an inspired attempt to help solve Milan's crippling traffic problem.

After a leisurely afternoon in the sun, I followed the Corso di Porta Romana through the south-eastern suburbs and saw the other face of Milan – the grim concrete blocks of workers' flats huddled beside a polluted canal, where filthy plastic bags, rotting cartons and tin cans lodged in the overhanging bushes showed how high the water had risen in that rainy season. I ate an ice cream outside a shabby café opposite the graffiti-covered office of the Italian Communist Party. Then I found the signpost for the Via Emilia.

4

The Roads to Rome

MILAN — PIACENZA — PARMA — BOLOGNA — RIMINI —
FANO — CAGLI — SCHÉGGIA — NOCERA UMBRA —
BEVAGNA — ACQUASPARTA — TERNI — NARNI — ROME

Stone, bronze, stone, steel, stone, oakleaves, horses' heels
Over the paving.

(T. S. Eliot)

THE Via Flaminia was Rome's Great North Road. Laid in
220 BC by the Censor Caius Flaminius, it ran north-east
from Rome across the Apennines to reach the Adriatic at Fano
(Fanum Fortunae), where it turned north-west along the coast
to Rimini (Ariminum). In 187 BC the Consul Marcus Aemilius
Lepidus constructed the Via Aemilia, to follow the Po valley
north-west from the end of the Via Flaminia; originally the road
went as far as Piacenza (Placentia), but it was later extended to
Milan and Aosta. The Flaminia crossed Roman Italy proper,
while the Aemilia ran across the province of Cisalpine Gaul
(Gaul on the nearer side of the Alps, as distinct from Trans-
alpine Gaul, which lay over the Alps from Rome). Ease of
travel along the Via Aemilia was the key to the extension of
Roman influence throughout Cisalpine Gaul and beyond. The
Via Flaminia was busy from its earliest days; and both roads
became even more important in the fourth and fifth centuries
AD, when the Imperial Court ruled the West from Milan or
Ravenna.

The Via Emilia, as it is now spelt by the Italians, is a clearly
marked highway, with a bright blue signpost every kilometre.
As in Roman times, much of it is raised on embankments to
keep it clear of marshes and rivers in spate; and it is so straight

that a traveller with magic eyes could stand on the outskirts of
Milan and see the road stretch in one direct line all the way to
Rimini. Today the parallel motorway takes most of the traffic
and the Emilia pursues a relatively tranquil course through the
cities and villages of Lombardy and Emilia.

The weather was hot now and I fell into the daily routine
which was to be mine throughout the rest of the summer. I slept
with my curtains open, so that I woke at first light and pedalled
off in the cool of the morning. As Italian bars open early, I
could be sure of finding my morning transfusion of coffee
within the first hour. Then I cycled steadily all morning, luring
myself on with the promise of refreshments at regular intervals.
I carried water for emergencies but a glass of mineral water,
straight from the refrigerator, was worth every one of the lire I
paid for it. I reached my target of 50 miles by early afternoon,
bought my lunch of peaches, apricots or cherries and looked for
a suitable hotel. After long, strenuous mornings, the Italian
siesta was a habit I slipped into most comfortably. I shut out the
blazing afternoon and rested on my bed with the local newspaper and a feeling of accomplishment. Then at four o'clock,
showered and changed, I wandered out to enjoy the best part of
my day.

Coffee and serious sightseeing came first, then I would sit
outside a café in the piazza, writing up my day's notes over a
glass of chilled white wine and watching the Italians out for
their evening promenade. The elegance of the shops, even in
the smallest towns, was a constant amazement to me and I
shared the delights of window-shopping with the locals. As I
had only two panniers for luggage and they were both full to
bursting, major purchases were out of the question, so my
gazings were not marred by the agonies of indecision. The
search for a few postcards or a replacement bar of soap filled
pleasant evening strolls.

It took me months to adjust to so much leisure. I always felt
that I ought to be *doing* something. I thought back to the frantic
years when I had rushed home from work, laden with groceries
and exercise-books, and shot straight into the kitchen to start
the family dinner. Then the days of non-stop trouble-shooting
as a headmistress; the evenings when I still had a concert to

attend, tomorrow's Plato to prepare and twenty letters to answer; and the nights punctuated, admittedly sporadically, with fire-alarms, appendicitis attacks and gangs of marauding youths. It had all been poor preparation for such a tranquil life and it was hard to accept it as a gift, even a reward, without feeling guilty.

An excellent dinner, accompanied by a small carafe of the local wine, crowned my evenings. It was my rule throughout my journey to economise on accommodation, when necessary, but never on food. I always ate as well as I could and I am sure this was one of the main reasons for my sustained good health. I never suffered anything worse than a cold in the head.

I had been told that the best value in Italy was to be found in small-town *trattorie con alloggio*, neighbourhood restaurants with a few rooms. These establishments survived on the quality of their cooking, so that I could always count on a good dinner, even if the accommodation was simple. As hotels near Milan are far from cheap, I was lucky to find the first of these *trattorie* in Melegnano, just ten miles from Milan's city centre.

The grumpy old lady in the kitchen, toiling over her home-made tagliatelle under the watchful eyes of six cats and a tame crow, was at first reluctant to let me have a room.

'Just look at you! On a bicycle, covered in dust, a woman of *your* age! You ought to be at home with your husband, not wandering about on a bike, like a vagabond.'

'Leave her alone, Mamma,' said her son. 'She's all right. In fact, I think she's very courageous. She won't cause you any trouble. Will you, signora?'

It took all my assurances and all her son's diplomacy to convince her that I should be a respectable lodger. Then she took me up to my room. I had to cross her kitchen several times on my way back and forth and I was relieved to see that the conclave of cats never ventured near the tagliatelle. They were probably as nervous of their owner as I was.

Melegnano's Sunday morning market was already in full swing when I pushed my bicycle out into the square. Overwhelmed by the scent of ripe cantaloups in the warm sun, I walked in a trance from stall to stall, luxuriating in their heady sweetness. Fruits and the roadside honeysuckle, elderflower, cypress and roses all have a stronger fragrance in the heat of the Mediterranean summer, providing one of the greatest joys of this passing cyclist.

Piacenza, the original terminus of the Via Emilia, was established by the Romans to guard a crossing of the Po; the city maintained its strategic importance as a member of the Lombard League, under the Viscontis, the Sforzas, the Church and the Farnese. I crossed the Po into the silence of Sunday noon, the only traveller to admire the Gothic town hall and the Farnese dukes on their spirited Baroque horses. I sat in the shade, contented and half asleep in the warm stillness, watching the swallows swoop round the red brick crenellations of the Farnese palace. For the first time in my life I was in a new city and yet I felt no obligation to trudge systematically round all the sights, guidebook in hand. I had a sightseeing policy which did not include Piacenza.

I had just embarked on a fifteen-month journey round a world that would be crammed with sights, scents, sounds, buildings, history, people, cultures – a kind of fruitcake of such richness that it would be impossible to digest it all. In general, I found the only way to enjoy sightseeing was to take one modest slice of this sumptuous cake at a time. The slice could be vertical, an in-depth exploration of one limited area; or it could be horizontal, a thin sliver shaved across the entire expanse of the cake. My method on this trip was the horizontal one, limited in each country to the study of one specific historical period. In Italy that period began and ended with the Romans so, on that warm Sunday afternoon, I was free to enjoy the monumental splendour of Piacenza with my eyes alone, without worrying about the exact dates of the palaces or the opening-hours of the churches and museums. The Botticelli Virgin could be left for another visit.

I found an unusual *trattoria con alloggio* near the Rococo theatre in Fidenza. Its small central courtyard bristled with bicycles: it turned out to be the evening haunt of the elderly men of the town and consequently my own arrival, on a bicycle, caused a sensation. It was clearly the most exciting thing that had happened for years to the pensioners of Fidenza and they were taken by storm. My dinner there, of chunky vegetable soup, guinea fowl with artichokes, strawberries and dolcelatte cheese, was truly memorable. I shall return to Fidenza one day.

Although the Via Emilia passes through interesting and important cities, it is not in itself a very interesting road. Between Milan and Bologna one industrial belt succeeds another, with flat fields between, where all the crops but the maize and sunflowers had already been harvested. Italians love the noise and vitality of cities. Unlike the English, they rarely choose to live in the country unless they have to and the dilapidated cottages and farm buildings along the Via Emilia were silent witnesses to this preference. Farm-workers now come to the fields on their mopeds or in their small Fiats and return home at night to their towns. I missed the English cottages with their lovingly tended gardens.

Fidenza, Parma, Reggio nell' Emilia. Although I knew Parma well, I stopped again in the city of ham, cheese and violets to look at one of my favourite groups of buildings. The fine Romanesque cathedral, with its even finer Romanesque campanile, spans the ages, from the Roman mosaics in the crypt to Correggio's *Assumption of the Virgin* in the dome. The neighbouring Church of St John the Baptist adds a touch of Baroque with its 1607 façade. But the jewel of the collection is Antelani's massive octagonal baptistry, built in a delicate rose-coloured sandstone, Romanesque at the bottom and soaring Gothic pinnacles at the top. I entered its cool dimness and gazed in renewed delight at the Byzantine frescoes and Antelani's twelve elegant pillars, each one carved in high relief to represent a month of the year.

There was a heat-wave now which left even the Italians gasping, and it was with great relief that I left my bicycle in the Cycle Depository near Reggio nell' Emilia Station and caught the train to Latisana. At Lignano, east of Venice, I spent an idle week bathing in the warm crystal waters of the lagoon, sleeping and enjoying the company and splendid cooking of my friend Minne. I had been cycling for a month.

Much restored, I had already breakfasted and was waiting outside the Reggio Cycle Depository when it opened at 6.30 a.m. By nine o'clock I was in Modena (Mutina), drinking coffee in one of the city's elegant arcades. The layout of the main streets still lies on the Roman grid and the Via Emilia runs straight through the centre. So straight was the road that the white marble campanile of the cathedral, the Torre Ghirlandina, was visible on that clear morning halfway from Reggio. At close quarters I was able to admire its Romanesque detail and the bronze garland on its weather-vane, from which it takes its name. I felt its massive presence towering behind me, slightly off the perpendicular, as I cycled on.

Emilia is a paradise for cyclists, perhaps the one place in the world where the interests of the motorist are subordinate. There are cycle-paths in all its cities and sometimes a whole lane in a one-way street is kept clear of cars and reserved for cyclists. Everyone cycles. Young, middle-aged, old, rich, poor, women shopping, women with babies in frilly cradles or children on little seats, with dogs on leads trotting beside, poodles in baskets, friends chatting alongside and eating ice creams, old ladies with sunshades, workmen with timber, old men clutching their walking sticks as they ride, even lovers holding hands and gazing harder at each other than the traffic. And the bicycles come in all shapes and sizes: small-wheeled shoppers, a small-wheeled tandem, elderly 'sit up and begs' ridden with solemn dignity, sleek racing multi-gears, mountain bikes and cleverly engineered tricycles of various designs for handicapped people. Cyclists are kings and queens of the road, allowed to go both ways up one-way streets or to take to the pavements when the cobbles are too proud. There are a few limits, however. A notice on the door of the Basilica at Forlì reminded us that we were not supposed to take our bicycles inside.

A long, stark, shadeless dual-carriageway led into Bologna, capital of Emilia. There was a strong headwind and the road was crowded with lorries. I entered the city through the Porta San Felice (St Felix Gate), a happy reminder of my old school, and was relieved to find shade and shelter in the narrow, arcaded streets. But unfortunately, the place was packed with tourists and tycoons and the hotels were full. I was too hot and tired to go on so I ended up paying a small fortune for a room in a marble palace, where I spent the night shivering under a pile of blankets. The air conditioning had no room regulator. A high price to pay for discomfort.

The Strada Maggiore (Via Emilia), with its arcade of shops leading down to the Porta Maggiore, must have looked very similar in the days of Roman Bononia. I wandered across the vast Piazza Maggiore and Piazza del Nettuno, overawed by the palaces, churches, basilicas and huge red-brick towers. There was so much to admire in 'Bologna la Grassa', but so little to love. It was my second visit to this wealthy city and my second failure of sympathy, so I was pleased to escape early next morning, even though I missed the expensive breakfast for which I had been obliged to pay in advance. The restaurant in the marble palace was not open to feed cyclists who rose with the sun.

Bologna was the last of the big northern cities and I returned gratefully to the small towns where the traveller is a welcome guest. The foothills of the Apennines, which had been visible in the distance from Modena, were now approaching the road on my right and there were a few gentle inclines on the Via Emilia itself. I cycled past orchards and vineyards. In Faenza I saw a row of porcelain factories and realised that faïence was Italian, not French, as I had always supposed.

In Forlì, I had been asked to doff my cap to St Peregrine, one of the saints dear to travellers, and I spent hours searching the basilica and churches of the town for his tomb or relics – without success. But I found another memorial there, which brought home once more the sadness and waste of war. Instead of the usual bleak list of names, this war memorial had a small snapshot of each victim. Most were dapper young men in 1940s style, with their small moustaches, wide-brimmed felt hats and Humphrey Bogart raincoats. But there were whole families portrayed – solid middle-aged men, whose name, age and physiognomy showed them to be the fathers of the two or three young men next to them in the rows; and husbands, wives and daughters, presumably members of the resistance movement. It was a poignant, personalised tribute.

War was on my mind, appropriately, as I cycled into Savignano sul Rubicone. The Rubicon river was the boundary between Italy and Cisalpine Gaul, the line at which Roman commanders under the Republic had to take leave of their armies before returning to Rome. Caesar arrived at the Rubicon with ten years of successful command in Gaul behind him and an army of seasoned veterans. He was a candidate for Consul, but his powerful opponents in the aristocratic party were plotting against him. His decision to lead his troops across the Rubicon on the night of 11 January 49 BC amounted to an act of aggression against the State. By choosing to retain the protection of his army rather than face the possibility of political annihilation, perhaps even death, at the hands of his rivals, he set in train the series of events leading up to the Civil War and the fall of the Roman Republic.

The Roman Rubicon has still not been identified with certainty, nor the point at which Caesar crossed into Italy, but the name 'Savignano sul Rubicone' has a splendid ring and I felt the excitement of participating in a momentous action when I crossed that small stream. Armour was glinting in the sunlight and the horses' hooves were clattering over the cobbles as the conqueror of Gaul, victorious Caesar, rode with his small but loyal band of 1,500 men to take on the might of Republican Rome.

I was the conquering hero myself in the next café. Two little boys on children's bicycles engaged me in conversation outside. When I told them that I was cycling round the world, their eyes opened wide with wonder. 'Che coraggio!' they exclaimed. 'E tutto da solita!' I was enchanted by the diminutive of *sola*. I was all on my little own! Inside the café, other admirers paid for my coffee and mineral water and the woman behind the bar said, 'Lei è forte – come la Signora Thatcher!' As I prepared to leave, I saw that my two small friends had assembled a squadron of junior cyclists and I rode out of the village in a cavalcade of honour.

Three miles before the end of the Via Emilia I completed my first thousand miles. I pedalled into Rimini past the umbrella pines and fir trees, with a fresh sea-breeze in my face, and rode straight to the Tourist Office. It was full of shorts, sun-tops, sandals and lobster-red faces enquiring about hotels and day-trips to San Marino, so my request for a plan of the Roman antiquities came as some surprise. I photographed the triumphal Arch of Augustus and the Bridge of Tiberius, two powerful reminders of the importance of Ariminum. As the stronghold at the junction of the Via Emilia and the Via Flaminia, it commanded the narrow strip of land between the Apennines and the Adriatic and was the key to Cisalpine Gaul. But Rome is forgotten today by the sun-seekers. Rimini's present fame rests on its sandy beach, the Riviera del Sole.

Rimini, Riccione, Cattolica – mile after mile of beach umbrellas and seaside hotels. The road turned inland for a stretch before entering Pesaro and I cycled through a changed landscape. The hills down to the Foglia Valley were covered with vines, fruit trees and the first olive groves of my journey south. Then back to the Adriatic, where the pale morning sun glittered on the sea as I rode along a causeway towards the massive battlements of Fano.

The Arch of Augustus stands within Fano's mediaeval walls; it spans the Via Flaminia with a broad central arch for road traffic, flanked by two narrower arches for pedestrians. Its crowning arcade, destroyed by Montefeltro's cannons, has been replaced by an elegant cinquecento loggia, running at right angles into the façade of the little Church of San Michele. Arch and church now combine to form a peaceful, harmonious corner, well away from the serious business of the Porta Maggiore, the gate in the city walls. Fano guards the point where the Via Flaminia from Rome first reaches the Adriatic and has a colourful history to prove its strategic importance. It was here that the army of Pope Pius II, led by Federico da Montefeltro, burst through the battlements in 1463 to end the rule of the cruel Malatestas; and in 1860 the Porta Maggiore was the scene of great rejoicing, when the people of Fano welcomed Victor Emmanuel II into their city and handed it over to join his united, independent Italy. I felt as excited as a child on Christmas morning. I was reliving history under the Arch of Augustus and the Porta Maggiore. I was setting out along the famous Via Flaminia to Rome.

When I am old and grey and have nothing more pressing to do with my time, I shall spend my summers cycling back and forth along the Via Flaminia. The autostrada to Rome and a Via Flaminia superstrada syphon off the traffic from the real Via Flaminia, helping to make its 209 miles a stretch of pure delight. The road is a miracle of engineering. The Romans planned the route so skilfully that even in the worst weather the highest reaches would never be impassable. And the surveyors who worked out the gradients were men of genius. The road from Fano climbs up and up but so gently that I never once had to get off and push, nor did I have to apply my brakes on the descents. The Via Flaminia is a road on a human scale, designed for people, horses, carts and beasts of burden, with a proper regard for their frailties.

I followed my nose out of Fano. The main road went off in a curve but there was no mistaking the original Via Flaminia, which made for the distant mountains in a straight line. For the first time, after weeks of cycling into the morning sun, I was heading south-west with its warmth on my back.

As usual, the Roman road followed the course of the rivers, up into the Apennines through the rugged scenery of the Marches. Shaded by woods of lime and mountain ash, it ran along beside trout streams, through spectacular gorges, round overhanging crags. It crossed Roman bridges, still in use, and in the majestic Passo del Furlo I experienced the wonder of cycling through a Roman tunnel, cut out of the rock in AD 76, in Vespasian's reign, and still the only passage for traffic along the edge of that precipitous gorge. (The superstrada bores its way under a mountain, avoiding the Passo del Furlo altogether.)

The surveyors on the Via Flaminia always took the easiest, lowest route. This was possible in Italy under the Pax Romana, when people could live on the plains and travel the roads without fear. In the violent days which followed the decline of Rome, the warring local princes had to build their cities on hilltops and surround them with battlements. Urbino, Gubbio, Perugia and Assisi all look down from their mountain fastnesses onto the peaceful Flaminia, meandering through the valleys below. I was pleased, in that hot summer weather, that my research was limited to the Roman road. Renaissance treasures on mountain-tops are distinctly unappealing to a warm cyclist.

Roses, oleanders, dahlias, geraniums and hibiscus bloomed in the village gardens along the way. In one small, undistinguished town with a row of eight mean shops, I was astonished to see the most elegant boutique imaginable, full of sumptuous wedding dresses: 'Everything for the Bride'. Two more shops displayed prams, pushchairs and cots, while another was full of corsets – steel and whalebone horrors of a kind I thought had long disappeared from the face of the earth. All of life in four shop-windows for a woman of Le Marche. Milan and Bologna were a world away.

From Cagli I climbed up through a pass leading from the Marches to Umbria, then up still higher to Schéggia. It was hard work, but even here the gradients were so comfortable that I managed to cycle all the way. When I came to sign-posts pointing to ski resorts, I was amazed to find that I had climbed so high.

Umbria was markedly different from the dramatic, craggy Marches. I was now on high rolling country with wide open stretches of farmland between the wooded hills. Harvesting was in progress, while grapes and sunflowers still ripened in the July sun. I was fascinated to cycle over the tops of the rounded hills which are always a distant feature in Umbrian Renaissance painting, and see their crown of wild flowers, broom, oak and pine at close quarters.

At night I stayed in simple country inns where they saw few visitors. In Nocera Umbra (Nuceria) I spent the afternoon writing a letter about my travels to date for the school magazine. The girls, who had bought me my bicycle, would be anxious to know how it was shaping up. I had woken that morning, 11 July, to bright sunshine and realised it was Parents' Day, the end of the summer term. I hoped that Southwold was enjoying good weather too and congratulated myself on having no speech to make. I wrote the letter instead. Detachment takes time. Afterwards, I went downstairs to the small restaurant.

'I'm sorry. Our menu is small,' said the signora. 'All we have today is wild boar in fresh sage and white wine – or you could have a steak.' Wild boar! Preceded by home-made pasta and washed down with Umbrian wine, it was the perfect end to the day.

The next evening, in Acquasparta, I sat in the warm twilight in the piazza in the shadow of the crumbling Cesi Palace, where Galileo was once a refugee from the wrath of the Vatican. There I wrote up my notes while the men of the town played cards.

POLAND

CZECHOSLOVAKIA

HUNGARY

YUGOSLAVIA

U.S.S.R.

ROMANIA

R. Danube

BULGARIA

BLACK SEA

TURKEY

Istanbul

Ankara

Kayseri

Gordion

ADRIATIC SEA

ALBANIA

Kavala

Thessaloniki

Gelibolu

Troy

Eskişehir

Afyon

Tarsus

Antioch

Bergama

Benevento

Brindisi

GREECE

Ioannina

Izmir

Sardis

Capua

Taranto

Igoumenitsa

Athens

CYPRUS

SICILY

CRETE

RANEAN SEA

MEDITERRANEAN SEA

0   500
MILES

London – Antioch 3,814 miles cycling
Dublin – London 328 miles

——— Cycle route   ------ Ferry

N

Across the square two men were playing, while eleven others shouted encouragement. On my side there were no fewer than 21 noisy, quarrelling spectators to a four-handed game. And not a glass or coffee cup in sight. The barman was surprised and gratified when I ordered a glass of wine. A paying customer at last!

In AD 69 the Romans changed the route of the Via Flaminia between Nocera Umbra and Narni (Narnia) to take in Spoleto (Spoletium), the route followed by the modern superstrada. I tried to keep to the original road through Bevagna, though it was sometimes hard to find. Sign-posts at crossroads labelled Flaminia Bis or Flaminia Ter pointed to Rome in different directions simultaneously. On one occasion I got myself so hopelessly lost that I ended up on the motorway at the mouth of a long tunnel through the mountains. Cycling through the tunnel was out of the question for me; there was a fence across the central reservation; so the only course left open was to cycle back, in the wrong direction, along the hard shoulder, with all the lorries and cars honking their disapproval of this dangerous (and illegal) activity. And all the time I had the frustration of seeing the real Via Flaminia running quietly through the poplar trees at a lower level. Eventually I succeeded in joining it.

In Terni (Interamna), the birthplace of Tacitus, I decided that something had to be done about my tyres. They had not been pumped since London and although they still seemed very hard, I was beginning to worry about them. Surely they must need attention by this time. I stopped at a workshop for cycles and mopeds, where all the mechanics downed tools to come and help, or just to chat and admire my bicycle. They managed to force in a little air with their pneumatic pump, but said the tyres would have been fine without it. After nearly 1,200 miles, I found that very surprising. I still had much to learn about the strength and reliability of my constant companion. Reassured, I explored Terni, a large industrial city, mostly rebuilt after the devastation of the last world war. I bought some sea-green espadrilles for my evening sightseeing and visited the Roman amphitheatre and the Porta Fuga, where Hannibal was put to flight. They are still great pursuers and huntsmen in Terni. I drank my morning coffee under notices of huntsmen's meetings and details of a hunting trip to Hungary.

I was descending now towards the plains of Latium. Rivers rushed down in cascades through narrow ravines, where hydro-electric plants harnessed their power, but on a modest scale, in sympathy with the landscape. From Narni, perched on its crag over the magnificent wooded gorge of the Nera, I swept down to cross the Tiber near Orte.

Orte was in fact a mistake, as I had taken the wrong fork after Narni, but I had no regrets. A group of locals gathered round me in the trattoria opposite the station, clearly the social centre of the town. When the proprietor heard I had cycled from London, he declared that no Italian would ever do such a thing. 'We are too lazy,' he said. One of his customers, a meek little simpleton in a flat cap, ill-fitting suit and scuffed shoes, countered that with: 'We are too rich. Italians have cars.' He spoke with pride and utter seriousness. I told him that I too had a car, but I enjoyed cycling. 'What sort of a car?' he asked suspiciously. 'An Alfa Romeo.' He received my reply in the silence of total disbelief. The *padrone* winked. He was a much travelled man, who understood the eccentricities of foreigners and pronounced on them with wit and relaxed good humour. Customers came and went, the dinner was good, conversation flowed and I was embraced in the social scene. It was a happy evening.

I had to toil over a great hill to Borghetto to regain the Via Flaminia, but it was a leafy hill in the cool of the morning. Alto Lazio, with its wide pastures and cornfields, seemed startlingly rural for an area so close to Rome. I stopped in the stillness under an olive tree for my lunch of peaches and had it not been for the heat and the chirp of cicadas, I could have imagined myself in one of the remoter Yorkshire Dales; yet I was less than fifteen miles from the centre of the Eternal City.

As I drew nearer to Rome, I began to see billboards advertising camping sites and decided to try out my new camping gear instead of struggling to find a hotel in Rome at the height of the tourist season. I selected Camping Tiber, just off the Flaminia, leaned my bicycle against a poplar tree and laid out my bivvy bag, mat and sleeping-bag in its shade to take my siesta under its

rustling leaves. I realised that night that the bivvy bag would be
of little use to me. With the sleeping-bag inside, it was far too
hot for Mediterranean camping and could serve only as a
groundsheet. But I was pleased with the self-inflating mat and
the lightweight down sleeping-bag and spent a comfortable
night under the stars, marred only by mosquitos and an overheard remark. Two young New Zealanders had pitched their
tent near to my poplar tree. Late in the evening, when I was
already tucked up, they arrived with two girls and the four of
them sat quietly chatting over a bottle of wine. I was stung into
instant wakefulness by the reply to an unheard question: 'Oh,
that's some old lady.' 'They can't be talking about *me*,' I said to
myself, pulling my sleeping-bag over my ears.

Dawn found me already up, packed and drinking my coffee
in the Camping Tiber bar. One of the most important days of
my whole journey lay ahead, the day when I should enter Rome
on the Via Flaminia and leave it on the Via Appia. I had already
travelled the Roman roads from Britain, the north-western
corner of the Empire; and now I was to cross the very heart of
that superb road network on my way to Rome's south-eastern
borders. The Romans were conquerors with an almost
twentieth-century appreciation of the importance of communications in controlling and civilising the conquered. All their
roads indeed led to Rome, to the centre of the spider's web; and
led there with remarkable efficiency and speed.

With mounting excitement and a sense of no time to lose, I
joined the early-morning queues of traffic on the remaining
nine miles into the city. The Via Flaminia led predictably to the
Ponte Flaminio, a grandiose bridge so crowded with eagles,
wolves suckling Romulus and Remus and mock Classical
columns that it had to be a Mussolini construction; the date on
its plaque – 1950 – was of its post-war rebuilding. Each town
along the Via Flaminia had its column on the bridge, inscribed
with Roman numerals. At first I was bemused by NARNI
KMLXXXII, until I realised that the K was not a modern
addition to the Roman system, but half of KM for kilometres.
The columns gave the distance of each town from Rome.

I was back again with the Roman generals, riding in triumph
into Rome. Across the Tiber they came, along the Via Flaminia

in their four-horse chariots, their manacled captives on foot before them and their soldiers marching behind, following the arrow-straight road to the heart of ancient Rome, the Forum; then across the Forum along the Via Sacra, the most ancient road in this ancient city, to the Temple of Jupiter Optimus Maximus Capitolinus on the Capitol, where they offered sacrifice and thanksgiving. Successive generations had embellished this route, setting up monuments to the glory of Rome, their visitors and themselves.

My own entry on a bicycle was more modest, but still exhilarating. I crossed the Piazzale Flaminio and cycled through the Porta del Popolo into the magnificence of the Piazza del Popolo. The inner face of the Porta, on the site of the ancient Porta Flaminia, was embellished in 1655 by Bernini for the State entry into Rome of Queen Christina of Sweden. The Piazza del Popolo itself is a breathtaking collection of monuments, from the central obelisk, brought by Augustus from Heliopolis after the conquest of Egypt (and moved to its present site by Pope Sixtus V as part of his city-plan) to the exuberant fountains and statues of Veladier, who laid out the Piazza in honour of the return of Pope Pius VII from France in 1814. The Borghese Gardens to the left and the Baroque churches of Santa Maria dei Miracoli and Santa Maria in Montesanto complete this overwhelming complex. I parked my bicycle outside a church door to take some photographs and received a stern reprimand from an anxious young man: 'Ten seconds is all it takes. You turn your back and whoosh! the bike's gone.' Despite his concern, I lost nothing more than a small compass in Rome or anywhere else until I reached America. There I had my Swiss Army knife stolen.

Still in possession of my machine, I swept down the Via del Corso, which corresponds to the Roman Via Lata (Broadway). Extremely narrow by modern standards, it is still a fashionable shopping street, boutiques filling the gaps between palaces and churches, and pedestrians jostling for pavement room. With Augustus' obelisk behind me, I looked south along the dead-straight line of the Corso to the glittering white marble confection of the monument to Victor Emmanuel II in the Piazza Venezia. Built to symbolise the unification of Italy, its style is as exuberant and flamboyant as the nation it celebrates. It may not be in the subtlest of taste but I always come to its extravagant overstatement with fresh pleasure. Here, in the geographical centre of the modern city, I sat down and wrote a postcard to a don of little faith at St Catharine's College, Cambridge. He had bet me £5 that I would never get as far as Rome. My postcard, with its odometer reading of 1,252 miles, was the triumphant claim to my winnings.

5

The Appian Way

ROME – ALBANO – PONTINA – TERRACINA – FONDI –
ITRI – FORMIA – SESSA AURUNCA – CAPUA –
CASERTA – BENEVENTO – AVELLINO – LIONI –
PESCOPAGANO – MURO LUCANO – RUOTI – POTENZA
– GRASSANO – MATERA – LATERZA – TARANTO –
BRINDISI

Minus est gravis Appia tardis.
(The Appia is less tiring if you travel slowly.)

(Horace)

THE vast bulk of the Victor Emmanuel II monument
blocked my path from the end of the Via Flaminia to the
start of the Via Appia and forced me into a perilous detour
through fleets of tourist coaches. I pedalled nervously along the
Via dei Fori Imperiali to the Colosseum, then turned right to
regain my proper route at the Piazza di Porta Capena. The
Porta Capena in the old Servian wall, south of the Forum and
adjoining the Circus Maximus, was the original start of the
Appian Way.

With great relief, I left the densest traffic behind me and
turned south-east through a wooded park beside the Baths of
Caracalla; through the Piazzale Numa Pompilio, where the
king of that name used to consult the nymph Egeria by her
fountain; and on to the Porta San Sebastiano, formerly the
Porta Appia in the Aurelian wall. Aurelian reigned from
AD 270 to 275 and it is the nine-mile enceinte of his wall
which defines the historical city and embraces its most
important monuments. The mediaeval towers of the Porta
San Sebastiano now provide a fitting entry to Rome from the
'regina viarum', the Queen of Roads. It was this proud gate
which in fact witnessed Rome's last triumphal procession,
when the Senate and people welcomed Marcantonio Colonna

II after the victory over the Turks at Lepanto in 1571.

I stood under the archway, gazing at the cobbled street ahead of me and at the 'Via Appia Antica' sign on a garden wall. I had cycled to Rome and survived its notorious traffic, but my route had all been through familiar and much-loved land. Now I was setting out into the unknown, bound for some of the wildest, emptiest mountains in Italy on the way to my next objective, Brindisi.

The Via Appia was laid in 312 BC by the Censor, Appius Claudius. At first it ran only as far as Capua but it was later extended to Benevento (Beneventum) and by 244 BC it had reached Brindisi (Brundisium), the port for Greece and Asia Minor. It was the most important of the consular roads during the centuries when Roman energies were directed southwards in Italy and eastwards beyond. Its importance as a triumphal and ceremonial way made it a favourite burial ground for the aristocracy and the first few miles out of Rome form a picturesque promenade between their ruined tombs and the cypress trees. The tradition survived into Christian times with the siting there of the catacombs. I had already done my duty years ago as a conscientious tourist, creeping among the towers and tombstones with my nose in a guidebook. This time I simply used my eyes and tried to put myself into the sandals of a Roman traveller, setting out from home on this 500-mile journey.

On this first stretch of the Via Appia the high garden walls, with their overhanging trees, gave the narrow cobbled street a village air. Traffic came along in waves, controlled by lights, so that half the time the road was completely empty of cars. As the cobbles were uneven, I pushed my bicycle along in the shadow of the eastern walls, enjoying the shade and the scent of flowers drifting over from the gardens. Then came an ugly stretch, full of workshops, filling stations and cheap cafés, then the first major crossroads and the little church of Domine, Quo Vadis?, standing on the spot where St Peter is said to have had his vision of Christ. Peter had managed to escape from prison in Rome and was scurrying out along the Via Appia in the dead of night when he saw Jesus coming towards him. 'Domine, quo vadis?' (Where are you going, Lord?) he asked. Jesus replied, 'Venio iterum crucifigi.' (I am coming to be crucified again.) Peter then understood that he was to turn back to Rome and face his own crucifixion. St Peter is my favourite of all the saints, the most human of the Apostles, with his fears and failings. He was Aristotle's truly brave man going to his martyrdom, not in the blindness and heat of bigotry, but with a clear appreciation of the agony to come. He was frightened and tried to run away, but in the end he found the courage to go and meet his death. I gave all the catacombs and the grand basilicas a miss, but I did call in, as always, to this modest little chapel.

Coming out into the sunshine again, I walked along the visually stunning stretch of road where cypresses and pine trees guard the crumbling tombs – a scene of romantic melancholy familiar from the canvases of the English landscape painters. The tombs came in all sizes, from touching little tributes carved with the likenesses of the dead to huge towers like the Casal Rotondo, some even fortified in mediaeval times to watch over this vital route into Rome.

At the corner where the Via Appia reaches the ring road, I found a lorry-drivers' pull-in – a caravan and two benches under a tree. I was greeted by two drivers and their elderly father, who had come along for the ride.

'Where are you going?'

'Round the world.'

'Madonna! You need a beer! Come and join us.'

'How far do you think you'll manage today?' asked the old man.

'I'm aiming for Albano.'

'Where are you going to stay? Have you booked a hotel?'

'Don't tell him!' (I had no intention of telling him.) 'He fancies you, the old devil! We can't take him anywhere. We have to watch him like hawks.'

The old man grinned. They insisted on treating me to a pizza and we sat in the shade together, relaxed and companionable. The sons chaffed the father and the father chaffed the sons, pouring out hilarious and highly improper anecdotes about one another with the slickness of a music hall act. They were kind, simple people and their mutual affection shone through their banter. I was included unreservedly in the fun. Once again, I blessed the humble bicycle's gift of approachability. The long-distance cyclist is right out of social and political context and no topics of conversation are barred.

Declining their offer of a third glass of beer, and promising to take great care of myself, I kissed them all goodbye and continued on my way. The Queen of Roads soon degenerated into a pathway through one of the city's major rubbish dumps. I would still have plodded on dutifully, despite the stench and the clouds of flies, had the driver of a dust-cart not given me the only acceptable excuse – that there was no exit at the far end of the dump. I left the Appia Antica and made my way with relief across to the Via Appia Nuova, the modern highway, which was only marginally better. Rows of factories lined its litter-strewn verges. Lorries thundered by and the afternoon sun beat down. Fortunately, this lasted only a short stretch and I soon regained the comparative tranquillity of the original road and began the long straight climb up into the Alban Hills.

I arrived at Albano at 5.45, shattered after almost twelve hours of intense concentration. I had covered 30 miles, some of it on foot over ankle-wrenching cobbles and the rest through the terrifying traffic of central Rome. As I strolled in the cool of the evening under the pines of the Villa Communale, the park once occupied by Pompey's villa, I looked down across the distant Campagna and understood Byron's love of these lush volcanic Alban Hills and Lakes. I was in Alba Longa, the most ancient town of Latium, predating even Rome. Here the Universal Church gave me another connection with home: Nicholas Breakspeare was Bishop of Albano before he went on to Rome as England's only pope, Adrian IV.

My solitude ended in Albano, for my friend and former colleague Katherine arrived from England with her bicycle to keep me company for three weeks. Always ebullient, she swept down the hill from Velletri to join me and we spent our first day together at Lake Nemi, a brilliant blue circle of water ringed with steeply wooded hills. Its groves, sacred to Diana, held the tree with the golden bough from which Sir James Frazer took the title of his book on magic and ritual. The scene was familiar from Turner's painting but Diana's Mirror, as the Romans called the lake, still had an air of ancient mystery. As we gazed out over the silent groves, Katherine, fresh from the end of term, rattled on about school and I listened quietly. I was interested but it was all beginning to seem remote, almost unmeaning.

When we set out next day, I was pleased to find that it was my turn to set the pace. After 1,250 miles and three mountain ranges, I had lost weight and was already a strong cyclist. Katherine, though an excellent golfer, was unused to cycling; the heat of southern Italy had inevitably come as a shock to her unacclimatised English system; and she was quite definitely plump. But she braved the Alban Hills and the Apennines, as I had braved the Alps, with the same hope and considerably better humour. Her disposition is sunnier than mine. As we crossed southern Italy, I was the one sitting quietly on the fences at the summits, while Katherine was the cheerful, red-faced struggler, toiling upwards and shedding weight so fast that the process was almost visible. She lost a stone in our three weeks, to her great satisfaction.

Once over the Alban Hills, the Via Appia Antica stretched out flat and straight between umbrella pines and oleanders all the way to the sea at Terracina. Tiny canals with their chorus of frogs criss-crossed rich agricultural land which was once the notorious Pontine Marshes. The draining of these marshes was one of Mussolini's proudest achievements, commemorated in grandiloquent terms in the square of Pontina, a 1930s New Town. There, a plaque on the town hall extolled 'the victory of Fascist Italy over the rebellious, deadly marshes, while the Legions of Rome, supported by the indomitable will of the Italian people, conquer for their native land, with spade, plough and pickaxe, a new province in the African Continent.' Stirring words for the shameful Ethiopian débâcle.

It was mid-July and a seaside weekend. In Terracina we were taken for Germans by the girl in the Tourist Office and booked into the last vacant room in town – in a pension run by Germans exclusively for Germans. The German landlady was not fooled but it was late evening and she let us stay. Formia was even more crowded. There nothing was available except the camping site, but the warmth of our welcome by the Italian holiday-makers made up for a rather chilly night in the sea air.

As soon as we arrived, a little boy was sent over by his mother with two canvas chairs, and when I started to write my notes, I was invited to use a neighbour's table. I sweetened my trainers by hobbling over the stones to dip them in the bay, but the clinging seaweed and plastic bags made for unpleasant bathing and my swim was a brief one. Katherine had no sleeping-bag, but she did have a tiny travelling kettle. Unable to sleep for the cold, she got up in the chilly hour before dawn and made us delicious hot coffee.

We left the sea at Formia to begin my second crossing of the Apennines. The Sunday morning traffic down to the coast was three abreast as far inland as Capua, where we were pleased to abandon the hot, dusty, fume-laden Via Appia for the hotel swimming pool. We passed a huge British war cemetery at Minturno and found a Norman fort in Capua, two reminders of the continuing strategic importance of our road.

The modern city of Capua, Santa Maria Vetere Capua (Roman Capua) and Caserta, the regional capital, all run together into one great conurbation. Capua was a monumental city with an air of neglect, where we watched an evening procession in honour of Santa Anna. The city band and the local dignitaries preceded the statue of the Saint, held aloft in all her finery cradling a tiny dolly Virgin in a glittering matinee coat and dainty baby shoes, lovingly knitted and threaded with ribbon. We entered S.M. Vetere Capua through a Roman arch with graffiti demanding the return of the Bourbons. The older Capua was, to our surprise, much livelier and better maintained, possibly because it was still a major garrison town. The Roman garrisons worshipped at the Temple of Mithras, the soldiers' god. We tracked down their Mithraeum to a hut in an alleyway, only to find that admission was by tickets to be purchased at the amphitheatre, which we had just visited at the other end of town. A typical tourist frustration. The custodian of the Mithraeum was the old lady in black who happened to live next door. I asked her what was in the temple. With supreme indifference she shrugged, turned down her mouth at the corners and said, 'Roba antica.' The 'old stuff' was evidently an altar with a channel for the sacrificial blood of the cockerel so we willingly forwent crossing the town twice in the heat of the morning in order to gain admission.

July 1987 was exceptionally hot in the southern Mediterranean. Every day the newspapers carried reports of old people and babies dying of heat as the thermometers soared to 111°F in southern Italy and 115°F in Greece. It was no weather for visiting the exuberant Bourbon palace at Caserta where Versailles, Tivoli and Chatsworth were all rolled into one gigantic landscaped park and where Adam, Fragonard and the Dresden China factories competed for precedence in style. The palace itself, with its marble floors, was enjoyably cool but the huge, open, treeless lawns were wholly inappropriate to the climate and wildly expensive to trim, water and keep green. Completed in 1845, the palace throne room was ready just in time to witness the downfall of the Bourbons.

We now entered ancient Samnite territory and toiled up a huge hill to Forchia (the Caudine Forks) where, in 321 BC, the Romans suffered one of the major defeats of their expansion south. The mountains were veiled in a heat haze but the Samnite trap was clear enough. The Romans learned a hard lesson in military strategy.

Benevento, in the heart of Samnite land, was a vital strategic crossroads. Lying in a valley where many rivers converge, it was the junction town for the Via Appia, the Via Latina and the Via Traiana. It was my crossroads too. Was I really bold enough to continue along the Via Appia Antica, the narrow Statale 7, as it twisted and turned through high, inhospitable mountains, or should I play safe and take the later route across to Brindisi via Canosa and Bari, the route used by modern traffic? After all, Horace, Virgil and Maecenas chose the more comfortable Bari route when they took their famous journey together, so it had classical respectability. My decision was made more difficult because I was no longer alone. On the one hand, the presence of a companion inspired a little confidence; but on the other hand I was worried about leading a friend into harsh, unknown territory where wild boar still roamed, where there might be nowhere safe to spend the nights and where arduous mountain cycling in the exceptional heat might well cause dehydration and sickness. It was one thing to take myself into difficulties but quite another to encourage someone else to take risks. In the end, though, caution and scruples were thrown to the winds. The Appia Antica was the Appia Antica, the Queen of Roads, and I should always be haunted by a sense of failure if I chickened out in Benevento.

The next day's ride to Avellino was so gruelling that I wondered if I had taken the right decision. The roads out of Benevento looked on the map like a tangled nest of worms and we took many wrong turns and backtracks before finally breaking clear at the start of a tremendous climb, just as the sun was reaching its zenith. The mountains were desolate and the one little shop we passed in the early afternoon could supply only cans of warm Fanta and a tin of pineapple. We had to rest for two hours under a tree, then there was another gruelling climb before Avellino. I was too hot and exhausted to eat my dinner that night – a bad sign. The Tourist Office told us there were no hotels between Avellino and Potenza, and Katherine depressed me further with tales of disasters on unsurfaced Italian B-roads. Should we turn back to Benevento and take the easier road after all? We rested a day before deciding. I had my hair cut by a coiffeur rejoicing in the name of Oreste and studied my maps, while Katherine went out to buy a sleeping-bag for our nights in the wilds. We decided to press on and were rewarded with five of the most interesting days of my whole trip.

The last two weeks had been packed with Roman history and I was beginning to wilt at the sight of triumphal arches and strategic crossroads. The simple life of remote mountain Italy would be a welcome change. I could feel the burden of classical antiquity falling from my shoulders and I left Avellino in holiday mood.

The cycling turned out to be much less arduous than we had feared, thanks to those brilliant Roman surveyors. Ascents were carefully gradated and height, once gained, was never lightly lost. It was instructive to see the Roman road winding from pass to pass, circling the valleys at a high altitude just below the summit of the mountains. For the traveller, the Via Appia was strategically safe, the views were spectacular, there was shade for at least half the day and long, long stretches were

blissfully, amazingly flat. What a contrast to the modern autostrada near Potenza! We paused in the shade and looked down
on it from our 3,250 ft mountain road. Following the dry bed of
the River Basento, it strode across the empty, treeless valley on
concrete stilts, attacking the hills head-on, then swooping
recklessly down again to the plain, wasting all the good altitude
it had gained. It was an ugly gash across the landscape, hot and
desolate enough for the motorist but impossible for the country
people with their carts, herds and donkeys. We passed them all
up in the mountains, watching their cattle among the oak trees
and driving their beautifully clean pinky-beige pigs along the
road to market. They never saw tourists up there and the
swineherds were as startled as their pigs to meet two foreign
ladies pedalling along, but we got a kindly 'Buon giorn' in the
local dialect which swallows its final vowels.

It was volcanic country, with fertile valleys where the craters
had been, and craggy, wooded slopes. In fact, the whole area
round Potenza had been devastated by the major earthquake of
1980 and was still struggling to recover. Potenza itself, built like
a modest La Paz across the floor of a giant crater, still had the air
of a ghost town, crumbling buildings boarded up and streets of
an evening deserted and sinister. In the small towns and villages
round about, many families were still living in prefabricated
huts or half-finished houses, and rubble lay everywhere. It was
hardly surprising that there were no hotels.

We arrived in Lioni late in the afternoon and cycled through a
scene of devastation still, seven years on, like a town in the blitz.
We bought a cold drink and chatted to the old lady in the corner
shop. Her home had been totally destroyed, so now she slept in
the back of her shop. And she confirmed what I had heard from
friends in Rome – that corruption was rife in the construction
industry and rebuilding had come to a virtual standstill. A price
would be quoted initially for the building of a house and work
would begin. But builders, joiners, electricians, plumbers were
all in short supply and the contractors could raise their prices as
high as they chose. So many homeless people put all their
savings into having a new house built only to find that costs rose
exorbitantly in the course of construction and that they ran out
of cash before the work was finished, left penniless and still

without a home. Hence the thousands of half-finished houses lying abandoned throughout the region.

I asked the old lady if she was not afraid to go on living in an earthquake zone. 'No,' she said, with great serenity. 'An earthquake is God's work. It happens. Then we all pick ourselves up again and life goes on. It's the Red Brigade that frighten me – those villains, bombing and shooting innocent people. You be careful, alone on your bicycles. The Red Brigade are everywhere.' From what I had seen and heard, it seemed that the Mafia or Camorra were more to be feared in those parts than political extremists, but we promised to take care. She solved our accommodation problem by directing us out of town, up an almost vertical hill, to a restaurant called 'Il Fantastico'. The proprietors had a couple of spare rooms but even if those happened to be taken, they would certainly let us sleep in their garden – and they had an Alsatian to protect us from the Red Brigade! In fact, the Fantastico had two small dormitories, one occupied by a team of building workers and the other vacant, so we were in luck.

From Lioni we climbed up to Teora, where the devastation was even more terrible, then cycled along a ridge between two spectacular valleys with a breeze behind us and a good flat road. Another climb to Sant'Andrea di Conza and yet another to Pescopagano brought us to an elegant promenade looking down over the most stunning view of woods and mountains imaginable. It must have been a summer resort before the earthquake. We had lunch in its newly rebuilt restaurant. The proprietor and his family had been living in a caravan and had just moved into their new premises, so they kindly offered us the caravan, free of charge, for the night and even got up early on Sunday morning to make sure we had a good cup of coffee before we set out to climb the pass above Pescopagano. At 3,600 ft it was the highest point between Avellino and Potenza. Fortunately, though the Via Appia was at its steepest here, it skirted most of the little mediaeval towns, perched on their pinnacles like eagles' eyries; they bristled with the battlements that Rome was too strong to need. In the late afternoon, we hurtled down the side of the crater into Potenza, windswept, sunburnt and exhausted after 43 miles of intimidating mountain road but elated with our success. We still had the pass at Valico Tre Cancelli (3,478 ft) to conquer and another 70 miles of mountain before we reached the comparative flatness of Matera, but we had crossed the widest, highest and least inhabited range. We had broken the back of the Apennines.

Looking back on our doubts and fears in Avellino, we saw how mistaken we had been. The road surface had in fact been excellent throughout and accommodation had come to us easily. We felt rather ashamed that we had so badly underestimated the kindness of the people on whom we were to depend. As I was to find throughout the world, it was the people who had the least who were the most willing to share what little they had. Earthquake victims, who have survived for months without a home, are the first to appreciate the value of a night's shelter and will never turn a traveller away.

Grassano, on the way to Matera, even had a small hotel. Two roadworkers in their little Vespa van guided us there through the narrow cobbled streets, since we found their directions too complicated. Foreign visitors were such a rarity in Grassano that I had to help the hotel complete all the necessary forms. I realised then how badly designed was the smart British passport in which I had always taken such pride. Details of bearer were handwritten in cursive script; months were given in words, not in internationally recognisable numbers, and abbreviations added to the problems; profession appeared at the top of the page, where the name might reasonably be expected; and who on earth chose Peterborough as a place of issue? Its spelling and pronunciation defeated hoteliers and passport officials in every country round the globe. No wonder our landlady found it all a bit daunting – and a bit of a joke.

We spent two days in Matera. I needed to get a pannier repaired. What would certainly have caused problems in northern Europe was simplicity itself here. I was directed by a cobbler to a man in a back street who sold hand-made luggage. Within the day, he had produced a beautifully crafted steel replacement for the plastic clip which had snapped. Ten thousand miles later, when I got back to London, that clip still gleamed in the sun and was the strongest, neatest part of my travelling gear.

Matera was an amazing place, a modern town surrounding a crater riddled with troglodyte dwellings. The houses of the upper town had pretty ironwork balconies and the grandiose public buildings were more reminiscent of Spain than of Italy, as was the preoccupation with death in the ornate Baroque churches. One had a carved doorway where rows of horizontal femurs alternated in a macabre pattern with grinning skulls, each one wearing a crown or a mitre. Memento mori. Another had paintings of the martyrs too gruesome to contemplate. Undeterred by their surroundings, two stalwart ladies were giving a spirited four-handed rendering of a Liszt Hungarian Rhapsody on the church piano, but I took one look at the screaming mouth and gory wound of St Agatha, whose left breast had just been cut off with shears and deposited in a bowl, and fled into the sunlight. Matera was a cheerful place for all that and we enjoyed our dinners on a terrace overlooking the subtly floodlit troglodyte town. Then it was downhill all the way to Taranto, leaving the oaks of the mountains behind us and pedalling past vineyards, citrus groves and ancient, gnarled olive trees.

Taranto was once a powerful Greek colony with a unique combination of natural resources. Its harbour, one of the largest and most sheltered in Italy, was especially valuable as it offered the only safe mooring of any size along an inhospitable coast. There was seafood in abundance; the richest murex-beds in the Mediterranean and the wool from the hinterland combined to make it a centre for fine textiles; and the local clay was ideal for the fashionable ceramics which were produced to Greek designs. The city was a rich prize, fought over and occupied by Romans, Phoenicians, Byzantines, Normans, Swabians, Angevins and Aragonese. Now the Republic of Italy used it as a naval base, its glorious ancestry visible only in the remarkably elegant and sumptuous displays in the National Museum.

As far as I was concerned, Taranto disgraced itself. We were charged 10,000 lire each to leave our bicycles in a garage overnight, almost as much as we had paid for our own accommodation south of Rome. It was the only place in the world where my bicycle was not accommodated free of charge. My other Taranto misfortune only came to light the next morning. It had been a hot, sultry evening. Service at the fish restaurant on the seafront had been slow and unwilling, and the white wine had been ice cold, dry and utterly delicious. Recklessly, we tossed it back and ordered a second carafe. The road to Brindisi was flat and ran due east out of Taranto into the morning sun. The asphalt gleamed with a harsh, reflected glare. I wore my sunglasses and pulled the peak of my cycling cap as far down over my eyes as safety allowed but there was no escaping the painful stabbing of the light, and my head crashed dully in time with the pedals. It was a long morning.

After an overnight stop at Mesagne, just ten miles out of Brindisi, we cycled at last into the city, the Roman gateway to the East. We pedalled in under Charles V's bastion, through the Porta Mesagna, and took photographs of each other standing at the foot of the column marking the end of the Via Appia. Gibbon is said to have spent twelve days travelling the road from Rome to Brindisi. Our journey had taken eighteen days, which we thought not too bad, considering that we had done it on bicycles, inspected all the Roman antiquities en route and crossed the Apennines in record-breaking heat. We had been cheered on our way by the roadside stones marking every kilometre, and even more by the tiny stone markers dividing each kilometre into ten. On slow, painful ascents, when even one-tenth of a kilometre seemed an eternity of leg-breaking toil, those little stones with their Roman numerals had been eagerly awaited. Only on the miserable journey from Taranto to Brindisi did they let us down. The road had been resurfaced and the workmen who had replaced the markers obviously had no idea of Roman numerals. The 100-metre stones had been stuck back higgledy-piggledy – a great pity, when they had marched in such orderly Roman fashion all the way from their capital!

In Brindisi, I collected a wonderful heap of letters from the Poste Restante and spent the afternoon reading and re-reading all the news from home. We booked our tickets on the overnight ferry to Igoumenitsa, watched a wedding, sent a clutch of exuberant postcards to friends and began to study the maps of Country Number Five. 'Don't go to Greece,' said the lugubrious waiter in the café. 'They're dying of heat there – and they'll steal your bicycles.'

6

Into Greece

From the dark barriers of that rugged clime,
Ev'n to the centre of Illyria's vales,
Childe Harold pass'd o'er many a mount
    sublime,
Through lands scarce noticed in historic tales;
Yet in famed Attica such lovely dales
Are rarely seen; nor can fair Tempe boast
A charm they know not.

(Lord Byron)

THE next official road on my itinerary was the Via Egnatia,
laid in 130 BC to take the Romans east. Unusually, it was
named, not after its builder, but after the city of Egnatia, which
lay opposite on the Appulian coast. The road began at the port
of Durres (Dyrrachium) and ran across modern Albania, so
that its first section was out of bounds: the Albanians were
beginning to open up to organised tours, but lone cyclists had
no chance of a visa. Katherine and I had to land instead at
Igoumenitsa and travel north-east over the Pindos Mountains
to join the Via Egnatia where it emerged from Yugoslavia.

The ferry-boat was filled to bursting. Hordes of students with
backpacks doing the mandatory Grand Tour on their Inter-
Rail cards got off the boat at Corfu. Unlike the students of the
'sixties and 'seventies, they were courteous and quiet. Most were
travelling in pairs – a robust, well-scrubbed, well-organised girl

leading a frail, timid youth with a straggly blond beard. I often watched these couples in restaurants and bus stations. As the girls dealt with the waiter or bought the tickets, I had the impression that Alice was taking Christopher Robin off on his holidays, and I wondered when and how these anxious, bearded boys turned into thrusting European executives.

We wove our way ashore between lines of new cars with German number-plates, driven proudly by Greek migrant workers. Their roof-racks groaned with consumer durables and lavish gifts for their families, who were there on the quayside to give them a rapturous, tearful welcome. A Ford with a Bunny Club sticker and an AEG washing machine were the reward for all those cold, lonely months in Düsseldorf or Frankfurt.

After the shadeless glare of Brindisi, we were struck by the green of Greece. Cafés were groups of white plastic tables and chairs under a canopy of vines and the road was lined with maples, olives, oaks, poplars, ilex, cypress and Judas trees. We were in Epirus, a wild, craggy, unexplored strip of land, cut off from the rest of Greece by the Pindos Mountains on the east and further isolated by the sea to the west and Albania to the north. Although assigned to Greece by the Congress of Berlin in 1878, Epirus was not wrested from Turkey until 1913, during the Second Balkan War, and assimilation had been slow. The only tourists were Italians, rushing through in cars on their way to the better-known parts of Greece. Yet this region had been renowned since antiquity for its beauty, its hospitality and its fierce independence of spirit. It was country dear to Byron, who considered it the most spectacular part of Greece, far surpassing Athens, Delphi and Parnassus in grandeur.

The air was less humid than in Italy, but the sun was stronger and the road rose dramatically from the sea. It was a day for taking things slowly. Roadside shrines guarded the nastiest corners and the most vertiginous drops, ranging in construction from miniature Byzantine cathedrals to rickety glass-fronted boxes with weather-beaten icons, rusty lamps and Pepsi Cola bottles for the oil. The favourite saint seemed to be St George of Ioannina, in a little white evzone kilt and pom-pom shoes.

There were no hotels and it was in Epirus that I began to develop my technique for finding accommodation. It would be rude, and almost certainly unproductive, to barge into a village and ask baldly for hospitality. The first essential was to establish a relationship with the local people, and what better way, on a hot, dusty afternoon, than to join them in the shade of the vines in the village café? In every country I crossed, natural curiosity soon overcame reserve and my bicycle provided the perfect introductory topic. Even where we had no language in common, mime and a list of place-names got the meaning across. After a while, someone was bound to offer a second cup of tea or another cold drink and the atmosphere noticeably mellowed. At that point I would ask innocently if there was a hotel or guest house where I could spend the night, knowing full well that the village could never run to such a luxury. Animated conversation would ensue and I would soon be escorted by a group of men to my accommodation. This approach not only secured me a bed; it ensured my safety. Half the village was involved in the process and by nightfall the entire population would know who I was, what I was doing and where I was staying. I was the guest of the village and would be protected. If I stayed in a private house and my hostess was poor, I would offer payment and it would occasionally be accepted. More often it would be refused and then I would leave a few notes on the kitchen table, pointing to the children and trying to indicate that the money was to meet their needs. On that basis it was welcome, as was a box of sweets or cakes from the village shop.

Our first night in Greece was spent in the spare room of an old lady's house in Nereida. The second night, in Soulopoulo, the owner of the village restaurant built a barricade of tables and beer-crates across the end of his terrace and we were able to lay down our mats and sleeping-bags out of view of the passing traffic. He and his family slept on the restaurant floor near at hand, in case of emergency.

I nearly lost my baggage twice in Soulopoulo. In the heat of the afternoon, we leaned our bicycles against the trees down by the stream and rested on the opposite bank, where the grass was lusher. I was awoken from a half-sleep by the tinkle of bells and saw a herd of goats taking an active interest in my panniers. I splashed in panic across the stream, waving my arms and

shouting, just in time to rescue my sleeping-mat and the pannier straps from their greedy jaws. Next morning the restaurateur's young labrador rushed to our haven behind the beer-
crates as soon as he was unchained from his kennel. A down
sleeping-bag was the most exciting plaything he had ever met.
He pounced on it, shook it, rolled in it and would have made off
with it had he not entangled his large, clumsy puppy's feet in
the zip. Thwarted over the sleeping-bag, he then made a dive at
my trainers, tossed them in the air by the laces and ran away
with them. A person with such exciting possessions could have
been his friend for life. He followed me on my morning expedition into the privacy of the bushes, where he twice knocked me
off balance by trying to sit on my lap, then he followed our
bicycles for miles up the road, undeterred by angry words and
smacks on the nose, until we were obliged to take him back to
his owner and ask for him to be tied up. He watched us set off
again, brown eyes peering out from his kennel with sad
devotion.

Ioannina, the capital of Epirus, provided our first good hotel
and our first shower for four nights. We took a short holiday
there, visiting the monasteries on Lake Pambotis – all crumbling and vacant, but tranquil among the trees. Ioannina was
conquered by Murad II in 1431 and rose to its greatest heights
under Ali Pasha, a man who knew his own mind. Though he
was nominally subservient to the Sultan, Istanbul was a long
way away and Ali Pasha pursued his own foreign policy, siding
with Napoleon in 1797 and forming his own alliance with
Britain in 1817. The Sultan eventually lost patience with this
independent spirit and had him executed in 1822. The old
Turkish quarter still endures, spilling down to the lake in a
maze of crooked streets and tiny shops. On our last day in
Ioannina we took a taxi out to consult the oracle at Dodona,
possibly the oldest and certainly one of the most venerated
sanctuaries in Greece, where Zeus prophesied to his believers
in the rustle of the oak leaves. The omens there were favourable, so we set off next day to scale the formidable Pindos
Mountains, cycling out of Ioannina in the grey light of dawn
and startling two sleepy storks in their nest on top of a telegraph
pole. Skirting Lake Pambotis, we soon left the tobacco and

cornfields far below as we climbed, sometimes very steeply, for over 35 miles along narrow shelves cut out of the mountainside. The scenery was spectacular but as I have no head for heights, it was entirely wasted on me: I couldn't look down and only learned what I had missed a year later, when Katherine showed me her slides. By late morning, dizzy with the climb, the strong sun and the scent of pines, we had reached the little town of Metsovo, clinging to almost vertical ground falling away from our road. We booked in at the first and highest pension and looked down from our window onto the steeply terraced village, where the local woollen rugs and colourful embroidery hung outside the shops to tempt the tourists – mostly Greeks escaping the heat of the plains.

Metsovo lay at 3,800 ft and we had another stiff climb up to the Katara Pass, at 5,545 ft the only route through the Pindos Mountains from Epirus to Thessaly. It was here that the Greek army repulsed the crack Italian Alpina Julia Division in the winter of 1940, a feat commemorated in small cafés throughout northern Greece. A popular poster shows the Greek troops hauling their artillery by man- and mule-power through snowdrifts and a raging blizzard up to the summit of the pass. It was noticeable that the Epirots maintained their end of the road to a much higher standard than the Thessalians. For the Epirots, it was their lifeline, their only overland connection with the rest of Greece; for the Thessalians, who naturally looked towards Thessaloniki and Athens, the road led only to wild Epirus. A tunnel is now under construction to ensure that the route remains open throughout the year.

From the Katara Pass, we swooped down to the plains of Thessaly, where the monasteries of Meteora looked down from their strange rock towers onto the rich fields near Kalambaka. The first monastic communities settled there in the early fourteenth century and provided a refuge throughout the Turkish occupation. Once thirteen major monasteries and over twenty minor settlements crowned the peaks of this geological oddity. Access was only by basket or vertiginous ladders until steps were cut out of the rock in the 1920s on the orders of Bishop Polykarp of Trikkala. Knowing my vertigo of old, I had to be content with viewing the monasteries from ground level. I

might just have managed to get up the narrow rock steps to St
Nicholas, but that would have left me on the monks' hands as I
should never have got down them again.

Our one night in Thessaly was spent under giant plane trees
behind a small family restaurant on the road to Grevina. Three
goats, a donkey, chickens and a dog, all fortunately enclosed,
shared the little grove with us. The grandfather, with his fine
face and splendid Balkan moustache, took the goats out to graze
in the early evening; and when we returned to our sleeping-bags
after our dinner of souvlaki and retsina, we found an ice-cold
watermelon with its peel already slit, a gift from the grandmother. There was a brilliant full moon in the cloudless sky. I
lay under the rustling trees and wondered what I had done to
deserve such good fortune.

The road from Katara and the corner of Thessaly had been
easy going. Soon we were back in the mountains again, with a
stiff ten-mile climb over a pass into Macedonia; the plain of
Thessaly below and the spectacular gorge of the Venetikos river
gave us a memorable morning's cycling. In Grevina, Katherine
and her bicycle boarded the bus for Thessaloniki, and home.

So far I had had quite a sociable trip, with companions for
two legs of the journey and friends to visit en route. Now I was
alone, with no prospect of company until I reached Ankara, and
I wondered how I should cope with the solitude. The journey
would be an exploration of my own resources as much as a look
at the world. That afternoon in Grevina I sat writing my notes
in a quiet bedroom where no one was rustling plastic bags or
running taps. I enjoyed company, especially in the evenings
over dinner, but I was to find that, for me, solitary travel also
had its pleasures.

Grevina, Kozani, Ptolemaida were all prosperous modern
towns where creperies and cocktail bars had taken the place of
the old coffee-houses. 'Snoopy's Dreams', 'Café Fiorino' and
'Maxim's' spread out their elegant white tables and chairs under
the shady trees, and the squares were lit up and thronged late
into the night with strolling friends and families and children
racing round on tricycles. Since my last visit to provincial
Greece, 'designer casuals' had transformed the population.
Gone were the ill-fitting tweeds which used to make the Greeks

look like western Europe's poor relations. Track suits and
T-shirts announced 'Life's a Beach in Florida'; bank clerks had
abandoned their ill-cut suits in favour of crisp cotton shirts and
slacks; and even the old ladies in black were venturing into dark
brown with microscopic patterns in green or beige. The region
prospered on its lignite mines and the expensive shops did good
business.

The Macedonians were proud of their military past. Statues
of generals and war heroes with impressive moustaches gazed
down on every public square, and Kozani, the barracks town of
the Macedonian Regiment, had a decidedly swashbuckling air.
Old Comrades' Clubs abounded and I was pleased to see that
they flew the Union Jack and the Tricolour alongside the Greek
flag. Old wartime friends were not forgotten.

Out of Kozani, I met the north wind which was to plague me
for the rest of my journey across Greece. It blew the dust from
the quarries and mines into my face as I pedalled across a dreary
plain, almost blinding me to the setting moon on my left and the
rising sun on my right. At Ptolemaida I stopped for a coffee and
a pastry at a café flying the Union Jack, where the young waiter
was full of admiration and keen to practise his English. 'What a
wonderful thing! To cycle to Greece at *your* age!' he exclaimed.
'In Greece the women stay at home. They do not make sport.'
His café, like many in Macedonia, had a mouth-watering array
of French patisserie, one of the legacies of the old alliance.

It was an exciting morning for me, as I was nearing the Via
Egnatia. A few miles uphill from the plain and I joined it at the
little village of Vevi. I should have liked to spend the night there,
as I was tired after my battle with the north wind, but the café in
the square was not the village social centre. It was patronised by
long-distance truck-drivers and no one could help me with
accommodation. Instead, one of the drivers encouraged me to go
on, explaining that it would be hard work for the first eight miles
up to the Kelli Pass (3,150 ft) but that after that it was all
downhill. 'Then you sit on your bicycle and you tell it to go. And
it goes – all the way down to Thessaloniki.' He told me there were
plenty of hotels in Arnissa on Lake Vegoritida and made it sound
like a pleasant holiday resort. So I took heart, pointed my bicycle
to the east and set out under the midday sun.

I was glad to be told the lie of the land. My Michelin road map was excellent on routes and distances but sparing on topographical information. I climbed up through the most desolate, barren, stony landscape I had ever seen, where not even a goat could find sustenance, keeping myself going by reading the miles on my odometer, converting them in my head to kilometres, calculating the proportion of the climb I had already covered and the proportion I had left in fractions and decimals – anything to keep my mind occupied through this weary, windswept desert upland. Walking or cycling, the climb was back-breaking and I should have despaired had I not known the exact length of the ordeal.

After nearly two hours' toil I reached the Kelli Pass. It was more an open road across the summit of a rising desert plain than a path through the mountains, and it was exposed to the full intensity of sun and wind. Scattered beside the road were the ruins of gun emplacements and dug-outs, left as reminders of the day in August 1916 when a Bulgarian offensive was beaten off by the Macedonians with the help of their French and Serbian allies.

I kept criss-crossing the railway, which took a lower, shorter route from Kozani to Arnissa, while the road ran over the mountains. Perhaps the lowlands with their lakes were once malarial, forcing the Romans to take the Via Egnatia across the healthier heights. The railway was built by the Allies in the First World War and played a key role in the Second, when Amindeo Station was used as the railhead to supply the Greek forces during the Italian invasion of 1940. Now it had lost its strategic importance and lay derelict in stretches. Traffic had returned to the Roman road.

The road-surface down to Lake Vegoritida was so bad that I had to keep my eyes on the potholes. To see anything of the pine forests and the blue waters below, I had to dismount at intervals, take a good look at the scenery, then mount again and once more glue my eyes to the intermittent tarmac. At lake level the embankment had collapsed in places, leaving gaping chasms skirted by sandy tracks to landward, which were unmanageable on my narrow touring tyres. When I finally arrived in Arnissa, it was not at all the elegant resort I had been led to expect. The

lorry-driver's 'lots of hotels' turned out to be one small establishment near the railway station – but what an establishment!

It was called 'The Great Greece' and its exterior plasterwork
had once been white with blue-painted doors and window-
frames, the colours of the Greek flag. And indeed a gigantic flag
was draped around a staff so huge that it was propped diagonally across the upstairs landing, making it almost impossible
to reach the lavatory. Altogether, I had no doubt that I was in
the home of a patriot.

The owner was aged, but very upright, with a splendid
Macedonian moustache. He and his wife lived on the dingy
ground floor, which did double duty as the station café. As a
hotel guest, I went up the outside steps to one of the four
bedrooms on the first floor and my bicycle was housed in the
wood-shed. The old man wheeled it in for me, leaned it gently
against a pile of logs, put his finger to his lips and whispered
'Ipno' (sleep). The walls of my bedroom were bright blue with a
white ceiling and white woodwork, the iron bedstead and
counterpane were white and so was the washbasin (waist-high,
with a shoulder-high cold tap and a mirror in which I could just
see my forehead and eyes if I stood on tiptoe – and I must be a
good foot taller than most Greeks).

The next morning my host offered me coffee and asked me if
I would kindly fill in the register and official form for him: the
information in my passport, in Roman script, was beyond him.
As I drank my coffee, I pointed to the inevitable poster on the
wall and said 'Katara.' He was thrilled that I had cycled over the
pass and knew about the battle; he had fought in it himself.
Over cup after cup of coffee, he described the campaign with
glowing animation, then went on to his father's exploits at
Kelli. For the fighting in Arnissa he got paper and pencil to map
out the disposition of the troops, the Greek artillery drawn up
on one side of the church and the Bulgars on the other. How I
wished I could speak better modern Greek! However, I was
able to follow the drift of the narrative and occasionally make a
suitable remark, thanks to my years of Homer and the battles of
ancient Greece. Military vocabulary has not changed very
much over the centuries. It was late morning by the time I left
the hotel. As the old soldier helped me load my bicycle and

came with his wife to the gate to wave me off, I felt, perhaps romantically, that I had met the epitome of all the traditional Macedonian virtues: pride and fierce war-like spirit tempered with gentleness, kindness and loyalty to friends.

The Via Egnatia showed little sign of its Roman past. Too many armies had marched, fought, sacked and pillaged along its route. 'Poli, poli polemo' (Much, much war), to quote the old soldier. Now it was the heavy trucks from Yugoslavia which roared along its rough surface, scattering grit and pebbles in their wake. Even major towns like Edessa had few remains to delay a Classicist, so I cruised on down through miles and miles of orchards, heady with the scent of ripe peaches. I stopped and bought two from a roadside vendor reclining in a deck-chair with a sandwich in one hand and one leg in a plaster cast propped up on his cart. He obviously thought I was out of my mind to stop and *buy* fruit, when I could have reached up from my bicycle anywhere along the road and helped myself. I had never eaten such delicious peaches. There were acres, too, of apricots, plums, grapes, apples and pears. I realised then why fruit salad is called 'Macedoine de fruits'.

I liked Macedonia and the Macedonians. Even alone in the desolate central mountains I had never once doubted my safety. I had felt welcome and protected. Near Nea Kalkidon a silent shepherd waved his crook in greeting and he and his dog watched me safely up the road, until I turned off to Pella, speeding to my rendezvous with the most famous of all the Macedonians.

7

In Pursuit of Alexander

Linger not on the way, stray not from your aim.
Always strive, always move on, always advance.

(St Augustine)

ALEXANDER was 22 when he set off with his Companions one spring morning in 334 BC to teach the Persians a lesson. He was already a successful general, King of Macedonia and Commander-in-Chief of the Corinthian League. Reams have been written about his motives for the task which was to occupy him until his early death, in Nebuchadrezzar's palace in Babylon, on 13 June 323. His determination to punish the Persians for having dared to invade Greece was only a part of a complex whole. Standing on his ruined acropolis in Pella that summer dawn, I felt his restlessness of spirit. A rough, invigorating wind swept over the hill from the north and the fertile plains of Macedonia spread out to the horizon. Beyond them lay the Persian Empire and the East. Greece was too small and too tame for Alexander. He needed adventure, danger. He needed to travel the known world – and then to find out what lay beyond it.

The jumble of stones, all that remained of Archelaos' splendid palace, and the archaeologists' tin hut gave little fuel to the imagination but I was alone on the remote hilltop in the morning sun, with a carpet of tiny blue flowers at my feet and the Via Egnatia crossing the valley below. I had my bicycle and I was going to ride with Alexander and his young Companions to the

furthest point of their great journey, to the east of Pakistan. I
saw them all in my mind's eye and shared their elation as we
dashed down from the citadel. I scarcely noticed the lorries on
the busy road into Thessaloniki. My dawn expedition to Pella
had been one of life's great experiences. 'O frabjous day, kaloo
kalay!' I wrote in my diary.

Thessaloniki, though a bustling modern port, is a place at
ease with its history. The Via Egnatia is the main shopping
street and is still called by its Roman name. It carries the
rush-hour traffic along beside great Byzantine churches, and
the Arch of Galerius still presides over its eastern end. A huge,
handsome statue of Alexander the Great, in romantic pose on
his prancing steed, points out to sea from the esplanade, and the
Archaeological Museum houses a stunning collection of
Macedonian treasures, including the contents of the tomb of
Philip II, Alexander's father. A gold chest holds his touchingly
small skeleton. Beside his skull lies a gold coronet in an exquisite oak leaf and acorn design and the lid of the massive gold
chest with its lion's feet bears the Star of Macedon. Diadems,
golden wreaths of myrtle, jewellery, gold and ivory armour, all
of the most delicate workmanship, mingle with more homely
grave objects, yet even these are elegant in their simplicity. I
was particularly charmed by two ivory bedknobs, carved in the
miniature likenesses of Philip and of Alexander. Here were
amazing wealth and sumptuousness held in check by the innate
fine taste of the Classical Greek tradition. My eyes popped. In
all my years of museum-haunting, I had never seen such a
dazzling display.

I spent three days in Thessaloniki, drinking hot coffee in the
open-air cafés beside the sea and enjoying proper continental
breakfasts – simple requirements which are very hard to satisfy
in Greece. I answered the letters which were waiting for me in
the Poste Restante and gave my dusty bicycle a good wash down
in the street outside my hotel, watched in the lazy afternoon
hours by half the men of Thessaloniki.

Although my general rule in Europe was to limit sightseeing
to Classical Rome and Alexander, I did make an exception in
Thessaloniki. I had waited for years to see the city's great
Byzantine churches and there they were, all lined up along the

Via Egnatia. The church I most wanted to visit, Agios Giorgos, a Roman domed rotunda converted into a church with fifth-century mosaics, then into a mosque, then back again into a church, was naturally encased in scaffolding and closed to the public. The girl in the postcard shop said it had been in that state for eight years. But I enjoyed Agia Sophia, with its unusual capitals of windswept acanthus leaves (very appropriate in Macedonia) and learned from an icon of the saint with three little girls that her daughters were Faith, Hope and Charity. The church of Thessaloniki's greatest saint, Demetrios, was flying the Greek flag and a standard with the golden eagle of Byzantium. It was clearly an important Church occasion, for a black limousine with fancy gold-embossed number-plates and an eagle pennant was parked outside. The verger told me with considerable satisfaction that it was 'the despotic motorcar'. Crowds were pouring out from morning Communion, casually chewing great hunks of white bread or wrapping them in tissues to take home.

To my relief, I managed to find the local Sunday morning duty chemist. An old cartilage injury in my left knee had started to play up on the Kelli Pass. Of all the team games I have played and hated, hockey on cold winter afternoons is without doubt the most loathsome. I damaged the cartilage when I skidded on the icy turf, keeping goal in my last ever compulsory school match at the age of eighteen. If only I had damaged it years before – I could have limped and got off games for the rest of my school career. Now, in pessimistic mood, I feared that the hated hockey was about to shatter all my plans. I hobbled into the shop.

'Could you give me something to rub on my knee, please?'

'What's the problem?'

'It's rather stiff and painful.'

'Have you been doing anything special to cause the pain?'

'I've just cycled from London.'

The chemist roared with laughter. 'If I tried to cycle from London, I should be *dead* before I got to Dover. And you worry about an aching knee!'

That put everything into perspective. We laughed and the gloom was dispelled. He sold me a tube of gel, which felt ice-cold and very soothing. After three days' treatment and a rest from cycling my knee was as good as ever.

On my last evening in Thessaloniki I treated myself to a fish dinner in a good restaurant, where the proprietor offered me brandy with my coffee and tried to make an assignation. He was my fourth suitor that day. As the reaction of most Greeks to my trip was to ask my age and then express astonishment that a person of such advanced years could still ride a bicycle, my successes in Thessaloniki worked wonders for my morale.

I was keen to be off on the trail of Alexander and made an early morning start eastwards along the promenade. There I had my first puncture and felt that fortune had smiled on me. It could have happened in the wilds of central Macedonia. Instead, it happened in the middle of Thessaloniki, just round the corner from a cycle shop. Twenty minutes later, I was on the road again with a new rear inner tube.

I took a last look at Alexander's statue before I left, and climbed northwards over the encircling mountains. Looking down on its superb situation, I could see why Thessaloniki, named after Alexander's sister, had been the capital of Roman Macedonia, second city in Justinian's great Empire and the capital of the Latin state of Thessaloniki. It stood at the Balkan crossroads where the Vardar river from the north-west met the Via Egnatia at a safe anchorage.

It was perfect cycling weather, sunny and breezy. The mountains of Chalcidice towered to my right; on my left lay the blue waters and sandy beaches of Lakes Koronia and Volvi. Both were completely still, with not a boat or bather in sight. After the lakes I climbed to a thickly wooded pass where the remains of a fortress guarded the narrowest point, then sped downhill to reach the sea again on the Gulf of Strymon. I passed through Apollonia, one of the original stations on the Via Egnatia, then on to Asprovalta, where the coast was at its loveliest. Here I was in tourist land again. Large lobster-coloured Germans stalked around in shorts and swimsuits, expecting all the Greeks to speak German to them – which they did. I fell for Camping Achilles, where the flags of the nations fluttered gaily over the swimming pool and smart restaurants, the Union Jack in pride of place beside the Greek flag. I was more patriotic than I had realised. The showers and toilet facilities in the camp were of good hotel standard, all marble and cream tiles. I disturbed a tiny lizard there. He was perfectly cream to match the decor and I spotted him only by his shiny black pinhead eyes.

But the night was not a success. I had found my bivvy bag far too hot in Italy and Thessaly but I decided to give it one last chance in the cooler air of northern Greece. I started by putting my mat and sleeping-bag inside it, then zipping it right up over my head, in the approved fashion. It was Goretex and supposed to 'breathe', but claustrophobia and the feeling that I was a kind of defenceless, blind, trussed-up chicken soon made me unzip it down to my neck. That left my face at the mercy of the mosquitos. Dogs barked, noisy campers arrived and left, and the Goretex bivvy and the down sleeping-bag in combination soon built up enough heat to withstand a night on Everest. I tossed, turned, rolled off the mat, tried different combinations of cover, tangled my arms and legs and finally woke up in a terrified sweat from a drowning nightmare. When dawn came, I rolled up the bivvy bag neatly and left it under a tree. My mat was waterproof, so I had no need of an extra groundsheet – all the bivvy bag was good for – and I was pleased to shed an item of luggage. As I cycled wearily on my way, red-rimmed eyes swollen with mosquito bites, I vowed never again to camp from choice.

Alexander did not, of course, follow the Via Egnatia. The Via Egnatia followed Alexander, or rather the ancient, obvious route he took along the coast from Thessaloniki towards Byzantium. Taking the line of least resistance, the modern road more or less coincided with the path of the old, though there were a number of digressions. At the River Strymon, for example, my road crossed a bridge near its mouth instead of turning upstream to make the crossing at Amphipolis, once a Greek and Roman port enriched by the gold of Mount Pangeion. The city's best archaeological find, the huge Lion of Amphipolis, stood sentinel over the modern bridge and I decided that the ruins of the actual site, said to be difficult to identify, were not worth the detour into the north wind.

Mount Pangeion was clothed in walnut and olive trees and masses and masses of vines, an appropriate crop for a mountain of Dionysus. On the lower slopes were tobacco fields, which also seemed to be very suitable; Dionysus would almost certainly have been a chain smoker, had he known about cigarettes. The Via Egnatia used to run to the north of Mount Pangeion, from Amphipolis to Philippi, but there was no existing road along its path. A new treeless highway ran across the flats beside the sea, so I chose the narrower road round the southern slopes of the mountain, following the pre-Roman route taken by Xerxes and his Persians in 480 BC and presumably by Alexander himself.

The Via Egnatia joined the modern road just before Kavala. A stretch of the original paving had been found at the summit of the hill overlooking the city and I was able to walk along beneath the cypress trees over Roman cobblestones. The view over Kavala Bay was spectacular: the island of Thasos lay in the middle distance and I could just make out the hazy bulk of Samothrace. Kavala was ancient Neapolis, the port of Philippi. Alexander's army had marched through it, Brutus' fleet had anchored there and St Paul had disembarked there on his arrival in Europe. More recently, it had been the scene of ex-King Constantine's landing in Greece when he had tried unsuccessfully to reclaim his throne. Its heights were dominated by its Byzantine citadel, supplied with water by the wonderfully preserved aqueduct of Suleiman the Magnificent.

Kavala was a patriotic city. The hill down to the harbour was lined with hoardings, 'Remember Cyprus' their slogan under a map of the island, with the Turkish North covered in dripping blood-red paint. Signposts in red and gold displayed the double-headed Byzantine eagle and gave the distance to Constantinople, not to Istanbul. This was Macedonia at its most imperial and I could well understand why ex-King Constantine had chosen the city as the base for his attempted come-back.

From Kavala I had to make the trip to Philippi. The fate of the Roman Republic had been sealed there in 42 BC, when Octavian and Mark Antony had defeated Brutus and Cassius. By that victory they had gained control of the provinces east of the Adriatic and had consolidated their hold on the Roman world. Brutus and Cassius had both committed suicide and the poet Horace, fighting on the losing side, had dropped his shield and run away. St Paul had preached his first sermon in Europe there and had been thrown into prison. But above all, the city bore the name of Alexander's father and Alexander himself had almost certainly passed that way.

I went along to Kavala Bus Station and was told to take a Drama bus and get off at Krenides for Philippi. Now Greek buses have a speciality: they all carry the name of their garage of origin, not their destination, which is fine if you happen to be travelling to their home base, but confusing if you want to go anywhere else. The buses were lined up in the station yard, every single one of them labelled 'Kavala'. I was led by an inspector to a bus which he assured me was destined for Drama. I was the first passenger and took the front seat. Everyone else who boarded asked me if the bus was going to Drama and I blithely told them it was. The bus was full when we set off. Had I been misinformed, or simply mischievous, 35 passengers would have found themselves travelling in the wrong direction.

It was grey and drizzly at Philippi. My mosquito bites itched and I had a cold. For once, I was glad not to be on my bicycle. I took some photographs of the misty plain and looked at the restored Roman theatre, where summer festivals were held. Most of the acropolis seemed to be buried under a car park, except for a few dreary lumps of Byzantine masonry. I was pleased to visit such an important historical site but even more pleased when my duty was done and I could catch the bus back to Kavala.

Shopping occupied the afternoon. I was horrified to have to pay more than double the English price for slide films. Relative to local prices, each film cost as much as a night's accommodation in one of the best hotels and I could see why there was still a market in Greece for the men with the tripod cameras and black cloths who took pictures of family groups in the parks. Photography was still the hobby of the rich. I also bought a tiny tube of toothpaste. It went against the grain after years of scouring the shops for economy-size bargains, but travel on a bicycle was giving me different priorities. I had started out from London with a special offer tube as large and heavy as a

policeman's truncheon and had hauled it all the way across
Europe, regretting its weight but too mean to throw it away.
Now I was careful to buy my toiletries in small sizes and always
in tubes, not heavy jars. Brand and price had become less
important than packaging.

After Kavala, cycling was much less agreeable. The weather
turned cold and I had to struggle against the north wind with a
runny nose and painful sinuses. I crossed the Nestos river, the
boundary between Macedonia and Thrace. It was such a sad
river in the rain that the notice prohibiting photography seemed
superfluous. Greek Thrace was little more than a narrow corridor between the Communist Balkans and the sea. In Komotini
I looked out of my bedroom window at the Rhodope Mountains; Bulgaria was only fourteen miles away over the ridge, and
the mosque in the foreground was a reminder that Greek
Thrace had a large Turkish minority and that Turkey still laid
claim to the region. Tension was in the air. Army camps were
everywhere and army lorries rumbled back and forth along the
Via Egnatia but there was scarcely any other traffic apart from
the big, inter-continental trucks. One day I counted only ten
cars in all – two Bulgarian, one French and seven German. It
was a region too of intense industrial activity. Quarries,
cigarette factories, agricultural research stations, sugar refineries and large petro-chemical plants were in operation or under
construction, as if the Greeks were trying desperately to boost
the working population of Thrace and so consolidate their
tenuous hold.

I struggled on under a leaden sky. Just as I thought I should
die of boredom on the flat, windswept embankment between
endless, empty marshes, I came to a ridge above Sapai and
found another excavated stretch of the Roman Via Egnatia.
Horace claimed that the Thracians were an intemperate lot, but
they looked very sober to me and they were noticeably less
sophisticated than their neighbours in the Macedonian cities.
Perhaps it was the birth of Orpheus in Thrace which accounted
for their wild reputation.

My last night in Greece was spent in Pheres near the border
with Turkey, where I gave up after only eighteen miles of a
losing battle with the wind and a painful sinus headache. I

found a smart hotel, only half-finished. The ground floor was
still a builders' tip but a few of the bedrooms were in good order
and I was accommodated in one of them. Over the best dinner I
could find, a soggy pizza, I watched my last evening of relatively comprehensible television – a film set in Southwold (to
my great astonishment) and some sensible Government propa-
ganda about cherishing the countryside, reporting forest fires
and refraining from throwing plastic bottles into the sea. No
one talked to me and I went to bed early, to try to shake off my
cold. I slept soundly, blissfully unaware that I was the sole
occupant of the unfinished, doorless building.

8

Aegean Turkey

iam seges est, ubi Troia fuit, resecandaque falce
  luxuriat Phrygio sanguine pinguis humus;
semisepulta virum curvis feriuntur aratris
  ossa, ruinosas occulit herba domos.

(There is a cornfield now where Troy stood and the
soil, rich with Trojan blood, is luxuriant with crops
awaiting the sickle. Curved ploughs strike the half-
buried bones of men and grass covers the ruined
homes.)

(Ovid)

IF I had a prize to award to the nicest, kindest people in the
world, it would go to the Turks. I left the dour Thracian
Greeks and their claustrophobia behind me. Turkish Thrace
was geographically broader, under a wider sky; I felt as if I was
emerging from a dark tunnel into fresh air and sunshine and the
mood of the people matched the greater expansiveness of their
landscape. The Greeks had, of course, expressed horror at the
idea of my cycling alone across Turkey: 'The Turks are terrible
people! They'll attack you. They'll steal your bicycle.' Now the
Turkish Customs were amazed that Condor and I had made it
unscathed across Greece to the safety of the Turkish frontier.
The clerk in the bureau de change came out to greet me. 'Very
good bisiklet,' he said, spinning a pedal round and taking all the
time in the world to examine my machine, while his customers

queued at the counter. I pulled up in Ipsala for my first glass of
the hot, strong tea which has been the national drink since
Turkey lost its Arabian empire and its coffee. It was given to
me, free of charge – the first of countless glasses of free tea all
the way across Turkey. Children in the fields shouted 'Ello'
(rhyming with yellow) and drivers tooted their horns in greeting. It was like Italy, only more so. I was back among the
extroverts.

Turkish men look very fierce. They have dark, flashing eyes
and large bristling moustaches and their smile, on meeting a
stranger, is not automatic. Yet beneath this alarming exterior
they are real softies at heart. It was not long before two of them
pulled up in a van and tried to give me a lift, an offer which
would be repeated every day by scores of drivers. My suspicions, born of our more violent Western society, soon melted
and I learned to take these persistent offers at face value: they
were kindly meant by drivers who simply could not understand
that a woman might choose to cycle alone over mountains and
plains when motorised transport was available. I always refused
their lifts, as gently as I could, and cycled on. And they always
stood in the road, watching me go, a mixture of bewilderment
and pity on their faces.

The Via Egnatia ran on to Istanbul to finish at Constantine's
'milion', the first milestone in his capital, from which all distances in his empire were calculated. But in Alexander's time
Byzantium/Constantinople/Istanbul was not the great city it
was to become under the Christian emperors and the Ottoman
sultans. It was still a small settlement of no great importance
and it lay off his direct route to Persia. He turned south-west
near modern Keşan and marched down the Gallipoli Peninsula
to cross the Dardanelles, the ancient Hellespont. I turned
south-west with him and finally left the Roman road network
which I had followed for almost three months.

Throughout northern Europe, my budget of £125 a week had
imposed severe restraints on my lifestyle. In France and
Switzerland I had just managed, assisted by the hospitality of
friends. The wealthy cities of northern Italy had pushed my
expenses through the roof, though I had managed more
comfortably south of Rome. In Greece I had been able to stay

within limits, even allowing for good hotels in the cities and wine every night with my dinner. In Turkey I realised that my financial problems were over. I settled into the best of Keşan's many smart hotels and still had almost half my daily allowance left in my pocket.

Keşan was a feast of flowers, trees and fountains. I spent the afternoon in a tea-garden, where I was mobbed by little shoe-shine boys. My espadrilles were of no interest to them; they were crowding round to gaze in delight at my pink, white and blue plastic watch.

A German couple in a camper drove up to talk to me.

'We saw you this morning cycling along near the frontier and assumed there was a man with you. But you seem to be on your own. Are you really?'

'Yes. I'm cycling across Turkey to Antakya.'

'Well, we think you're very courageous. We just wanted to stop and tell you that. There we were this morning thinking that *we* were brave and adventurous, the two of us coming to Turkey together in a camper. But you're on your own on a bicycle! That beats everything.'

It had never occurred to me that I was doing anything specially daring. I had once owned an independent travel company and had organised tours of Classical sites in Turkey. I spoke some Turkish and was so used to the place that I had quite forgotten how apprehensive people could be on their first visit. Quite without cause, as they soon realised. Western Turkey was a Mediterranean country like any other. There was not a Grand Vizier, a janissary, a bashibazouk or a flashing scimitar in sight; all that remained of the Empires of Basil the Bulgar-Slayer and Selim the Grim was their dazzling architecture. Nor was Muslim fundamentalism a problem.

My bicycle was an object of wonder. The Turkish bicycle, the Bisan, is a heavy-duty machine with thick tyres, double cross-bars for strength and no gears. My Condor was deemed so precious it was carried lovingly, like a baby, up to the safety of my bedroom every night. In Keşan, the bell-boys helped me load it up in the morning, pumped up the tyres for me and, as their reward, were allowed to wheel it across the hotel vestibule and guard it while I settled my account. They refused a tip. The honour of serving such a splendid machine was payment enough.

My first full day's cycling in Turkey was a joy. I had turned south-west, so my old enemy, the north wind, was behind me. Now he gave wings to my pedals and I scarcely noticed that the road was rising until I came to the Koru Dağı Pass through the mountains of a national park. Tiny blue flowers, which were everywhere in Greece and Turkey, carpeted the pine forests. I freewheeled down to the bluest blue sea imaginable, in the Gulf of Saros. The colours, the sun and the strong scent of pine were intoxicating. For a while there was marshland, teeming with wild fowl. A stork flapped lazily across the road, just a few feet in front of me at head height, the first time I had seen a stork at such close quarters. And I had all this wonderful world to myself. Then I climbed the hill at the neck of the Gallipoli Peninsula and stood looking down at a strip of land so narrow I could see the Gulf of Saros on one side and the Aegean Sea on the other. In the early afternoon I arrived at the little port of Gelibolu, to give it its Turkish name. There I threw away the hotel guide from the Turkish Tourist Office. It had listed no hotels at all in Gelibolu and worry about my accommodation there had been the one cloud over my day. I now discovered that there were at least a dozen hotels, not tourist palaces with swimming pools and saunas, but good, clean hotels patronised by Turks. My bedroom with private facilities down by the harbour had everything I needed and cost me less than £4. I also discovered that Eurocheques could be cashed quite easily at Turkish banks and that was another load off my mind. I celebrated my newly restored tranquillity by taking a siesta.

The young travellers in Gelibolu were mostly Australians and New Zealanders who had come to visit Anzac Cove and the cemeteries of the First World War. The thwarted attempt to land on the Gallipoli Peninsula cost over 100,000 Allied and Turkish lives. I had seen so many memorials to gallant, wasted youth in the north of France that I had no heart to visit their replicas on the shores of the Dardanelles.

I raced out of Gelibolu, literally. My first challengers were two little boys on tiny bicycles, who pedalled like mad to overtake me. Then I decided to take on a Russian tanker,

AEGEAN TURKEY 87

steaming beside me down the Dardanelles. I was under a considerable handicap, as the tanker's route was straight and flat, whereas mine was hilly and curved in loops, but the contest amused me and kept me pedalling briskly. I arrived in Eceabat and ate a lunch of grapes and peaches as I waited for the ferry across the Straits of Çannakale.

The Dardanelles control the traffic from the Black Sea, Istanbul and the Sea of Marmora through to the Aegean. At Çannakale the straits are little more than a mile wide, and the ruins of Byzantine and Ottoman fortresses look down on the inevitable theatre of war. The village on the European side of the narrows is named Kilitbahir, 'the lock on the sea'. Cynossema to the Greeks, it was the scene of the Athenian naval victory over Sparta in 411 BC. In Inci Liman, ancient Aegospotami, just a little further up the straits, the Spartans finally wrested control of the sea from the Athenians in 405 BC, at the end of the Peloponnesian War.

I had paused at Inci Liman on the way from Gelibolu to Eceabat. It was a lovely peaceful inlet, 'the harbour of the pearl', as the Turks appropriately call it. Ancient Sestos stood there, where Hero held up her lamp every night to guide her lover, Leander, across the Hellespont from Abydos. Byron did the same swim in 1810 and wrote a poem about it. And it was there that Xerxes' Persians landed, when they invaded Greece in 480 BC, watched by their king from his marble throne on a hill in Abydos. Alexander turned the tables on Xerxes by sending his army across under Parmenion from Sestos to Abydos. He himself embarked at Elaeus, which I was easily persuaded to identify with Eceabat.

Scholars throughout the centuries have argued merrily about the size and composition of Alexander's army. Faced with conflicting evidence, I have chosen to follow Alexander's chief biographer, Arrian. Although he wrote almost 500 years after the death of his hero, he took most of his military information from Ptolemy, a participant in many of the battles. Arrian states that Alexander crossed into Asia Minor with 30,000 infantry and 5,000 cavalry. Included in the cavalry were the Companions, his crack force of 1,800 troopers and the 300 members of the Royal Squadron, Alexander's personal bodyguard, who led the battle charges. It was a modest army for such a major undertaking, but money was a bit short.

The army was proof of Alexander's military intent; his intellectual curiosity and his urge to explore the world were demonstrated by his choice of other companions. He took philosophers, men of letters, historians, geographers and botanists, as well as the engineers, surveyors, interpreters and the secretariat he needed for his campaigns and the subsequent administration of conquered lands. His tutor, Aristotle, was too old by then for such a long trip and retired to Athens, but he sent his nephew, the philosopher and historian Callisthenes of Olynthus, in his place. Alexander never forgot his debt to his old teacher; throughout his campaigns he had botanical specimens collected and sent to Aristotle in Athens.

Alexander himself took the helm of the admiral's ship and halfway across the straits sacrificed a bull to Poseidon and poured wine into the sea from a golden cup in honour of the Nereids. He was the first of his army to leap ashore, fully armed, on the Asian side and, after more dedications and sacrifices, he set off in the direction of Troy. His troops meanwhile were making the crossing in 130 triremes and a convoy of merchant vessels. I crossed with my bicycle on the Çannakale ferry. I had cycled 2,343 miles across Europe.

Anticipating the trip and my feelings back in London, I had imagined this crossing into Asia as a significant, even rather alarming, stage of my journey. How different was the reality. I stood in the sun on the deck of the creaking ferryboat, eating the last of my peaches, while the local tradesmen smiled at me and admired my bicycle. Then we arrived. The ramshackle vans were coaxed into spluttering life and the ponies made a quick escape up the oily ramp, pulling their carts onto dry land with sprightly relief. As I wheeled my bicycle along the waterfront, eyeing the line of hotels, I felt cheerful, confident and completely at ease. I had crossed into Asia, but Çannakale was a town like any other.

In Alexander's time, Troy was under Persian control, as was the rest of Asia Minor. He reached the city with his characteristic lightning speed and took his enemies by surprise, entering without difficulty. First, he made a sacrifice in the Temple of

Athena, offering up his armour to the Goddess and taking in exchange some weapons from the Trojan War, which were still hanging on her temple walls; ever after that, the shield from Troy was carried before him when he went into battle. He laid a wreath on the tomb of Achilles, declared Troy a free city, set up a democratic government, abolished the tribute paid to Persia and then rejoined his army. It was a visit full of symbolism. It was also his challenge to Darius and the Persians.

It took me rather longer to pedal along the coast to Hisarlik, ancient Troy. The site is an archaeologist's delight. There are nine major layers of habitation, some of them subdivided. More precisely, Professor Blegen and his team from Cincinnati claim to have identified no fewer than 46 strata, dating from the early Bronze Age (c. 3,000 BC) to the decline of the city after the Turkish conquest of 1,306 AD. To the layman, the site at first seems disappointing – just a jumble of stones – until Homer begins to cast his spell. The romantic can identify the Scaean Gate, through which Hector and the Trojan heroes rode down to the plain to meet Agamemnon, Menelaus and Achilles. Troy in Homer is always 'windy Troy' and it was in a strong, buffeting wind that I stood on the height once crowned by Athena's Temple, in the middle of the ruins where Alexander had sacrificed. I looked across the plain and the glint of the River Scamander towards the Dardanelles, where the Greeks had moored their ships for the nine long years of the Trojan War. It was a clear day and I could see Mount Ida in the far distance, where Paris had once been a shepherd boy and where Zeus had sat on his throne, a spectator in the theatre of war. An evocative site, but it needed the *Iliad* to bring it to life.

After Troy, my itinerary in western Turkey coincided only roughly with Alexander's. I continued to cycle down the coast while he rejoined his army at Abydos to fight his first pitched battle against the Persians on the River Granicus (modern Kocabas). This was a crazy young man's battle, which he won through sheer effrontery against all the military odds. The Persians had 30,000 cavalry to Alexander's 5,000. The combined armies of Lydia, Phrygia, Ionia and Cappadocia were massed on the opposite side of the river, where the bank was high and in places sheer and they assumed their position

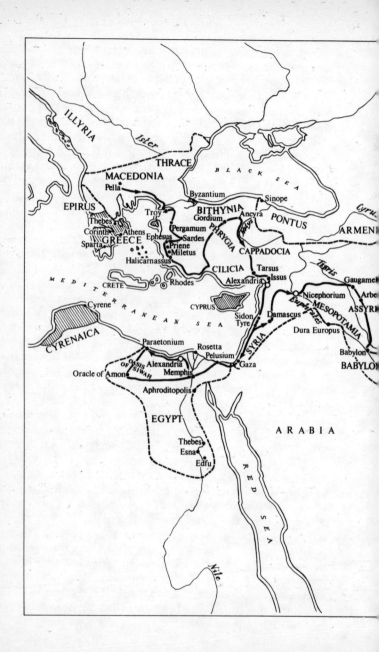

ARAL
SEA

Jaxartes

Oxus

CASPIAN SEA

MASSAGETAE

○ Alexandria Eschata

SOGDIANA

Samarkand

○ Alexandria
Margiane

Bactra

Alexandropolis

BACTRIA (HINDU KUSH)

Alexandria

Hecatompylus

Alexandria
(Herat)

Ortospana
(Kabul)

Taxila

Bucephala

Ecbatana

PARTHIA

ARIA

Alexandria
(Ghazni)

INDIA SUPERIOR

Hydaspes (Jhelum)

DRANGIANA

Susa

Prophthasia

Alexandria
(Kandahar)

Indus

SUSIANA

Persepolis

Alexandria
Sogdiana

Alexandria

CARMANIA

Alexandria

INDIA INFERIOR

INDIA

PERSIA

Alexandria

GEDROSIA
(BALUCHISTAN)

PERSIAN GULF

Alexandria

INDIAN OCEAN

EMPIRE OF ALEXANDER THE GREAT

—————— Alexander's route 334-323 B.C.
— — — Voyage of Nearchus 325 B.C.
○ Cities founded by Alexander
- - - - - Greatest expansion of the empire
▨▨▨▨ Areas dependent on Alexander

0   750
MILES

was unassailable. As usual, Alexander triumphed through the unexpected. The Persians and their allies watched in amazement as the battle cry went up and Ptolemy charged into the river at the head of the first squadron, leading across in an oblique line to the current. Alexander followed, in command of the second wave. Despite the rain of Persian lances from the bank above, the Macedonians somehow managed to gain a foothold and in no time Alexander had sighted and speared Mithridates, Darius' son-in-law. The Persians were routed and fled with the loss of thousands. Alexander lost 25 of his Companions, who died leading the charge, a further 60 cavalry and about 30 infantry. It was a stunning victory.

As Alexander's first objective was to free the Greek cities along the Aegean Coast, he left Calas to hold the Dardanelles and swept south though Aeolia, Ionia and Caria, picking off the cities and their pro-Persian rulers one by one. In each case he supported the democratic party, who overthrew the pro-Persian governments with his assistance. Pergamum, Ephesus, Priene, Miletos and Halicarnassus all welcomed him as their liberator. Wisely he refused to meet the Persian fleet off Miletos and in fact sent his own fleet home, to cut costs, concentrating instead on depriving the Persians of their harbours and the pine forests behind them, their source of timber, tar and pitch.

In the winter of 334, he sent all newly married soldiers home on leave. While Parmenion led the heavy troops and their baggage into what is now central Turkey, with instructions to meet him in the spring at Gordion, Alexander himself undertook a swift campaign in the south of Turkey. Winter was not the normal campaign season, so once again he caught his enemy off balance, marching along the south coast through Lycia, Pamphylia and western Pisidia, freeing the Greek cities and taking control of their resinous pine forests. By the time he rode north to rejoin his army at Gordion, he had achieved his twin objectives: the Greeks were free and the Persians had been deprived of all their naval bases round the west and south coasts of Turkey. It had been an outstandingly successful campaign, but he had still to meet Darius, the Great King, in person.

My own journey south was less strenuous. The road was good and the going easy, even though it was a windy coast;

sometimes I had to struggle and sometimes I flew like a bird with the wind behind me. Cycling was always a pleasure. The magic combination of mountains, pine forests, blue sea and sun never failed to enchant and south of Edremit I came to the olive belt. But I knew that hardship lay ahead. The view of lovely Lesbos to my right was counterbalanced by the vast bulk of the Anatolian Plateau to my left and I knew that, sooner or later, I had to scale it.

Bergama (Pergamum) was the only western Greek city I had time to visit. I took a taxi up to the acropolis, as the ascent was too long and precipitous even to contemplate on a bicycle. It was probably Alexander's first significant conquest in 334 and I could imagine his satisfaction as he stood on that giant rock, which rises sheer from the plain on three sides and commands it in all directions. Its heyday was to come later, under Eumenes II (197–159 BC), when sumptuous buildings descended the mountain in stepped terraces to the rivers below. The most astonishing feature was his theatre, which exploits a curve at the summit of the rock and seems to hang in mid-air. The Romans built its marble stage, but in Eumenes' day it had a wooden platform which was taken down between performances: the aesthetic refinement of the Greeks could not allow a stage to ruin the harmony between the theatre's fine architectural line and its niche in the landscape. Significantly, the city developed in the plain below under the Pax Romana and it was only when Rome's power was in decline that the Pergamenes shrank back into the safety of their rocky fastness.

Continuing down to Izmir, I avoided the tourist palaces on the shore and stayed a little inland in small Turkish towns. In one of these, my hotel was part of a cheese factory, over the cheese shop to the left and the factory to the right, where Condor spent the night reclining among the churns. I entered up a narrow staircase through a room filled with men playing backgammon. My Turkish was limited but there was usually someone around who could speak German. In this hotel it was Mohammed, an attentive boy who seized my hand and kissed it whenever we met. I was getting used to hotel staff who showed me to my room, then perched on the bed for a good long chat, or just to stare with unashamed curiosity. Mohammed was one of these. In his best school German, he informed me that he was the hotel masseur and offered his services free of charge, as I must be tired after my journey. I busied myself with the contents of my handbag and tried to look impassive.

To get away from Mohammed, who came up with tea during my siesta, I went for a walk round the town, and followed the sound of pipes and drums to the start of a circumcision feast. Two boys of twelve or thirteen were decked out in the usual costume for these occasions – a white suit, a royal blue velvet cloak with silver embroidery and white fur trim, topped with the white and silver plumed shako of a toy-town general. The street and the balconies above it were crowded with family, friends and local spectators. The taller of the two boys was a born showman and was thoroughly enjoying the party, joining his friends in one of those traditional Turkish dances where the men progress together in a solemn line. The smaller boy sat on a stool in the background, whey-faced. Soon the white horses appeared and both boys, even the little one, began to jump with excitement while their chargers were decked out in coloured scarves, white streamers and silk Turkish rugs. Then they were up and off. The band led the procession, piping and drumming in an open lorry, followed by the two pocket generals on their white horses. Then came the photographer, standing in the back of an open van shooting cine film; then a stream of cars, each with a coloured towel attached to a windscreen wiper. Bringing up the rear was another open lorry full of shouting, squealing children. It was a cheerful procession, with much waving, and hooting of horns. I bitterly regretted not having my camera with me.

My bedroom had soft pink harem lights of suggestive dimness. I locked myself in the bathroom that evening to write my notes under the fluorescent strip and escape the attentions of Mohammed. Undaunted, he arrived at dawn with a glass of tea, swearing eternal devotion. He was a tiresome lad, but artless, and I had to give him full marks for effort.

I pride myself on being a wily old fox and I got myself into real difficulties only once in western Turkey. I was sitting outside one evening, having dinner at a fish restaurant. The man at the next table was obviously a great cat-lover, surrounded by about

twenty strays who were getting most of his meal. I had to smile
at the way he orchestrated the cats and their appetites, feeding
them in turn, ensuring fair shares for all, coaxing the timid and
smacking the greedy ones on the nose. I joined him for cheese
and a melon. He was a florist named Ünal, travelling on business, and he had picked up reasonable German during his spell
in a Düsseldorf car factory. When he learnt I would be cycling
through his home town later that week, he handed me his card
and invited me to dinner. I thanked him politely, but of course
had no intention of taking him up on his invitation.

I duly arrived in his town and booked into a hotel on the
waterfront. Emerging after my siesta from the landward
entrance to the hotel, I was horrified to find myself directly
opposite a florist's shop – with Ünal sitting outside. I tried hard
to avoid the dinner date but we were soon surrounded by his
assistants and neighbours, who had heard all about me. He
would clearly have lost face in his little community had I turned
him down. After a lavish dinner with Ünal and his friend who
ran a newspaper stall, it was suggested that we should adjourn
to his shop for a final glass of beer. The shop seemed safe
enough and it was opposite my hotel, so I agreed, especially as I
could see that the lights were still on there and an assistant was
working late into the evening on a wedding display. Then the
unexpected happened. Ünal invited me to look at his workshop
and I was astonished to find myself in one huge, magnificent
bower of roses and gladioli. In the middle of it all stood a
marquee of silver foil, festooned with tiny pink fairy lights and
furnished with Turkish carpets and a divan. I fled and next day
was careful to leave by the waterfront exit. I slunk out of town
feeling rather ashamed of myself. At my age, I should have
handled things better.

Izmir was a disappointment. I had intended to use it as my
base for a visit to Ephesus, but I cycled round the city for two
hours without finding a hotel room. It was a bigger city that I
had thought, filled with smog and diesel fumes; in one suburb
the reek of goatskins drying on all the roofs was indescribably
nauseating. As Greek Smyrna, it had once been one of the most
splendid cities of Ionia, but the great fire of 1922 at the end of
the Greek–Turkish War had completed the annihilation of its

past. Its Greek population was expelled and it became a busy
port and industrial centre, home to 1.5 million Turks. Abandoning my plan to visit Ephesus, I consoled myself with the
argument that its spectacular ruins were mostly Roman in any
case and that the buildings would not have been there in
Alexander's day.

Alexander's winter loop along the southern shore of Turkey
had never been on my itinerary: there were too many cities
there for the time available to me and the craggy mountains of
Caria and Lycia were hardly cycling country. In fact, I filled in
the gaps the following year, for most of this book was written in
Antalya (Attaleia) between visits to Perge, Aspendos, Side,
Phaselis and other Greek cities freed by Alexander. My next
cycling objective on this trip was Sardis, former capital of Lydia
and the start of the Persian Royal Road.

The main road eastwards out of Izmir, the E23 towards
Uşak, led directly to the ruins of Sardis but I took a different
route, the ancient one up the valley of the River Gediz
(Classical Hermos). It followed one of the easiest climbs up
from the sea to the heights of central Turkey and was used long
before the Greeks settled in Ionia. To take it, however, I had to
cycle back northwards to Menemen.

The journey from Menemen to Izmir and back again, my
vain search for an Izmir hotel and my ride up the Gediz Valley
to Manisa gave me my longest day's cycling to date – ten hours
and 77 miles. But the beauty of the olive groves, vineyards,
poplars and pomegranates soothed the frustrations of Izmir.
Sultanas were everywhere, mile upon mile of grapes laid out in
the sun to dry. And the Gediz flowed beside me as I followed
the winding, ancient path up through the gaps in the mountains. By the time I reached Muradiye in the late afternoon, I
was hot, weary, dying of thirst and longing for a *vişne suyu*,
that delectable drink of mineral water and morello cherry juice
which kept me going across Turkey. The centre of Muradiye
was a deserted square with a tree in the middle, four tea-houses
full of old men, and one shop. Trade in Turkey is so specialised
that a tea-house will rarely have soft drinks, so I tried the village
shop. It was a dusty little place, run by a rough-looking character with one eye. It was too poor to run to a refrigerator and I

was about to turn wearily away when the proprietor rushed round from behind his counter, held out a chair for me and switched on an electric fan. He then zipped off to each of the four cafés in turn, failing to find me a *vişne suyu* but returning with an ice-cold Coke. He offered me a cigarette. When I declined, he went to one of the old-fashioned glass-fronted biscuit boxes that I had not seen in England's grocers' shops since my childhood, took out three custard creams (his best biscuits) and placed them on the counter before me, neatly arranged on a little square of paper. Meanwhile, we communicated. He had no word of anything but Turkish, yet his miming was so brilliant that I understood everything he said. He told me about the sultanas, for which the region is famous. Then we discussed my itinerary. At the mention of Greece, he made aggressive boxing movements, then a sly look came over his face as he crept away with my invisible bicycle. Although he never travelled himself, he knew a lot about Turkey and every place name produced an appropriate mime. The highlight for me was Konya, when he closed his one eye, stretched out his arms and began to rotate with supreme dignity. He was a Whirling Dervish warming up for his mystic spin.

When I indicated that it was time for me to leave, he put out a staying hand and went out of the shop again, returning with a stainless steel platter laden with wonderful seedless grapes, beaded with icy water. I ate as many as I thought polite under the gaze of his one benevolent eye; the rest he put into a plastic bag and slid into my pannier, along with more custard creams. He accepted money for the Coke, as he had had to pay for it himself, but the rest were gifts. The entire stock of his shop amounted to little more than twenty packets of cigarettes, three packets of Knorr soup, four kinds of loose biscuits, sultanas, candles, rice and a few tins of sardines. It was a humbling experience to be given so much, with such evident joy in the giving, by someone who in Western terms had so little. His father came out with him to wave me off. As I turned out of the square, I saw them both rushing into the nearest tea-house. Strangers are a great event in Muradiye and they could scarcely wait to tell their story. The reward for all that kindness would be the prestige they had gained in the village.

I soon reached Manisa (Magnesia of Sipylus), where the hotel manager greeted me with iced mineral water and a glass of tea, another simple act of kindness to a weary traveller. I stayed for two days, as my knee was troubling me again after my long ride, and I needed a haircut. I was given one with a vengeance: ignoring my halting phrase-book Turkish, the hairdresser gave me a drastic 'short back and sides' with a gel-stiffened cockscomb on top – the sort of style I had complained about very forcibly in my days as a headmistress. For a cyclist, it was a disaster – it left my neck and ears unprotected and I had to resort to a headscarf instead of a cycling cap – but the scarf turned out to be a great success. In a Muslim country, my decorum met with approval, while on dusty roads I could copy the country people of both sexes and draw the end of my scarf across my nose and mouth to protect them. I left Manisa, a pleasant city on the Gediz, without realising that there was a Sinan mosque there – which gives me as good a reason as any for a return visit.

9

The Royal Road and the Cilician Gates

> I love roads;
> The goddesses that dwell
> Far along them invisible
> Are my favourite gods.
> *(Edward Thomas)*

THE Royal Road. What a magic name for a road-lover. I had
always wanted to travel along it and one day, when Iran can
be trusted again, I shall ride it from end to end, from Sardis all
the way to Susa, the ancient capital of the Persian Empire.

Cyrus the Great of Persia conquered Sardis in 546 BC. At
that time it was not only the capital of Lydia; it also controlled
Phrygia and the flourishing Greek cities of Ionia. The Lydian
king was powerful, yet wise and benevolent. And he was the
richest man in the world, his capital adorned and his coffers
filled with the gold which flowed down the Pactolus River from
Mount Ptolus. His name was Croesus. It was inevitable that
Cyrus should cast a covetous eye over such a wealthy kingdom
and at a battle on the Halys river, Croesus was defeated and led
away into captivity. Soon afterwards, all the Greek cities of Asia
Minor fell under Persian rule.

With such an extensive empire to control, the Persians
needed swift, reliable communications, and laid the Royal
Road. Its surface was well maintained and regular relay-
stations enabled royal messengers to change horses and speed
on without delay. In its day it was the fastest road in the world.

Its route across Turkey was an arduous one. The later Graeco-Roman road, which was used chiefly for trade in more peaceful times, followed an easier, more open path through Laodicaea (Denizli) and Archelais (Aksaray), then south of the Great Salt Lake to Caesarea (Kaiseri) for Persia, or by Tyana, near Bor, for the Cilician Gates and the Mediterranean. The Royal Road, on the other hand, described a northerly arc through Ancyra (Ankara) over very difficult terrain. Its route can only be explained if the Persians incorporated older, existing roads through previous power centres. In fact, most of the cities along the route had old Phrygian names and the major junction of the Royal Road with the north–south trade route between the Black Sea and the Mediterranean (from Sinope to Tarsus) was Hattusa (Classical Pteria; modern Boğazkale), once the capital of the Hittite Empire. As might be expected in those dark, war-like days, sites of cities were chosen for their military strength and their water supply. Most stood on precipitous hills, or ones whose sides could easily be scarped. Trade was important, but commercial convenience was clearly subordinate to strategic need.

All this made for strenuous cycling, though the ride began easily enough, as I continued up the Gediz valley from Manisa to Sardis. The acropolis came into view long before the city, an impressive, sharply pointed mountain with ruins crowning its summit. The capital of Lydia could not have been better sited: the smiling valley, where the golden River Pactolus flowed into the Gediz, was protected by its superb natural bastion. With all those advantages, it was surprising to find that the modern village of Sartmustafa was just a depressing little hole, where I was pursued by a horde of screaming, barefoot tots. Alexander had freed Sardis from the Persians in 334 BC and it had continued to flourish under Greeks, Romans and Byzantines, but Tamerlane destroyed it utterly in his sack of 1401 and it never recovered its glory. Most of the excavation there was of recent date. Fifteen graceful Ionic columns stood again in the Temple of Artemis and the substantial ruins of Roman baths, gymnasia and shops lined the highway, as they must have done in the great days of Sardis. I was pleasantly surprised. There was already far more to see than I had expected and excavation was continuing.

In Salihli I stopped at a newspaper kiosk to enquire about hotels. The other customer was a restaurateur, who had prospered in Munich and now had his own restaurant there, as well as the one he ran in Salihli. A minion was cleaning his Mercedes across the road. First I was treated to a *vişne suyu*, then I was driven in the Mercedes to the cleanest hotel in town, while the minion wobbled behind on my bicycle. My friend wanted to know why Westerners were so mistrustful of Turks. In Germany they were not very kind to them, though they relied on their labour in the factories. And Western tourists only came to Turkey for the beaches; they never wanted to talk to the people or try to understand them. I was the first foreigner he had ever met who had attempted to speak Turkish and had been willing to sit down and have a chat. My hotel was a wing of a Turkish bath. It was certainly clean, if a little steamy, but I retired to bed in misery. I had another cold, despite the huge quantities of fruit and vegetables I consumed every day. Clearly my recent Greek cold had given me no immunity from Turkish cold germs.

The modern roads follow the route of the Royal Road only in stretches, as highway technology has the skill to take more direct routes across difficult country. Ancient roads are more likely to be found along the railway tracks, as both had to be laid to follow the lie of the land. There had been no choice of route up the narrow Gediz valley; river, road and railway had all run along together. At Salihli they divided: the river and the railway looped south of the mountains, while the main road ran over them to Uşak. I had to take the main road to find accommodation. In any case, the villages listed by Sir Arthur Ramsay in his *Historical Geography of Asia Minor* as lying on the route of the Royal Road were too small to appear on my maps. Even if I left the modern road, the ancient one might still have eluded me.

After a flat section, I had a twenty-mile climb up to Kula, then lost most of the altitude gained in a steep swoop down into the town. Although I was only about a hundred miles inland, I

was already in a different, Levantine world. The men wore
baggy Turkish trousers, like exaggerated black or brown jodh-
purs, and sat in the tea-houses smoking and playing backgammon. There was not a woman to be seen in the streets;
presumably they were all at home, busily knotting the carpets
for which Kula is famous. Yet, despite appearances, it was
generally the women who were the domestic tyrants. I was told
of one old lady who hid her husband's false teeth when she
suspected him of philandering. The Kula Palas Otel failed to
live up to its name and the one restaurant in the town was basic
and dry. It was now September and darkness fell before 8 p.m.
The streets were unlit and the shops closed. An early night in
the Kula Palas was my sole option.

Next morning my cold was considerably worse but I dragged
myself out of bed and onto my bicycle. Another 24 hours in
Kula were not to be contemplated. Uşak was 50 miles away over
barren steppeland. The road would climb to a high ridge,
descend a little to a fertile valley, them climb to an even higher,
stonier elevation. It was a dusty, shadeless road with lorries
roaring by, half of them stopping to offer me lifts and all of them
tooting their horns. In my low physical state, I found their
jollity irritating and started to snap at them. There was one
cheerful sight. A man overtook me on a small motorcycle,
obviously going hunting, as he had his gun slung over his
shoulder. A cardboard box was strapped to his pillion and in the
box sat a young brown spaniel. He travelled so proudly behind
his master, conscious of the important work which lay ahead of
him. As they puttered past me, he turned his head to stare and
his gaze never wavered until he disappeared over the crown of
the next hill, craning his neck to get a final view. In Uşak I
found an excellent hotel, where I stayed for three days, resting
and trying to shake off my cold. A notice in my bedroom invited
me to make full use of my 'burial balcony'. I have still to
discover the original Turkish phrase which was so quaintly
mistranslated.

The cashiers in the bank and the hotel receptionist had colds
too. They said it was the change in the season; autumn was
coming. I strolled round the bazaar. It was market-day and all
the country people had come into Uşak to buy and sell. The

women were brightly, even hectically, dressed in layer upon dazzling layer: baggy trousers in luminous floral prints were topped by a long-sleeved dress in a different but equally luminous pattern, then a vivid sleeveless cardigan and a floral-patterned pinafore, all in the most brilliant, clashing colours. Round their heads and throats they wore a sort of white muslin wimple with a large white square flowing down their backs, the whole secured by a plait of multi-coloured wools. The market stalls were fascinating too, with their hand-made saddles and bridles and their beautifully crafted tools and ironmongery. I took my camera to the bazaar next morning, only to find it deserted. I never seemed to have my camera at the right time.

I was now in Phrygia, the ancient realm of King Midas. He was not as rich as Croesus but the legend of his golden touch must have had its roots in the wealth of his state. From his capital of Gordion, he controlled the trade routes through to central Anatolia from the north-east Aegean coast and Lydia. The modern cities of Phrygia were dull industrial towns which owed their prosperity to their railway junctions. The great centres of the old Phrygian civilisation, with their rock monuments and temples, lay off the present highways across endless-seeming miles of desolate steppe. To explore them, I should have needed a four-wheel drive, or at least a cross-country motorbike. I could not possibly locate them and cover such great distances and rough terrain on a bicycle.

I always relied on my current hotel for advice on my next night's stop. My average of 50 miles a day was well within the radius of their personal knowledge. In Uşak they told me that there were no hotels on the direct route to Kütahya: it was 92 miles of secondary road across empty country, with only two tiny hamlets on the way. I was advised to take the main road along two sides of the triangle. It was further to cycle, but I could be sure of food and a bed. I still felt under the weather, with a stuffy nose and a sinus headache. When I left Uşak, hoping that the fresh air would clear my head, I cycled straight into a north-east wind sweeping the dust in clouds over the arid steppeland. I swathed my nose and mouth in my scarf, but my eyes still streamed and my throat was raw. After sixteen miles I

gave up, at Banaz. I was the only guest in the town's surprisingly large hotel, with its long, echoing, tiled corridors.
The proprietor had his office down the village street, where he
doubled up as the Calor Gas dealer. When I tried to go out for
lunch, I found that the catch on my bedroom door had jammed.
I rattled it, twisted it, shook it, hammered on the door and
shouted, all in vain. There was nobody in the hotel. Three
small children were playing ball under my window, but they
were too young to understand anything but Turkish. In desperation, I turned to my Turkish phrase book. There, to my
astonishment, in the middle of all the useless phrases with
which such books tend to be crammed, I found 'Fetch the
manager! My bedroom window is jammed.' Hastily substi-
tuting *kapı* (door) for *pencere* (window), I leaned out and
screamed my heaven-sent sentence at the children below. They
duly scampered off and returned with the manager, who forced
the catch and transferred me to another bedroom. A lunch of
kebabs, salad, beer and delicious melon restored my
composure.

Just beyond Banaz I accepted my only Turkish lift. The road
was up for repair and I had to push my bicycle over rough,
unsurfaced rocks. Even with my scarf over my nose and mouth
I was almost asphyxiated by the dust thrown up by passing
lorries. I was plodding resolutely up a hill when a minibus
driver pulled up and told me in German that the road was
unsurfaced for the next six miles and I would choke to death if I
tried to walk that distance through the dust cloud. I gratefully
accepted his lift. It was not cheating: the road was physically
impassable, except in a closed vehicle. The surface improved at
the bottom of a huge mountain up to Dumlupinar and there I
got out, to the astonishment of my friend, who simply could not
understand why I refused a lift to the top.

Afyon, or Afyonkarahisar, was notable only for its name, 'the
black castle of opium'. Its fortress on an outcrop of black
trachyte towered over a plain once famous for its opium poppies. The villages in the region were oases in the mountain
hollows. They had enormous village greens, commons where
horses, donkeys and cattle grazed and children with sticks
drove their flocks of strutting geese. Families worked in groups,

some winnowing grain in the age-old fashion, others sitting cross-legged on the grass sorting fruit and vegetables into piles for market. They were busy rural scenes, full of colour and variety. I thought how Breughel would have enjoyed painting them.

The 62 miles from Afyon to Kütahya had to be covered in a day as there was not a single village on the way. The mountain air was crisp and clear and I bowled along the kind of smooth, balding asphalt which bicycles love, through miles of rolling grassland, the distant mountains pink, then mauve, then plum as the day progressed. Kütahya (ancient Cotyaeum) is famous for its faïence, so I was disappointed to find that the Great Mosque was painted, not tiled. But it was a splendid building nevertheless, begun by Sultan Bayezid in the fourteenth century and restored by the great architect Sinan in the reign of Suleiman the Magnificent. I stood admiring its forest of marble columns when the aged sacristan, in a striped woolly hat, came across for a chat.

There is one Turkish phrase which always goes down well: 'Çok güzel.' It means 'very beautiful' and it can be applied equally happily to people, buildings, food, weather – anything nice. I smiled at the old man. 'Çok güzel,' I said, embracing the mosque in a wide sweep of the arm. He beamed. 'Çok, çok güzel,' he replied. 'Would you like to take a photograph of it?' The interior was dim, lit only by the high stained glass windows under the dome, and mosques are in any case notoriously difficult to photograph. Their beauty lies in their tranquillity, their symmetry and the subtle relationship between their spaces. I doubted if any photograph of mine could do justice to Sinan. But I snapped it, so as not to give offence. The sacristan hesitated and looked a bit shy. 'Would you take a photograph of me?' 'Of course. I'll take your photograph in your beautiful mosque.' He was delighted. 'Just wait a minute,' he said. He hobbled out as fast as he could go and came back with his friend, a tiny man in a flat cap above a kind old face wrinkled and brown like a walnut. 'We were at school together,' said the sacristan, 'and he's been my best friend ever since.'

The two old friends stood side by side in their mosque, backs straight, unsmiling, staring straight into the camera with the intensity of people for whom a photograph is a great occasion. Just as I was about to press the button, they reached out to each other and stood holding hands, like the two little boys they had been in school, so many years ago.

Kütahya, Eskişehir, Siyrihisar. I felt as if I had a job again, getting up each morning at the same time and working hard all day to put miles beneath my wheels. The landscape gradually changed from open grassland to rocky desert, but it was equally featureless, the journey only made tolerable by the sociability of the drivers in the tea-houses. I reached one tea-garden at the end of a particularly dry and dusty stretch and saw two lorry-drivers with a cool, sliced honeydew melon in front of them. Melon was just what I needed, so I ordered a half, only to discover that the lorry-drivers had brought their melon in themselves. To my embarrassment, they overheard my request and immediately, with typical Turkish generosity, sent half of their own melon over to my table. It was delicious. I went over afterwards to thank them and they invited me to join them for a glass of tea. They had passed me some way back and had been worried about me because, they claimed, Turks were notoriously wild drivers. With not a word of English or German at his command, the more extrovert of the two then detailed all the fearful road accidents that might befall me, illustrating his warnings with teaglasses and matchboxes, his lorries, which he pushed energetically all over the table. I was always the bread basket. The climax of each dramatic incident came when the poor little bread basket was violently overturned and its contents sent flying in all directions.

My one detour off the main road took me to Gordion. When Alexander met Parmenion there at the close of his winter campaign in southern Turkey, the city was under Persian rule and an important staging-post on the Royal Road. He took it without opposition, then went to look at the cart of King Midas, which stood in the Temple of the Phrygian Goddess Cybele. An ancient prophecy told that whoever untied the difficult knot would be Lord of Asia. With his gift for the unexpected, Alexander simply slashed it through with one stroke of his sword. That same night, as Arrian reports, there was thunder and lightning, heavenly confirmation that the prophecy would be fulfilled.

The road to Gordion was a track across eight miles of stony desert. First the railway ran on my right, then I crossed it and it ran on my left, the only feature in that flat, empty landscape. I cycled through the dusty little village of Yassilhöyük, where ganders hissed and tried to attack me as I passed their flocks. This was the site of Gordion, on the River Sakarya (Classical Sangarios) near its junction with the Porsuk (Tembris). I walked round the ruins of a megaron, said to be the Temple of Cybele, and entered the tumulus known as 'Midas' Tomb', though it probably predated him. In view of my recent encounter with the ganders, I was amused to find that the museum had Phrygian vessels shaped and painted to represent geese, with beaks for spouts. It must have been a great area for poultry even in Midas' day. The River Sakarya was low at the end of the summer and I saw no sign of the reeds into which Midas' barber had whispered the secret of his master's ass's ears. Of all the sites I visited, Gordion was the most difficult to imagine in its former glory, probably because it was deserted in 278 BC when the Gauls invaded Asia Minor, and consequently had no impressive Roman monuments. I was pleased when my desert excursion was over and I could relax in Polatlı – inevitably, in the Midas Hotel. The dryness and dust of the desert continued to play havoc with my throat and sinuses, already sensitive after my cold. By the end of each day's cycling I was reduced to a choking, spluttering wretch. I was relieved that I had only one more day of arid mountain country before I followed Alexander into Ankara.

I found that I had enjoyed travelling alone. People hesitate to intrude when friends are journeying together but a solitary cyclist is always approached and entertained. Across Greece and Turkey I had met some marvellous characters and learned a great deal about their way of life and their perspective on events. I was never lonely. Yet struggling through the language barrier was always quite hard work and after six weeks of it I was really looking forward to a few days' easy chat with a native English-speaker. Shirley's flat in Ankara would be my haven from dust and the difficulties of communication.

ANKARA – KIRIKKALE – KIRŞEHIR – AVANOS –
ÜRGÜP – KAYSERI – NIĞDE – POSANTI – TARSUS –
ADANA – ISKENDERUN – ANTAKYA

A blue Renault screeched to a halt in a cloud of dust beside me.
'You must be Anne! There can't be *two* mad women on bicycles
on the Eskişehir road!'

It was Shirley, with a car-load of Turkish ballerinas. We had
never seen each other before but we met in laughter and I knew
that I was going to have a good time in Ankara. She dashed
ahead to deposit her ballerinas and put the kettle on, while I
found my way more slowly through the centre of Ankara and
out to her flat in Gazi Osman Paşa.

Shirley's brother was the link. He was a governor of St Felix
and had put me in touch with his sister, who had immediately
invited me to stay. I could not have been more fortunate. I had
all sorts of jobs to do in Ankara and Shirley was the ideal person
to help me with them. She was a ballerina who had gone out for
a tour with the Turkish National Ballet, married a Turkish
tenor and settled down. Moving as she did in two worlds and
being gregarious by nature, she seemed to know everyone in
Ankara and of course spoke Turkish like a Turk.

A new face in a foreign land is always an event and for the first
few days I was fêted by expatriates avid for news about
England. Then we got down to business. First came the injections. As cholera and hepatitis B vaccinations give only a six-
month immunity, there had been no point in having them in
London. Through her hospital contacts, Shirley arranged an
appointment for my cholera injection but I was advised, unofficially, against having the hepatitits B in Turkey, as it was a
blood serum and might not have been tested for AIDS. Hepatitis was not a problem in Turkey so it was suggested that I
should wait until I got to Pakistan and then approach the British
Embassy. The staff there would certainly be immunised
regularly and safe serum would be flown from London.

Then Shirley took me shopping and we managed to replace
my black cotton cycling trousers. These had been growing
steadily shorter, as I had patched the seat three times by cutting

strips off the ends of the legs. Quite apart from their general shabbiness, they were beginning to look a bit too much like shorts to be acceptable in the remoter regions of a Muslim country. My new pair were identical to my old ones in the shade, but they had a subtle, Turkish touch; in bright light they revealed a Paisley pattern and looked almost like black brocade. Plain fabrics are not to the Turks' taste.

Next I turned my attention to visas and the real frustrations began. I had tried unsuccessfully to get an Iraqi visa in London. In Ankara, after numerous phonecalls and a visit to an embassy as closely guarded as Fort Knox, I drew another blank. The Iraqis would be happy to give me a visa if I had a sponsor in Iraq. Given time, I could probably have found a sponsor but time was not on my side. So I tried Syria instead. As Britain had no diplomatic relations with Syria, a visa was technically out of the question. My only chance, according to the British Embassy, was to cycle to the border near Aleppo and stand there obstinately. The frontier post might just issue me with a visa on the spot, if I was resolute enough in my approach. They thought a British car had got in that way recently. All this sounded most unpromising. I was even disappointed in my enquiries about possible sea passages from Mersin or Iskenderun to Egypt. It was beginning to look as if I might not be able to follow Alexander across the Middle East after all.

I was interested that neither the Foreign Office in London nor the Ankara embassies were concerned for my safety if I cycled through Iraq; they were concerned only with the visa situation. My proposed route down the Tigris was not in the Iran–Iraq war zone. Their reaction would no doubt have been different had the Iraqis already begun to use chemical weapons in the north.

Feeling rather despondent, I decided to forget my visa problems in a spell of map work and went out in search of the British School in Ankara. They had moved from the first address I tried but after a weary morning, three taxi-rides and much leg-work, I finally tracked down their new premises, only to find them closed; presumably the archaeologists were still away on their summer excavations. That was a great blow, as I needed to consult Sir Arthur Ramsay's authoritative book to

work out my route from Ankara along the Royal Road: I had
not had time to research all the world's roads before leaving
London and was counting on access to relevant books en route.
At that time I was unaware that the Royal Road continued to
Boğazkale, and consequently took the wrong road out of
Ankara. It was the only major route mistake of my trip.

Between all these administrative tasks, I had a wonderful
time. Shirley was a flautist, I was a pianist and Shirley's upstairs
neighbour, Akte, a shy but extremely talented girl, played the
violin. We worked together on a C.P.E. Bach trio and Shirley
and I polished up a Satie suite and put it on tape. She was an
enthusiastic and generous hostess. We entertained, went out to
parties and dinners and saw *The Importance of Being Earnest* at
the British Council. My silk suit certainly earned its place in my
luggage. Mornings were more tranquil. While Shirley exam-
ined at the Conservatoire, I rested in the leafy suburb of Gazi
Osman Paşa, recovering from catarrh, answering all my letters
and enjoying the luxury of modern English novels from the
British Council Library. I even did a little sightseeing.

Ankara is a much more interesting city than is generally
supposed. A small regional centre, away from the main east–
west trade routes and famous only for the soft wool of its
long-haired goats (angora), it was chosen by Ataturk in 1923 as
the capital of modern Turkey and has been growing ever since.
A city of wide boulevards, elegant shops and rather stern public
buildings in 1930s Teutonic, it is dominated on one side by the
austere floodlit mausoleum of Ataturk himself and on the other
by the ancient citadel. Climbing up its steep volcanic rock to the
Byzantine walls is like entering another, gentler world. There
are Ottoman houses with their overhanging wooden balconies,
leafy squares and small tea-houses, where old men smoke their
hookahs and play backgammon. I saw an old lady sitting in the
sun on her doorstep, lovingly combing the pale beige coats of
two sleek angora goats. She also had a giant of a fat-tailed ram,
of which she was extremely proud. Though she smiled
indulgently and invited me to stroke him, I kept my distance. I
visited the superb Hittite and Phrygian collections in the
Anatolian Museum and marvelled at the city's enthusiasm for
Western European art and culture. It seemed surprising in an

enclave cut off from the West by endless tracts of barren steppeland – or perhaps its very remoteness made its citizens so eager to keep in touch.

Shirley borrowed a bicycle from the American air base and accompanied me for three days out of Ankara. This was the time I failed to follow Alexander. We cycled out up Elmadağ, 'Apple Mountain', then freewheeled down to the green banks of the Kızılırmak (Halys) river, where we were invited to join a family picnic. They were all very merry, as two of the young people had just got married. The newly-weds danced for us, first alone, then with the bride's brother, while the mother plied us with watermelon in the shade of the poplars. They were a family of plumbers from Ankara and I was pleased to be able to take photographs of their party and send them as a souvenir. Travel with Shirley added a new dimension, as she was able to join in the conversation and interpret for me.

Had I been alone I should have played safe and stopped for the night at Kırıkkale, especially as Turkish winter time had just begun. But Shirley, extremely fit and lithe as only a ballerina can be, was keen to go on, and her exuberance made me over-confident. Darkness overtook us on the way to Keskin. We had no lights and the road was busy with thundering lorries. A lone shepherd called out plaintively, 'Let's make an evening of it! I'm lighting a fire,' and made drinking motions with his right hand.

We were rescued by Başol, the young driver of the Keskin–Kırıkkale minibus, who took us the last three miles into Keskin. There was no hotel in the little town, so he invited us to spend the night in his home, if we had no objection to sharing a room with his children. Yildiz, his wife, was understandably a little taken aback when he appeared with two strange lady cyclists, but she soon recovered her composure and gave us a delicious supper of pasta, homegrown tomatoes, olives, cheese, homemade cherry jam, fresh bread and endless glasses of tea. The neighbours came in to pay their respects and the landlady's elder daughter entertained us in French with great poise and charm for a fifteen-year-old. Her younger sister was showing signs of turning fundamentalist: she wore an enveloping headscarf and had opted for the religious stream at school,

choosing Classical Arabic instead of a modern European language. They teased her that she wanted to be a *hodja* (religious
teacher) when she grew up, but underneath their teasing was a
genuine concern. Turkey is a secular state, keen to be considered modern and European. Islamic fundamentalism is not
widespread but it surfaces now and then in small ways and
worries the families of those involved.

Ercan, the three-year-old son of the house, slept on a divan in
the living room, where he just curled up under a blanket when
he felt tired. It was all so simple, with none of our Western
bed-time dramas. His baby sister was asleep in her cot. Shirley
and I would have been quite happy on divans with Ercan and
Leila, but Yildiz insisted on giving us the short, rather narrow
matrimonial bed, perhaps because Ercan was convinced that
Shirley had come to give him an injection. They were a
charming family, living happily with their neighbours round a
common courtyard. I was grateful to Shirley and her inter-
preting for such an insight into ordinary Turkish lives.

After an elaborate yet leisurely breakfast and a photo-session,
we set out rather later than usual to the sound of the local imam
summarising the day's news over the mosque loudspeaker for
the benefit of villagers who had no radio or television. It was
bleak steppe landscape all the way to Kırşehir, mile upon mile
of stones and coarse grass. We were cheered on our way by a
lorry-driver who tooted his horn and shouted, 'Hello, kittens!'
as he drove by. That was the one event of the cycling day. In
Kırşehir, a spa town, we recovered from the dust and
exhaustion of the road in the local Turkish baths, fed with hot
volcanic spring water – another experience for which I have to
thank Shirley. I should never have ventured in there alone. The
locals were thrilled to have foreign patronage and the masseuse,
a cheerful, hefty girl, kept patting me on the head and beaming
with delight.

Ankara in late September had been pleasantly warm but as
we went south into Cappadocia across the shadeless steppes we
felt the full force of the southern sun again. At Avanos we
stayed with friends of Shirley's in traditional Turkish houses
they had refurbished and made into an hotel. It was in a back
street, surrounded in Middle Eastern fashion by a high wall;

without Shirley, I should never have known what delights were hidden away there. The rooms were furnished with kilims and hand-carved wood and all looked out onto courtyards full of flowers and shady trees. In the evening we sat round a fire in the main courtyard, eating supper and talking until midnight, when we put Shirley and her bicycle onto the bus for Ankara.

I took a bus tour next day to see the sights of the Göreme valley before cycling through Ürgüp to Kayseri. In the ninth century, Cappadocia was one of the greatest monastic centres in the Byzantine Empire, its rocks riddled with churches and monasteries, decorated with mediaeval frescoes. At Kaymakli I visited one of the underground cities hewn out of volcanic tuff to a depth of ten storeys, the upper ones for dwellings and the lower ones for storerooms, all splendidly ventilated and inter-connected by underground streets which could be sealed off at strategic points with huge mill-stones. These cities were places of refuge, possibly pre-dating Christianity, and were used as late as 1839, when the local people hid from Ibrahim Pasha's invading Egyptians. But more amazing than these was the landscape. Erosion had worn away the soft tuff into fantas-tic spires, columns, pinnacles and cones, which stood in for-ests across the valley floors. Some had blocks of harder stone perched on top that had resisted erosion, while their supporting columns had continued to wear away. They were known as 'fairy chimneys'. Some of the larger ones had been hollowed out and inhabited, while the largest of all, Uçhisar, contained a whole vertical troglodyte village crowned with a citadel. The soft colours of this weird moonscape, yellows, greys, pinks and mauves which paled and deepened with sun and shadow, added to its magical beauty.

I took the wrong turning out of Ürgüp and found myself climbing up to the Pass of Topuzdağ (5,050 ft), then descending in vertiginous hairpin bends to a salt lake and the flat Kayseri road. It was a spectacular detour, but it took time and I realised that I should never reach Kayseri before dark. At a lonely cross-roads in the middle of nowhere I met two Dutch cyclists on their way to China. When dusk was falling and there was no hotel at Incesu, I gave up and took the Kayseri bus. It was not cheating, I told myself, as I should be cycling back

down the same road out of Kayseri and I was not, after all,
obliged to cycle the world's roads more than once.

In Kayseri I met up again with Alexander, who must have
marched through this important city on his way to the Mediterranean: as Hittite Mazaka and Roman Caesarea, it had been a
vital strategic cross-roads throughout history. I was not at ease
in Kayseri. The mosques overflowed at prayer-times and
women were nowhere to be seen. I was stared at and plagued by
young men who followed me in the streets wanting to practise
their English, or blatantly propositioning me. I was even pursued into an Aile Parki, a garden reserved for ladies and families. My refuge was the pastry shop next door to my hotel,
where the younger son, who was reading French Philology at
Erzerum University, was a charming boy with excellent
French. He and his father watched over me, giving me a
secluded table at the back of the shop where I could read and
write in peace, while they warded off interlopers.

It would take at least a week to see all the Seljuk and Ottoman
buildings in Kayseri so I had to content myself with a morning
in the Archaeological Museum, the Ottoman bedesten and a
mausoleum or two. In the morning I sought every possible
patch of shade from the burning sun but at lunch-time it
clouded over and began to rain. By next morning the temperature had dropped from 95° to 45° and I needed pullover,
cagoule and cycling gloves. Autumn had come to Anatolia and I
would have to race out of Kayseri if I was to get across the
Taurus Mountains before the winter snows began.

My haste was appropriate, as Alexander too had passed
swiftly down the same road, not attempting to conquer Cappadocia. He was keen to join battle with Darius, but first he had to
pass with his army through the Cilician Gates.

Even today there are few passes through the rugged, inhospitable Taurus Mountains and of these the Cilician Gates is still
the most important. Until a wider path was dynamited by
Ibrahim Pasha in the mid-nineteenth century to make room for
his artillery, the Cilician Gates were so narrow that a laden
donkey could scarcely pass through. In Alexander's day it was
virtually the only practicable route down to the Mediterranean
from central Anatolia. The Crusaders called them 'the Gates of

Judas'. Whoever held them held the key to the Mediterranean and the Middle East.

The Persian army was in control of the Gates in 333 BC. Alexander left his heavy infantry in the valley and made a forced march by night to take the defenders by surprise. His approach was in fact observed by the Persians, according to Arrian, but the sight of Alexander in person leading his crack regiments in such a swift, bold move was too much for them, and the guards turned and fled. So Alexander took the Cilician Gates without the loss of a single life. Coastal Cilicia lay before him. He had cleared the last major obstacle separating himself from the Great King.

For almost three days I pedalled across empty land under a grey sky. Each day was colder than the last and the north wind was icy, but at least it was behind me, helping me along in my flight south. I passed the salt lake again and its dreary flats, noticing a senior school with boarding houses. What a desolate place for children to board. Goatherds and potato pickers crouched over fires and I saw a few women winnowing grain. Otherwise there was nothing but the road and the railway track unwinding before me into empty distance. Yeşilhisar, Niğde, Bor. There were times when I felt like a microscopic insect, toiling with lonely determination across the immense expanse of the world's crust. The days dragged and I wished that I still had Shirley to cheer me up and act as pace-maker.

One day I climbed to the top of a desolate ridge from which I could see my road crossing the grey plain below until it disappeared over the next mountain pass. In the whole expanse of 30 miles or so there was one filling station. No houses, no people, no traffic. Eventually I reached the filling station and asked the attendant if there was any tea. 'Yok,' he said, using that unmistakable Turkish negative. I must have looked a poor dejected creature as I started to push my bicycle back to the empty, windswept road because he came running after me, shouting 'Var, var!' (There is! There is!) and led me into his office. His name was Ali. He was 22 and very proud to be in sole charge of a filling station at such a young age. While the kettle boiled on his paraffin stove he set out a tray with tea-glasses and biscuits and even took the sugar-lumps out of their box and

arranged them neatly on a saucer. Then he poured out the tea
and offered it as graciously as any tea-party hostess. There was a
map of Turkey on the wall, which was very useful, as my
Turkish was just about adequate to explain my route. Ali's one
customer was an old man who arrived on foot (Heaven only
knows from where) for a litre of paraffin in a can, and joined us
for a glass of tea. When I left, Ali declared that I was his great
friend and enveloped me in a big bear hug before waving me off
to the road. That small incident gave me a new understanding
of Turkish hospitality. In that huge, harsh, barren landscape, a
warm by the fire, a glass of tea or the offer of a lift was more than
a politeness. It could mean the difference between life and
death. In my case, Ali's tea was the only refreshment I found
that day until late afternoon and it encouraged me in my climb
over the highest point of the Taurus range, the Çaykavak Pass
at 5,200 ft.

After the pass came a steep descent. The Kayseri road joined
the highway from Konya and I began to glide gently downhill
along a silky-smooth road through beautiful scenery, a narrow
valley with high blue mountains on either side protecting the
apple orchards and olive groves. The railway now ran close
beside me through the narrow defile and a small tributary of the
Seyhan river went back and forth under the road nine or ten
times before the valley broadened out at Posantı. There was
blue sky and sunshine now, but the air was still sharp.

In Posantı I was joined at dinner by one of the many local
pharmacists (Turkey has more pharmacies than any country in
the world and they all do a brisk trade). Fethi had worked in a
German factory to save up for his chemist's shop. He spoke
German, which he said was a difficult language compared with
Turkish. 'Take this,' he said, lifting up a glass. 'Turkish –
bardak – an easy word; German – *Glas* – very difficult to
remember.' As I found words like *bardak* singularly un-
memorable, I was obliged to differ.

Fethi invited me home to meet his wife and mother. I had
nothing else to do that evening so I accepted without a
moment's hesitation and set out gaily enough, but it was further
than he had suggested. As he led me down ever darker and more
deserted alleyways, right away from the lights and the people, I

began to take fright. My imagination worked overtime. Robbery, rape, the flash of a knife at the throat, murder! My heart pounded. I must have been out of my mind. How *could* I have accepted an invitation from a total stranger? But my instinct had been right. Eventually we arrived at a brightly lit house, where his wife, his mother, his sister and his niece, who was also a pharmacist, all threw their arms round me and kissed me. We were joined by his uncle, a retired schoolmaster. We sat round the kitchen table in a warm, cosy glow. Fethi peeled and sliced apples for me and we drank tea together.

Although Turkish women are little seen in village streets, they rule their homes with authority. It was interesting to see the garrulous Fethi of the restaurant transformed into the subdued, dutiful member of a female establishment. It was his mother who dominated the proceedings, laughing, joking, talking merrily and asking me a thousand questions. Fethi was only her modest interpreter but I could see that he was proud of her vivacity and the warmth and ease with which she entertained me. As a woman traveller, I had an enormous advantage in Muslim countries. I met the women and saw the domestic side of the men. Male travellers are generally excluded from ordinary homes: they are entertained outside, or they eat and sleep in special guest quarters, right away from the women.

The uncle was keen that I should pay him a visit and rushed off to make his preparations while Fethi, his niece and I strolled there in leisurely fashion. I was appalled by what I found. The uncle lived in a sort of brick lean-to, no larger than a garage. There was an entrance section, where a fridge, table, television, food stores and packing cases were stacked from floor to ceiling. The 'living room' had whitewashed brick walls, bare floorboards spread with newspaper, a mattress on the floor, an old divan and a bookcase with nine tattered books. His clothes hung on nails round the walls, covered with newspapers. He said it was all he could afford on his teacher's pension. He and his nephew were the first Turks I had met who were critical of Özal and would vote Socialist in the next elections.

Despite the poor surroundings, we were entertained with customary Turkish generosity – rakı, Pepsi Cola, nuts, sliced tomatoes, aubergines and crystallised rosewater. I could scarcely do justice to this feast as I had eaten a large dinner followed by two apples at Fethi's. Uncle drank more rakı than was good for him and became over-animated. There was quite a scene when Fethi got up to escort me back to my hotel; his uncle wanted to take me. Fethi was clearly very unhappy at the suggestion but I assured him that I could easily cope. We must have looked a fine pair, picking our way round the potholes through the dark streets, the tiny, elderly uncle tottering along beside me, just keeping upright with his arm round my waist. Fortunately I had my bedroom key handy in my pocket. As soon as we reached the hotel, I thanked him for his hospitality, gave him a friendly peck on the cheek, then sprinted up to my room and locked the door. For fifteen minutes there was a plaintive calling, knocking and trying of the door-handle but he finally went away and I settled down to a cold night. A strong wind had sprung up and one of the window-panes was missing. I stuffed the hole as best I could with plastic bags and crawled into my sleeping bag under the blankets. I was glad when morning came.

Next day was one of my great days. The Cilician Gates – the route taken not only by Alexander but by Sennacherib, Seleucus I Nicator, Pompey, Hadrian, the Crusaders, Selim the Grim and Ibrahim Pasha, to name but a few of the world's conquerors who had led their armies through that pass. My excitement mounted as I climbed out of Posantı. The way was very narrow now. The railway ran along a ledge on the east side of the cleft while my road, the old road, ran along a corresponding ledge cut into the western wall. There was a new motorway set on piles over the river below – a sign of peaceful times, as its situation was a strategic disaster. I ascended through poplars, maples and mountain ash until I reached the pine belt, passing through a few small villages perched on the mountain-side. My one disappointment was that so much of the road had been widened that I failed to identify the crucial narrows and I began to wonder if I had passed through them the previous afternoon, on my way to Posantı, without realising it. The locals were no help. They had never heard of the Cilician Gates and my Turkish was not up to a detailed explanation.

The highest point was the Kandu Sırtı (4,500 ft), though the main pass was the Gülek Boğazi (3,500 ft). The sun was strong and I was able to take off my cagoule, but I still needed all my other layers. Then I began the descent to Tarsus. I had succeeded in getting across the heights of the Taurus before the snows came, so when I found a smart roadside restaurant I decided to celebrate with a good lunch. As I sat on the terrace with a kebab and a beer before me, gazing out over the pine forests to a distant valley, I was conscious of one of those rare moments in life. I was supremely happy – brimming over with happiness, and I knew it. I could think of nothing more perfect than that moment.

After the pinewoods the land opened out to a bleak plateau. The descent was very gradual, the road by no means all downhill, and it was late afternoon before I saw the rich green Cilician Plain. My descent was memorable chiefly because I was leaving the harsh Anatolian autumn behind. First the cycle mitts, then the pullover, then the extra pair of trousers, then the long-sleeved shirt were packed away in my panniers and by four o'clock I was back into summer again, pedalling along in a T-shirt and my cotton cycling pants. I entered Tarsus and just downstream from Justinian's Bridge I crossed the Tarsus river (Classical Cydnus), where Alexander nearly died of a chill and Cleopatra sailed in her golden barge with silver oars and purple sails to her fateful meeting with Mark Antony.

The Taurus Mountains were behind me. I felt utterly drained by the effort of crossing them. I had lost 22 lb of my London weight and I was conscious of my pounding pulse as I lay in bed that night, a sign of stress which I had not noticed since I gave up my job. As Tarsus was a small town with a Middle Eastern feel and no good hotels, I cycled along the coast to Mersin, a more sophisticated modern port, for three days' rest.

The shipping offices there confirmed the information I had been given in Ankara. There were no sea-passages to Egypt; only a car-ferry to Turkish Cyprus. Egypt had been my last hope of staying with Alexander. Visa problems aside, I was not keen on Syria as Alexander had only rushed through it; and it was not possible to cross from Syria into Iraq, as Syria supported Iran in the Middle East War and had closed its frontier.

I had been much more interested in entering northern Iraq direct from Turkey and following the Tigris down to Gaugamela, scene of Alexander's great battle with Darius. But in Mersin I heard rumours that Iraq was now using chemical weapons in the north against the Kurds and so I was finally reconciled to abandoning that project. Politics preventing me from following Alexander overland from Turkey, I booked a flight to Karachi, to meet him again in Pakistan. But my Turkish journey was not yet at an end. After my short rest in Mersin I returned to Tarsus, where Alexander had recovered from his chill, and we set out together in pursuit of Darius, the Great King himself.

As I crossed the Cilician Plain between Adana and Ceyhan, my relationship with the Turkish traffic police reached its happy climax. I knew that they had kept a paternal eye on me from the moment I had crossed into Turkey and I had appreciated their care. The officers in the first squad car over the border, seven weeks ago, had tooted and waved, then spoken into their car radio. After that, I was obviously passed on from district to district. There was always a friendly wave when I pedalled into view and my arrival was reported into the car radio. If the squad car had a loud-hailer, I would often get a Turkish greeting and once I heard 'Good morning. Have a nice day!' On the road to Ceyhan, a squad car overtook me, then pulled up.

'You should be cycling on the hard shoulder,' said the officer. I frowned at the stones and gravel and said in my best Turkish, 'The hard shoulder is difficult. Stones, stones. My bicycle is *çok güzel* and it will get punctures.'

'Sind Sie Deutsch?'

'Nein. Ich bin Englisch, aber ich spreche Deutsch.'

Then we were well away. The officer had worked in Munich and had good German, while the constable even spoke a little English. They wanted to know all about my journey and told me what I had already guessed – that they were not a bit concerned about the hard shoulder. They had just used it as a suitable excuse to stop and find out about me. Turks are engagingly and unashamedly nosey. We chatted for a good twenty minutes in the shade of a tree; they would have gone on

all morning had I not excused myself and pedalled away. Two
hours later, as I passed a Shell station, I found them waiting for
me. A table was already laid outside the restaurant and they had
ordered lunch for three. They told me what a boring job they
had, cruising up and down the same stretch of highway day
after day, looking for traffic offenders. My bicycle and I were
the most interesting things they had seen on their road for
years. As they waved me off the constable shouted after me, in a
mixture of Turkish and English: 'I'm going to travel too – but
not on a bike. I'm going to buy the most powerful car in the
world and drive it at top speed all the way across Europe and
America! Brrrm! Brrrm! I'll come and see you in London.'

After Ceyhan I turned south round the top of the bay and found
myself on the Plain of Issus. This narrow strip of land between
the Amanos Mountains and the sea led down to Iskenderun and
the Syrian Gates (Belen Pass), which was the main route into
Syria. To Alexander's knowledge (a rare failure of military
intelligence), it was the only route and he marched across the
plain and through the Syrian Gates knowing that Darius was
waiting for him on the other side of the mountains. But Darius,
with his huge army, was growing impatient. Alexander's chill, a
number of skirmishes and a bad storm had delayed him, so
Darius unwisely abandoned his position on the wide Syrian
plain where his vast numerical superiority, particularly in
cavalry, could have been used to devastating effect and led his
hordes through the Amanian Gates (Bogtche Pass), to the
north of the Syrian Gates, and descended to the Plain of Issus,
searching for his adversary. Alexander, startled to learn that
Darius was now at his rear, astride his line of communications,
rushed back through the Syrian Gates to do battle. On the
narrow plain the greater skill and flexibility of the Greeks under
the courageous personal leadership of Alexander completely
overwhelmed the 600,000 Persians, crammed together into too
small a space for manoeuvre. Darius himself was no hero and
soon fled the battlefield, first in his chariot, then on horseback.
Darkness saved him, but Alexander took possession of his
chariot, his royal mantle, his shield and his bow. More importantly, he captured Darius' wife, children and mother, whom

the Great King had abandoned in his flight. Alexander was greatly admired in antiquity for his generous treatment of these hostages, to whom he always accorded royal respect.

Alexander had achieved his stated objectives: he had freed the Greeks in Asia Minor and humiliated the Persian king. He was now faced with two alternative strategies. He could be satisfied with his achievements and adopt a defensive policy, simply consolidating his hold on Asia Minor against Persian attempts to recapture it; or he could go on the offensive and try to conquer the entire Persian Empire. With the wind of fortune in his sails, his course was inevitable. He would fight the Persians to the end.

His decision was not surprising but, as always, his strategy was. Instead of pursuing Darius into his heartland, he continued south to Egypt, capturing Phoenicia on the way. So the Persians lost their last Mediterranean ports and their fleet disintegrated after their defeat at Sidon. Alexander was accepted as Pharaoh of Egypt. He traced the outlines of his new city of Alexandria, then returned to take Syria and Iraq, defeating Darius again on the Tigris at the Battle of Gaugamela. Only then, when the Levant was secure behind him, did he pursue the Great King into Persia itself.

I took photographs of the Plain of Issus and pedalled along to Iskenderun, founded by Alexander as Alexandria ad Issum and later called Alexandretta. He would have been disappointed. Although it was a major Turkish naval base, it was a dull provincial town. I felt so weary when I arrived there, that I lay down for a short siesta and slept until long past dinner-time.

My last day's cycling in Turkey was one of the most gruelling. The climb from Iskenderun up to the Syrian Gates was more than eleven miles on a dreadful road surface into a strong headwind. It was a windy corner of the Mediterranean, as I could see from the wretched, twisted trees by the roadside. The altitude of the pass was only 2,430 ft, but the ascent was so difficult that I had to push my heavily laden bicycle most of the way. From the top, though, the view was spectacular. It really was the gateway to Syria. I could see the Syrian plains spreading out before me to the far horizon. On the way down to Antakya (Antioch) it snowed and I was almost jolted to death on the stony road. I feared for Condor's tyres. If the state of the roads into a city is an indication of its importance, Antakya has fallen sadly since the days when it was the fourth city of the civilised world.

Although Antioch was important from Hellenistic times, it is best known in the West for its role in the history of the Christian Church. I visited the Crusader church in the cave used by St Peter for worship, where it is said that the followers of Christ first decided to call themselves Christians. The Church of St Peter in Antioch therefore claims to be the earliest Christian church. In Antioch, St Peter united the Church by drawing together Jews and Gentiles, and in Antioch, in 341, the bishops began the process of tearing it apart. By accepting Arianism at their Council, they sowed the seeds of the eventual schism between the Eastern and Roman Churches.

For all its Christian connections, Antakya was a Middle Eastern city. My hotel was full of Saudi Arabians and Syrians, mostly wholesalers in Turkey to buy fruit and vegetables. They huddled in dim corners of the hotel lobby, clicking their worry beads, wheeling and dealing in mysterious whispers. My particular friend was a debonair Saudi in dazzling white robes who looked a portly 40 but was in fact only 24. (A Syrian from Houston, Texas, was our interpreter.) I was his mother's age and he collapsed into helpless laughter whenever I mentioned my bicycle. He had a vision of his mother donning T-shirt and cycling pants and riding a bicycle round Jeddah. When he heard of my visa problems, he suggested that I should cycle across Saudi Arabia instead and was genuinely astonished to learn that Saudi visas were the most difficult of all to obtain, and would never be given to a solitary woman.

I had cycled 3,814 miles from London, 1,471 of them across Turkey. Now, having travelled to Antakya in the far south-east, I had to go all the way back to Istanbul in the far north-west to catch my plane to Karachi. I went by bus and was pleased to find that my bicycle caused no problems. I simply rode it into the bus station and, free of charge, it was laid in the luggage compartment, in a comfortable nest among the suitcases.

I had a fortnight to spare before my flight and I badly needed a holiday, so I broke my journey at Kızkalesı, not far from

Mersin, where I had a quiet, restful time by the Mediterranean. In late October it was still warm enough to sit on the beach and bathe, though darkness fell by five o'clock. I ate three hearty meals a day, trying to put on weight in preparation for the rigours of Pakistan and India, where I knew that the diet across-country would be poor. I love my food and it was a delightful experience, after years of prudent weight-control, to be able to eat as greedily as I liked. I felt a new woman by the time I caught the Istanbul coach. The bus began its climb up to the Anatolian Plateau and I looked in amazement at the stark bastion of the Taurus range. Had I really crossed such fearsome mountains on my bicycle? Already it seemed unreal. Turkey was already receding. My mind was now on Pakistan. I was ready, both physically and psychologically, for the next stage.

10

The Indus Valley

KARACHI – THATTA – HYDERABAD – LARKANA –
SUKKUR – MIRPUR – RAHIMYAR KHAN – KHANPUR –
AHMADPUR EAST – BAHAWALPUR – MULTAN –
KABIRWALA – SHORKOT – JHANG – FAISALABAD –
CHINIOT – SARGODHA – MALIKWAL – JHELUM

. . . You will not meet
The Laestrygonians, the Cyclops or fierce Poseidon
Unless you carry them in your soul,
Unless your soul sets them in your path.

(C. P. Cavafy)

I flew into Karachi on 31 October. I had enjoyed everything about the flight, especially the cycle ride out to Istanbul Airport along the notorious Londra Asfalt. The hotel manager had been so worried he had wanted to drive me there, but I scarcely noticed the traffic. I went first to the square in front of St Sophia and found the very centre of Constantine's city, the site of the milion from which all roads in the Byzantine Empire were measured. A fire hydrant now stands on the spot. The square was full of tourists, mostly German and Japanese with cameras. They grouped round me in perplexity.

'Was fotografieren Sie?'

'This fire hydrant,' I said mischievously, without explanation. They watched anxiously for a while, then *their* cameras started to click too. I left them photographing they knew not what and set off along the Via Egnatia once again, following its route through the gap in the Theodosian Walls and past the Edirne Gate. I was delighted to be able to trace the road I had followed across Greece from the heart of Byzantium, even if I had to fight with lorries all the way.

As my flight was not until 3.20 a.m., I followed the example of the young backpackers in the airport, spread out my mat beside theirs in a secluded area of the concourse and had a good sleep. I had cycled less than 4,000 miles but in myself I was light years away from the headmistress in the Hardy Amies suit. I had no 'image' to preserve and my needs were simple. On the half-empty PIA jumbo, I had three seats, pillows and blankets. I knew nothing of the flight until the hostess woke me with breakfast and I looked out of the window at the frigates patrolling the war-torn Persian Gulf. Though not timid by nature, I must confess to feeling greatly relieved when the Strait of Hormuz was behind us. Soon I looked down on Karachi and saw a desert city. There were a few dots of green inside its boundaries, then the desert began. Strips of asphalt radiated out into a blank, sandy immensity beside the Arabian Sea. What terrain to cycle through! From the air it looked impossible.

Pakistan was my seventh country and my first new one. I had no idea what to expect. What I found in the airport was efficiency, kindness and, above all, people who spoke English. After three months of battling with difficult tongues, I could have real conversations again. I made a present of my English–Turkish phrase book to a group of struggling Turks.

I was a little apprehensive, as I had never flown with my bicycle before, but there it was by the luggage carousel, with a porter standing guard. All was in order except the handlebars, which had been turned so firmly to save storage space that I was unable to straighten them out again. I wheeled my problem to the manager of the baggage department. He was doing his best to calm four distraught Pakistanis who had lost their luggage and I had by this time been long enough in the East to know that nothing is ever achieved there by pressure. I sat down in a corner of the office and waited quietly. When he had dealt with the hysterical passengers, I told the manager what a difficult job he had. It was not a tactical move – I did feel genuinely sorry for the poor harassed man – but it served as one. He blossomed under my sympathy, explaining his Bagtrac Computer Program and talking proudly of his responsibilities. The head porter was summoned, a large, upright figure of a man with a white beard and the bearing of a regimental sergeant major. He took infinite trouble with the realignment of my handlebars, tightened the rest of the nuts, checked the tyres and held the bicycle while I loaded it, checking and tightening the straps after me. He refused a tip. 'No problem. A pleasure,' he said. With my bicycle in excellent order, I set out into the hot, humid morning.

It was strange to be on the left-hand side of the road again. As I cycled the eleven miles into the city centre, everyone stared. I was used to that after central Anatolia; the difference here was that the Pakistanis smiled and laughed much more readily than the Turks. A little boy on a bicycle called to me and gave me a smart military salute.

The first thing that struck me about Pakistan was the colour. The buses, lorries and scooter taxis looked like rides from a Victorian fairground. Green or red, they were painted all over with pictures and patterns in primary colours, trimmed with gleaming filigree chrome – chrome coronets crowning the drivers' cabs, rows of tiny chrome hearts or diamonds dangling on chains from the bumpers, and pennants flying from every projection. There were prayers and slogans, brilliant landscapes, lions, General Zia, houris, palm trees, menageries, everything the imagination of man could invent. Not a centimetre was left undecorated. Horns blared and the bus conductors banged on the sides of their buses, touting for more passengers when their buses had already overflowed and crowds were clinging to the outside. Motorcycles sped by with whole families aboard – one small child in front, father driving, mother riding side-saddle with cool, calm elegance, a baby in her arms and another small child squashed between herself and her husband.

Despite all this frantic activity on the roads, it was easier to cycle in some parts of town than to walk on the pavements, for these were crammed with tradespeople. There were not just the usual street vendors. There were opticians, watch repairers, barbers, ear-cleaners, palmists, Vespa mechanics, masseurs, typists, all plying their trade by the roadside under brilliantly coloured placards.

Then there were the clothes. Both men and women wore the light cotton baggy *shalwar* trousers with a long, loose shirt, called a *kameez*, over the top. It was a most elegant outfit, well suited to the heat and humidity. The men's suits were all of one colour, usually white, cream or beige but sometimes in beautiful shades of lavender or palest green. The drab grey Western suit was little in evidence; it was banned for Government employees. The women tended to mix and match bright colours and finished off their ensembles with the *dupatta*, a long, flowing georgette stole which they wore over their heads or draped over their shoulders.

But all was not gaiety and colour. Karachi was a troubled city. Two bombs exploded there the morning I arrived and the police found various caches of weapons in house-to-house searches. With its large migrant population, come from all parts of Pakistan to seek work, there was tribal rivalry as well as political disaffection; and there were religious quarrels between the majority Sunnis and the minority Shi'ites. A curfew had just been lifted but it was soon to be reimposed. Because of this tense situation I was careful to choose a hotel with its own restaurant, so that I had no need to go out in the evenings.

I had an introduction to a couple of influential Pakistanis, which was a great help. I saw them only once, as they were leaving next day for Lahore to watch the World Cup Cricket, but they gave me the names and telephone numbers of friends of theirs in every major city in Pakistan, so that I should always have someone to turn to in an emergency.

Zuhra and Masud were very vocal about the law and order problems in Sind and advised me strongly against cycling between Karachi and Sukkur. Not only was Sind Separatism a violent movement, but Sind was also the heartland of Benazir Bhutto's opposition party. There was bombing, shooting and kidnapping. Even trains and buses were attacked by armed gangs, some politically motivated, other simply *dacoits* (gangsters) taking advantage of the unsettled situation. They made an appointment for me to discuss my route with the British Consul-General himself, when I went to get a letter of support for my Indian visa.

Zuhra offered me the use of their house during their absence in Lahore, but my hotel was central and it was convenient to stay there. But I gladly accepted Masud's offer of the services of his secretary and driver. Karachi was a large, hot, dusty city and it took experience of Pakistan to deal with officialdom. Three days and five visits were needed to acquire the Indian visa. And we never found the Department of Archaeology, despite an afternoon's search. For some bureaucratic reason, I was supposed to go there personally to pick up a chitty confirming my telephone booking of accommodation at their Rest Houses. Then I searched for two days before tracking down a bank, the Habib, which had a proper overseas section and would cash my traveller's cheques. (Hotel exchange rates were abysmal, presumably because the hotels had to devote the same amount of time and labour to recouping their rupees.) Finally, there was the difficulty over postcards. There were none on display and it took me another whole morning to find a stationer with a stock of dusty cards. Then I queued for stamps in the packed post office. Having discovered the price of a stamp to Europe, I asked for twenty but the clerk would sell me only three, for the cards I actually had in my hand. Then I queued at another counter to see them franked: I had been told that this was essential in Pakistan and India, as unfranked stamps were likely to be picked off for re-use and the cards thrown into the bin. In total, I spent almost a day on those three postcards. The literate classes all have servants, drivers and clerks to stand in the endless queues and probably have no idea of the time it takes to perform the simplest tasks. If they had to do their own chores, efficiency would improve overnight, though unemployment would certainly rise.

I went to parties in Karachi where the Scotch flowed. Alcohol had been made illegal in Pakistan as General Zia was bringing the law into line with the strict Islamic *shariah* laws which operated in Saudi Arabia, Kuwait and Iran. I was told that Pakistanis who wanted to drink still drank, but they did it behind locked doors and the profits went to the bootleggers, not to the Government. The *shariah* penalties of stoning women to death for adultery and chopping off hands for theft had been introduced, but the old British legal traditions died hard and no court had yet been callous enough to impose such sentences. The Government had banned bank interest, as usury is forbidden in the Koran, but Pakistan was still not a paradise for borrowers; they paid 'mark up' instead. Altogether, it seemed as if the fundamentalist zeal of General Zia was being thwarted at every turn by the kind, easy-going Pakistanis.

I was lionised at the parties and given useful advice about my food en route. I must always go where the trucks were parked, as most long-distance drivers were Pathans, who were very particular people. If a stall-holder served bad food, or tried to overcharge, he was likely to wake up in hospital, riddled with bullets. A picturesque exaggeration, but I found it contained a kernel of truth.

The Consul-General confirmed and elaborated on what I had already been told about Sind. The situation had deteriorated so badly over the past two years that he no longer allowed his staff to go there. He had visited the area himself, but under the protection of the local Ameers, the big land-owners, who had their own private armies; the police and regular militia were powerless by comparison. So there was no question of my cycling across Sind. If I refused to fly or take a train, he would have to ask the Ameers to look after me – and they would simply put me in an armoured truck and drive me across. The risk was kidnap rather than robbery or gratuitous violence. The political factions would like nothing better than to seize a Western hostage, as their grievances would then be brought sharply to the attention of Western governments. He smiled ruefully: 'Sorry to rob you of the most exciting chapter in your book!'

In the end we reached a compromise. If he would let me cycle from Karachi to Hyderabad, I would take the train from there to Sukkur. He was a little unhappy, as Hyderabad itself was a hotbed of insurrection and the Sukkur region was troubled, though not so downright dangerous as central Sind. He sent me to meet the young man who would have to come personally to my rescue if I got into serious trouble. I tried hard to convince everyone that I was enterprising, but not foolhardy.

Karachi was a creation of the British Raj, a fishing village which had grown into the great industrial centre of Pakistan. Under the Victorians it was graced with splendid Gothic monuments, usually 'erected in gratitude and esteem by the people of the Province'. Later Emperors of India were celebrated in a ponderous mixture of neo-Classical and Moghul. Karachi's most famous modern monument was the Mausoleum of Jinnah, the Quaid-i-Azam, 'Father of the Nation'. With his Savile Row suits and his penchant for champagne, Jinnah would have been startled at the turn his country was taking under General Zia. I went about my sightseeing in an unusually subdued frame of mind, worried for the first time about what lay ahead.

I was determined not to fly up the Indus. International politics had prevented me from following Alexander across the Middle East but I would follow him through Pakistan, whatever the difficulties. As I had been unable to enter the country, as he did, from Afghanistan, I would have to take his route in the opposite direction, cycling up the Indus and Jhelum rivers, then heading for the North West Frontier. It would all be an approximation to Alexander's journey, as the rivers had changed their course across the flat lands of the Punjab and Sind and the cities stormed by Alexander had disappeared without trace, but I should be travelling along the same general route, through much the same kind of country.

When I met Alexander again on the shores of the Arabian Sea he was a changed man. He had marched through Persia, Bactria and southern Russia, conquering all before him and founding a multitude of Alexandrias. Then he had entered Pakistan through the Hindu Kush and fought his way down to the Punjab. The entire Persian Empire was now under his control but he was still not satisfied. He wanted to battle on, south through India, exploring unknown lands and finally reaching the ocean, which bounded the earth. His men felt differently. After eight years of ceaseless campaigning, they had achieved their main objective and lost their taste for war. They wanted to go home. In November 326, they mutinied.

Alexander agreed to turn back but not by the way he had come. Never short of ideas, he decided to sail down the Jhelum (Hydaspes) and Indus rivers to the Arabian Sea, then find a route from there to Persia. There was fighting all the way to the coast and Alexander himself was pierced in the lung during a siege. His courage had now turned to recklessness. Sending Nearchos off with the fleet to the Strait of Hormuz, he marched his men across the Makran Desert, an act of outrageous folly.

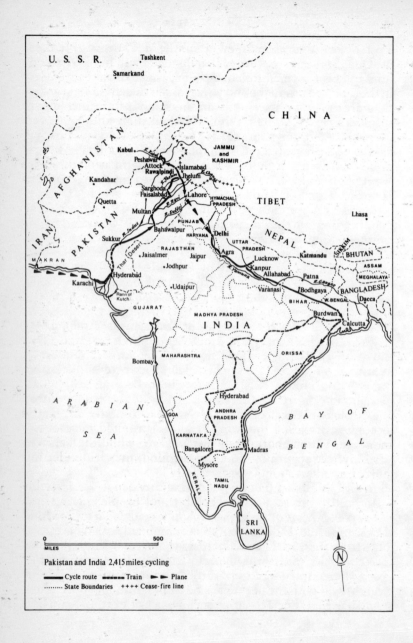

U.S.S.R.

Tashkent

Samarkand

CHINA

AFGHANISTAN

Kabul

Peshawar
Attock
Rawalpindi
Islamabad
Jhelum

JAMMU
and
KASHMIR

TIBET

Lhasa

Kandahar

Quetta

PAKISTAN

Sarghoda
Faisalabad
Multan
Bahawalpur

Lahore

HYMACHAL
PRADESH

NEPAL

SIKKIM

BHUTAN

IRAN

Sukkur

R. Indus

PUNJAB

HARYANA

Delhi

UTTAR
PRADESH

Katmandu

ASSAM

MEGHALAYA

MAKRAN

Thar Desert

RAJASTHAN

Jaisalmer

Jaipur

Agra

Lucknow

Kanpur
Allahabad

R. Jumna

Patna

R. Ganges

BANGLADESH

Karachi

Hyderabad

Jodhpur

R. Ganges

Varanasi

Bodhgaya

Dacca

Rann of
Kutch

Udaipur

GUJARAT

MADHYA PRADESH

INDIA

BIHAR

W. BENGAL

Burdwan

Calcutta

Bombay

MAHARASHTRA

ORISSA

ARABIAN

Hyderabad

BAY   OF

SEA

GOA

ANDHRA
PRADESH

BENGAL

KARNATAKA

Bangalore

Madras

Mysore

KERALA

TAMIL
NADU

SRI
LANKA

0   500
MILES

Pakistan and India 2,415 miles cycling

———— Cycle route   ┅┅┅┅ Train   ►━► Plane

········· State Boundaries   ++++ Cease-fire line

N

Even today the Makran is untamed, a burning, roadless, waterless wilderness. Despite night marches, his troops suffered intolerable hardships and the sick and exhausted were left in the sand to die. Virtually all the animals died of thirst, sank in the burning sand dunes, or were slaughtered for meat. Only a tiny, desperate band of men reached Hormuz and continued into Persia. Arrian claims that the nature of the terrain was known to Alexander but that he wanted to cross it, as no previous ruler had ever succeeded in getting an army through. He paid off his few remaining veterans and sent them home. He himself, weakened by his wound and the desert crossing, returned to Babylon, where he died of a fever, still dreaming of his next campaign. Ambition and restlessness had driven him over the edge.

The Makran Desert spread west of Karachi. To the east lay the Great Thar Desert, that I had to skirt all the way to Bahawalpur. I rode out early past the airport, past 'St Solomon's Cambridge High School and College' above a row of sparse little shops, on the old road to Hyderabad, via Thatta, as it would take me up the Indus. In any case, the new direct highway to Hyderabad was a cyclist's nightmare – 110 miles across desert with not even a village on the way.

It was good to be back on my bicycle after my three weeks' break and my spirits rose as I bowled along the dual-carriageway past all the factories. It was not unlike the Great West Road in England and that comparison gave me confidence. Anticipating the worst, I had distributed most of my money in various corners of my luggage, while the balance, with my passport, hung in a purse round my neck under my shirt. I also had a loud whistle handy.

In fact, my first day out of Karachi was not the least bit frightening. It was a public holiday and people, not lorries, were on the move. A huge procession was forming just outside the city. Buses and camel-carts were crammed with passengers, a chanting mob with green banners lining up behind. As their chant was in Urdu, I had no idea what they were shouting, but the rhythm was international: 'What do we want? Fish and chips! What do we want? Fish and chips!' I pulled up to take a photograph of a camel-cart overflowing with excited, waving children and was most alarmed when a policeman rushed over, shouting at me. In such a politically sensitive area, I assumed that photography was a crime and waited to be arrested, or at least cautioned. Instead, he called over his colleague and the pair of them posed for me in front of the cart.

Soon I was out in the desert, cycling through sand and scrub. The sun beat down and my water supply diminished. Cold bottled drinks were out of the question, as the small roadside tea-stalls had no electricity. So I made do with Pakistani tea – leaves boiled up in a mixture of milk and water with a mountain of sugar. Drunk piping hot, it goes down surprisingly well and is very sustaining – a safely boiled drink, which I came to enjoy. I always filled up my water-bottle at the stalls, then stopped at a discreet distance to drop in a Puritab.

There were plenty of cyclists on the road, gangs of young men travelling towards Karachi. They rode heavy black bicycles and had their bedding-rolls tied to their rear-carriers with string. At Gharq, where I did find chilled Pepsi Colas and drank three in rapid succession, a cheerful group came up for a chat – they in Urdu, I in English – and we had a photo-session with our bicycles. I realised then that Pakistani men were desperate to have their photographs taken and resolved to keep my camera out of sight. Another bad moment was my first encounter with a police roadblock. I was flagged down by a stern, well-armed figure in immaculate khaki – only to be invited into the hut and entertained to tea. This turned out to be the pleasant custom all the way across Pakistan.

I passed near Lake Haleji, said to be the largest wildfowl sanctuary in Asia, with over 70 species of Siberian migratory birds, but it was over two miles from the road and the only wildlife I saw were two carrion crows picking at the squashed carcass of a huge lizard, or small crocodile, on the highway. It was so large I was glad to have met it dead, not alive.

As I neared Thatta, electricity began again and I was able to get two cold Sprites in a village. I was hemmed in there by at least 80 men and boys, one of whom acted as interpreter. They just couldn't believe that someone like me, from London, had come to their village and they hoped that I was not afraid of such a big crowd. They bombarded me with questions, asking me to find them jobs in England, offering me tea and wanting to take me off to meet some important personage. It was all a bit overwhelming late in the afternoon after 60 miles of desert, but they meant well and I managed to smile through it all.

At Makli Hill, just before Thatta, there was a huge necropolis with some Moghul tombs in blue faience and carved sandstone. More importantly, there was an Archaeological Society Rest Home where I had a telephone booking, though not the official chitty confirming it. The young Archaeological Officer knew nothing of my booking, but he let me have a room nonetheless, sparsely furnished but with a cold shower. I was glad of my sleeping-bag and large cotton square, as the bed had no top sheet or pillowcase. With my clean cotton square wrapped round the cushion, I could zip myself snugly into my sleeping-bag and sleep in hygienic comfort.

Holiday-makers and pilgrims had come in droves to the Makli tombs. There was a full moon, drums were beating and the necropolis swarmed with praying, chanting Muslims: there was strange howling and motorbikes whizzed round the Rest House until the early hours. I was the only overnight guest and it was all so unnerving that I locked and bolted my door and decided to go without dinner, afraid to venture forth into the dark. I managed on an apple and a packet of ginger nuts, and forced myself to consume three litres of disgusting Puritab water, to get my dehydrated kidneys working again.

I stopped in Thatta for breakfast and viewed my surroundings with dismay. The café was open to the street and in the gloom behind the tables were rows of sleeping men, rolled up in their blankets on charpoys (string beds). It was my first experience of a *muzzafir khana*, a local guest house. An unkempt individual joined me at my table, calling me 'Sir' throughout the one-sided conversation. After Pakistani tea and a dry chapatti, I restored my spirits in the beauty of Shah Jehan's blue-tiled mosque and gardens. Thatta was once the capital of Sind and may have been Alexander's port of embarkation, but its former glory had faded and I found only a poor, depressing little town with packs of pie-dogs asleep in the dust.

It was another 60 miles to Hyderabad, but there was a village marked halfway where I planned to stop for lunch. I soon

reached the end of Thatta's scant sugar cane and entered the
real desert with the wind, inevitably, against me. There was
nothing there – no houses, no tea-stalls, no cyclists and scarcely
any traffic, the empty immensity made even more forbidding
by rocky outcrops which could have hidden kidnappers or
dacoits. My whistle was useless. There would be no one to hear
it. I pedalled doggedly on, looking forward to Jhirk with its
people and its Pepsi Colas. Just as my water ran out, a man
appeared from a roadside lean-to with a glass of water. I drank
as little as I could without appearing rude and poured the rest
into my water-bottle, so that I could treat it with a Puritab later.
The ten minutes I had to wait for the tablet to do its work
seemed an eternity and I spurred myself on after that by
promising myself three gulps of water every quarter of an hour.
After another anxious two hours, when my water was long since
finished, I approached Jhirk. There were no buildings on the
road, just a narrow dirt track leading to a small cluster of houses
in the distance. There was unlikely to be even a tea-stall there. I
could only press on.

I saw a patch of shade beside a bridge over a dry river-bed and
crouched there to eat my last apple. There were three shacks
nearby and I was soon surrounded by their male inhabitants.
They stood in a silent circle, watching me eat my apple. I
already knew the Urdu for water: it was the first word I had
learned in that parched land. 'Pani,' I said and a small boy ran to
one of the shacks, returning with my water-bottle full of gritty
brown liquid. Two Puritabs for that! Then they pointed to
their mouths, miming an offer of food, but I pointed to my
apple and smiled. There was relief all round.

The afternoon seemed endless in the eerie silence and my
pace was slow against the burning wind. What little traffic there
had been in the morning had dwindled to nothing in the baking
afternoon sun. I was utterly alone, equidistant from Thatta
and Hyderabad, in the dead centre of the wilderness. I worried
about my slow progress and wondered if I should reach the
safety of Hyderabad by nightfall. I started to see dacoits and
kidnappers behind every rock. For the first time on my trip, I
smelt real danger. I could be robbed, raped, even murdered,
and no one would ever know. The vultures would deal with

what was left of me and the wind would cover my bones with the desert sand. When I heard a heavy lorry approaching from behind, my heart started to thump. I was completely defenceless and I had worked myself up into a state of terror at my vulnerability. Then the nightmare came true. The lorry pulled up beside me and there, in that bleakest, loneliest, most desolate stretch of the desert, three wild-looking men in turbans and filthy *dishdashas* jumped out and rushed towards me. One was armed with a rifle and wore a bandolier of cartridges. He seized my bicycle by the handlebars, while the other two men grabbed my arms and tried to push me towards the lorry. This was it. Kidnap! The Consul-General had been right.

The lorry was flying black streamers. These had been variously explained to me – mourning for President Bhutto, opposition to General Zia, boycott of the forthcoming local elections, Sind separatism, Shi'ite fanaticism. Whatever they stood for, it was trouble, and they were a terrifying sight in the middle of nowhere.

I was still astride my bicycle. I clung on grimly and somehow, with the strength of desperation, I managed to wrench it away and pedalled off at furious speed. The lorry came in pursuit and again the three men leapt out, shouting loudly at me as they grabbed my arms and my bicycle a second time. By now, I was shaking with fright, but my terror only heightened my resolve. Screaming at them to let me go, I again broke free. I heard the lorry start up and soon it was cruising beside me, but this time the men only beckoned from inside the driver's cab. Then one of them held up a can, pointed to the bottle on my bicycle and said 'Pani.' I desperately needed water, but was it a trap? He smiled, then climbed down alone from the lorry. I hesitated, still uncertain, then decided to risk it. I stopped and handed over my water-bottle. He filled it, then pointed to the lorry with a puzzled expression. I suddenly understood and my knees went weak with relief. They were only doing their best to help a poor, crazy woman on her own in the middle of the desert under the fierce afternoon sun. They were offering a lift, not a kidnap! When I shook my head, they drove off with anxious, bewildered looks and waves. It was just like Turkey, except that the men were rougher and we had no language in common. I had only reacted differently because my head had been filled with notions of disaster. As I sat on the empty asphalt, trying to control my trembling limbs, I decided that even in troubled Sind I would relax and trust the innate goodness of the people I met. I would not have embarked on my trip had I not felt sure that 99.999 per cent of the world's population were good, kind, helpful people; and the 0.001 per cent of robbers or rapists were just as likely to turn up in Shepherd's Bush or Walberswick as on the edge of the Great Thar Desert. More often than not, danger lies in the imagination. I would never again let suspicion poison my mind. I would be prudent, but unafraid.

Perils apart, I was of course only playing at survival in the desert. I could at any time have begged a lift of a lorry or paid my fare in one of the Suzuki vans which swayed past wildly from time to time with eight seats, 30 standing and luggage on the top. But it was a challenge to get across the desert unaided, surviving on an apple and my water-bottle.

As I approached Hyderabad, I understood why the Consul-General had called it a centre of insurrection. Tea-stalls, mosques and houses were flying the black flag or the red, black and green banner of the opposition PPP (Pakistan People's Party). There were photographs of Benazir Bhutto everywhere, often beside a photograph of her father decked with a martyr's garland. There were a few Pakistani flags but I felt it took courage to fly them. I was welcomed and treated with kindness everywhere I stopped, so the problems were General Zia's, not mine. Revived by four Pepsi Colas, I just got over the double Indus bridge and past the police roadblock into Hyderabad by nightfall. It was at Hyderabad or Bahmanabad that Alexander is thought to have built his dockyard.

The train journey to Sukkur was quite an experience, and one which started in the station. Tickets were kept in a dark cupboard and the myopic clerk in thick pebble spectacles had to use an oil-lamp to locate the appropriate ones. I finally got to the front of the very slow queue and bought a ticket to Moenjodaro, as I wanted to stop off and visit the ruins of the city where the Indus Valley Civilisation (3000–1700 BC) had reached its zenith. Then I went to register my bicycle. With the registration clerk as my interpreter, I sat in the middle of an admiring crowd of porters and station officials, telling them about myself and my bicycle ride. 'In Pakistan,' they said, 'ladies of your age are resting.' I discovered from them that the train was not due into Moenjodaro until 6 p.m. and that the site and tourist bungalow were a long way from the station. So I changed my plans. Moenjodaro was not relevant to my ride and I had in any case seen the best artefacts from the site in the Karachi Museum. I booked through to Larkana instead, this time jumping the queue with my retinue of station officials. After numerous cups of tea, my procession escorted me to a first-class ladies' compartment, carrying my bags and wheeling Condor to the guard's van. They queued up to shake hands and refused tips or payment for the tea.

I climbed aboard. The carriages lined up behind the shiny black steam engine were wooden boxes, painted green and yellow. It looked like my old Hornby train-set. My travelling companions were all in purdah. Two were obviously wealthy, wearing beautiful silk clothes, topped with an enveloping black silk cloak and hood. They travelled with their maids. The women all uncovered their heads when the train was on the move, but shrouded themselves in stations or when one of their husbands called in from the next-door compartment. It was unbelievably dusty in the train and I soon produced the sea-green *dupatta* I had bought in Karachi and swathed my own head and face. That was a great success, especially as my *dupatta* exactly matched the *shalwar kameez* of one of the ladies, and we all became very cheerful. We were joined later by a woman with seven children, six boys and a girl, who were all terribly rowdy and uncontrolled by Western standards. The youngest boy was already running around and had two fine rows of teeth but his mother breast-fed him whenever he grizzled – which was often.

I tried to read but it was too hot and noisy. Sometimes the train ran along beside the Indus or one of its canals and I saw water-buffalo bathing, wildfowl, small donkeys, camels and bullock carts with solid wooden wheels. But the aridity between the green patches seemed endless. People and animals kicked up dust and everyone and everything was smothered in it. The small villages were of baked brick with thatched roofs and later on, towards Larkana, they were built of reeds. The pale bricks of 'major' buildings were engraved in intricate patterns or laid in designs with gaps to resemble filigree work. Sometimes the train halted at a platform where there was no village at all, just footpaths leading off into the empty sand. The rains in that area had failed for the last two seasons, but some parts of the Thar Desert had been without rain for seven years. I read later that Sind had been declared a disaster area. Looking out on that abomination of desolation, I was secretly rather pleased that circumstances had prevented me from cycling through it. And I was even further tempted: if Alexander had taken a fleet of boats all the way down the Jhelum and Indus, why should I not take a fleet of trains all the way up them?

The beige monochrome of the landscape was relieved by the people's brilliant clothes. Magenta, scarlet, orange, shocking pink, purple, dazzling turquoise and an almost luminous leaf-green were the favourite colours. Most of the men wore magenta hats like upturned cake tins, sometimes with scalloped edges, sometimes simply cut back over the forehead, but always embroidered and gleaming with mirror-work. They strode along, a brilliant shawl slung elegantly over one shoulder; their shoes, again embroidered and covered in mirror-work, had pointed, turn-up toes. The women and children wore startling combinations of colours and even the *burka* of the women in strictest purdah (the enveloping garment with a grille over the face) was more likely to be turquoise than black or white. Both sexes covered mouth and nose with a scarf or the end of a turban to keep out the dust, and looked as if they were veiled.

When I arrived at Larkana in the dark, my bicycle was unrideable, as the front wheel had been buckled under a moun-tain of sacks. The inevitable crowd of men collected round me on the platform while I tried, tired and flustered, to get my wheel to turn. At just the right moment a station official appeared. He led me over to a bench and brought me a cup of tea while a porter was sent to find a horse-drawn tonga large enough for me, my luggage and my bicycle. He had no English but he smiled reassuringly, held up imaginary reins and made a 'clop clop' sound. Meanwhile the crowd of starers grew and grew until finally the police arrived to find out the cause of the disturbance.

I had the name of a hotel from my guide book but the tonga-driver had never heard of it and when he enquired in the town, we were told that it had closed down three years before. The streets were dark and crowded, there were no hotels to be seen and my driver spoke no English. But as usual, just as panic was beginning to set in, salvation arrived, this time in the shape of a young man named Stephen, who jumped up beside me on the tonga and announced in good English that he was a Christian and a schoolmaster and had come to help his sister. After trying two hotels, he found me a room in the third. Its sign was in Urdu only; there were two beds in my room with filthy sheets, a lavatory and washbasin black with grime and the curry was inedible. But my door had a lock and the manager spoke English. It was a haven for the night.

Slogans on the wall opposite the hotel: 'Destroy Pakitan' [sic] and 'We want Sindhoodesh.' The manager asked if I had heard of Benazir Bhutto and his eyes lit up when he told me that she lived in Larkana. He was already a B.A. and a B.Sc. and was studying for his Ll.B. I learnt later that the extra degrees would secure him more dowry in the marriage market. He managed the hotel in the daytime and worked at night as a dispenser at the hospital. A busy young man.

I slept well, laying down my mat on top of the well-used sheets before I unrolled my sleeping-bag, and wrapping the dirty cushion in my cotton square. The waiter who brought breakfast to my room sat on the other bed smoking, smiling and watching me eat. In such a closed society, men saw no women outside their own families and I was a great novelty. Everyone was amazed and impressed that I was travelling alone.

The cycle shop next door opened at nine o'clock but they were unable to repair my wheel. At 9.25 I thought I had missed the 9.30 train to Sukkur, but the hotel *chowkidar* phoned the station and was told I still had plenty of time: the train was nowhere in sight. The hotel manager helped me get my damaged cycle to the station and handed me over to last night's friendly official. Tea was brought for me while my ticket and cycle registration were organised. 'Long Live Bhuttoism with Blood of SPSF' in the waiting room; 'We fight for Sindhoodesh' and 'Sacrifice for Sindhi Nation' in the railway compartment.

The train finally left at 10.20. I was told that we should reach
Sukkur at 6 p.m., then had a frantic rush when the train drew
into the station at 1.15. I knew there was a first-class hotel
beside the Indus and I pushed my bicycle into its cool, clean
interior with enormous relief. I had a tray of 'separate tea',
showered and took a siesta between clean white sheets, listening
to three of the most irresistible sounds I know – rushing river
water, the passionate muezzin and the jingle of rows of tiny
camel bells. I regained my resolution. Of course I was going to
cycle up the Indus! It might be harder work, but it would
certainly be less complicated than the train – and safer for my
bicycle.

I rested for two days in Sukkur while the hotel staff had an
excellent job done on my bicycle. They were most apologetic
that it had cost 10 rupees (32 rupees = £1) but explained that
the repairer had had to remove all the spokes before he could
straighten the rim and the work had taken him all morning.
They refused a tip. 'You are our mother and we want to help
you.' I was moving in a totally male world where men had no
concept of a woman friend and could express respect or liking
only in family terms. I was always their mother, daughter or
sister.

So far, I had travelled up the west bank of the Indus. At
Sukkur I crossed over, riding along the top of the magnificent
Sukkur Barrage, the largest irrigation scheme in the world,
designed by Mr A. A. Musto (no relation) in the 1930s. Its 46
spans fed seven main canals, irrigating 2½ million hectares of
previously desert land. Together with the English language and
the railways, it was one of the most useful legacies of the Raj.

It was beautiful cycling weather, sunny but not too hot, for
the mature trees by the roadside made a tunnel of shade.
Brilliant green parrots flew overhead and kingfishers were
sudden flashes of blue in the rushes. A young man on a
motorbike kept me company for a few miles. He was an army
captain, a Pathan, stationed on the Indian border. His family
on both sides had been army for generations and many of his
ancestors had died fighting 'the foreigners' on the North West
Frontier; he was tactful enough not to say 'the British'. I said
that many ancestors of the British had died on the North West

Frontier fighting the Pathans, who had a formidable reputation. That pleased him and he bought me a tea at the next stall. The usual crowd gathered and a boy lit a joss stick and stuck it on my handlebars.

The bicycle (called 'cykel') was the most common means of transport and my fellow-cyclists could be a source of great irritation. They always travelled much more slowly than I did, dreaming along with their saddles far too low and their knees and toes sticking out sideways. I would inevitably overtake them and that roused their competitive spirit. I heard their unoiled, heavy-duty machines clank into action until, with a titanic effort, they overtook me. Then, exhausted, they pulled in about three inches in front of me and slowed down to their original speed. I had to overtake them and the whole boring process started all over again. Any idea of stopping to let them get ahead was doomed; they would stop too and wait with me until I was ready to go on. They never cycled alone through choice and would often keep me company, conversing in Urdu or just being there. One real ruffian in a turban and curly Ali Baba shoes cycled with me for miles across a desert stretch. There was no one else in sight yet I felt extraordinarily at ease. I just knew in my bones that he meant no harm; in fact, he probably thought he was looking after me. At a certain point he rang his bell, smiled, waved and veered off the road down a dust track that seemed to lead to nowhere.

My Condor was generally an object of wonder. No one had ever seen a sea-green bicycle with two pairs of brakes, ten gears, an odometer and specially designed baggage. When I stopped in a village, it was the bicycle they crowded round first, feeling the tyres, testing the brakes and spinning the pedals. I was just a woman and its minder, quietly sipping my tea and keeping an eye on the situation. I worried when they fiddled with the gear-levers, the one part of the mechanism I knew I could not get repaired in Pakistan. Their own bicycles were one-speed only. The country people were shy, almost farouche, and I had to learn how to treat them. The first time I shouted at a man who was tugging at my gear-levers he snatched his hand away as if he had been stung, jumped back and stood looking down at his bare feet like a naughty child. The whole group fell silent,

looking down and shuffling their feet in the sand. I had used a
sledgehammer to crack a walnut. Embarrassed in my turn, I
spoke gently, smiled and pointed to my bedding with an appropriate explanatory mime. The sun came out again. They smiled
back shyly and turned their attention dutifully to my sleeping
mat. I had learned my lesson. A wave of the hand in the
direction of the gears was all that was ever necessary.

The road from Sukkur ran beside the railway track, which was a
great comfort: if there was absolutely nowhere to stay, I could
always catch a train to the nearest big town. I thought I might
have to do that on my very first day out of Sukkur, as there was
no hotel in Ghotki, where I had planned to spend the night. I
cycled on to Mirpur, ordered a Coke in the main street and
enquired of the inevitable crowd of spectators. They pointed
across the road to a gleaming white building. I cheered up
immediately, but my hopes were dashed when it turned out to
be the bank. They led me instead to the *muzzafir khana* and
negotiated on my behalf. There was nowhere else for me to go
so I was allowed to stay there, which was unusual for a foreigner
and quite unheard of for a woman.

My first sight of a *muzzafir khana* in Thatta had appalled
me. Now, after only four days' experience of rural Pakistan, my
perspective had changed so radically that I could contemplate
spending a night in one with supreme equanimity. Condor and
I were installed in a private room. It had a concrete floor, the
unplastered concrete walls covered with a pale blue wash.
There was a recess, painted cream, which served as a shelf; no
window; a plank door with gaps wide enough for the children to
peep through; and a charpoy with an unspeakable mattress and
quilt which I discarded and replaced with my own bedding. On
the plus side, there was a bright electric bulb, a ceiling fan and a
lack of wildlife: in such a bare, inhospitable room there were no
cosy corners where little creatures could make their nests.
There was one other little kennel like mine; everyone else slept
on rows of charpoys in the gloom behind the restaurant tables.
The staff were delighted to have me there and I was delighted to
have solved my first real accommodation problem. How
shaming it would have been to have taken the train to comfort!

I was watched over by one of the policemen guarding the bank next door. He took me to the post office, treated me to tea in my 'hotel' and told me that he would be on duty all night in case I had any difficulties. I was just to blow my whistle and he would come. 'If a man asks you to follow him, day or night, you don't go,' he said. He repeated this solemn warning three times and I promised to be careful. He called in first thing next morning to check up on me.

Visits to the communal latrine on the roof were made bearable by the view of a golden sunset, hazy with dust but wide and glorious, and a spectacular misty red sun rising over the desert. The vegetable curry was the best I had tasted in Pakistan and I followed it with a bag of fresh tangerines. The manager showed me his ear, which was badly infected and must have been horribly painful. It needed a course of antibiotics but I was not prepared to part with mine. I could only offer aspirin and murmur sympathetically. I thought how terrible it would be to fall ill in such a place.

Mirpur, Rahimyar Khan, Khanpur, Ahmadpur East. A new highway to Lahore lay nearer to the Indus, but it had no towns. I took the older road along the edge of the Great Thar. I had once ridden a camel across the Indian side of the desert; cycling was harder work but my Brooks leather saddle was considerably more comfortable. The kilometre stones gave the place names in Urdu and the distances in Arabic numerals. A few miles out of Mirpur I crossed the border between Sind and the Punjab and was entertained to coffee, my first in Pakistan, by the Punjab police at the checkpoint: three officers, twelve constables and a cook. A chromium coffee service was produced, with china cups, and a plate of custard creams, and I was assured that there were no troubles in the Punjab, that I could cycle in complete safety all the way to Islamabad. The three officers were from Lahore. 'Here we are in jungle,' said the Superintendent grandly. It seemed like a Somerset Maugham jungle, with servants handing round custard creams on china plates. I declined their invitation to lunch.

The road ran near to the Indian border and at Khanpur the only main road into India struck out across the desert towards Jaisalmer, 125 miles away. Khanpur was a bazaar town with a huge covered market thronged with brilliantly clad desert folk trading their handicrafts for provisions. Tongas, donkey carts, camel carts, cycles, motorbikes and milling pedestrians churned up the dust while gigantic swarms of flies coruscated on the food-stalls. Everyone crowded round to stare. The pharmacist looked worried when I asked about accommodation and directed me to the Roman Catholic church. I had heard that the Christians could be relied upon to help European travellers but I was reluctant to slip comfortably into their network. They were a minority group and I preferred to make my way through mainstream Pakistan. For the same reason, I had recently declined the offer of an Inspector of Schools to arrange accommodation for me in Department of Education Rest Houses. In Khanpur two elegant young men with excellent English came to my rescue. Holding hands, as was the custom for men, they led me through the middle of the bazaar where I should never have ventured alone. A surprisingly modern hotel appeared, with 'Dilkusha Building' on the façade. The rooms faced onto a central lawn and I had my own private hole in the ground and a tap, bucket and ladle for my ablutions. I was welcomed as a guest and accommodated free of charge. That evening I sat watching the television in the restaurant, surrounded by dusty, unshaven men in magenta caps, turbans and shawls. I was quite alone in that tiny town on the edge of the Great Thar Desert and no one knew my whereabouts. Yet I never doubted my safety. I felt that I was watched over and protected.

If my accommodation up the Indus was spartan, the floors were usually clean. The exception was the hotel in Ahmadpur East, where my room was littered with cigarette ends, matches and general filth including a large turd under the bed. Fortunately, it was elderly and well dried, so that the reek of stale cigarette smoke had no competition. Had I arrived there straight from my beautiful house in Southwold, I should have swept out in disgust and caught the first plane home. But my tolerance had risen and my wants diminished as I had travelled slowly south-east. I had learned to be content with little and was just grateful to have found a charpoy and a padlock on the door.

That evening, my bicycle had fallen over as I was asking the

Above: The Appian Way makes a tranquil start to its 484-mile journey from Rome to Brindisi.

Below: Early morning light picks out the lonely, winding road over the Pindos Mountains.

Above: The Wooden Horse of Troy.

The two old friends in the Grand Mosque at Kütahya.

The vertical village of Uçhisar, carved out of the soft, volcanic tuff of Cappadocia.

Below: The Crusader façade of St Peter's Church, Antioch, the oldest church in Christendom, protects the cave where the Apostle preached.

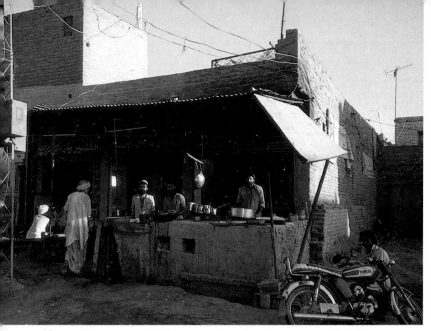

Above: The *muzzafir khana*, my hotel and restaurant in Mirpur.

Below: The cricket enthusiasts of Kabirwala.

Above: The massive tomb of Sher Shah Suri, the Afghan ruler who laid the original Grand Trunk Road, broods over its artificial lake in Sasaram. *Below:* Two young Buddhists receiving instruction in a Penang temple.

Above: The Taj Mahal, Shah Jehan's masterpiece, at Agra.

Below: Pilgrims flocking to wash away their sins at the Sangam, the sacred spot where the waters of the Ganges and the Yamuna merge with the mystic, invisible Saraswati.

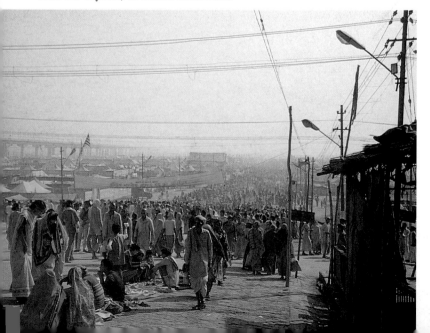

Above: A fossil quarry at Dinosaur National Museum, Utah.

Below: Front Street, Ogallala, Nebraska. The end of the trail for cowboys who drove their cattle from Texas to the railroad.

Above: Memorial to a Wild West legend. The Pony Express statue in Marysville, Kansas.

Below: A family of Amish, the strictest of the Pennsylvania Dutch sects, drive to church in the seclusion of their horse-drawn buggy.

way and had torn a gash down my left calf, which was bleeding profusely. As usual, Providence had come to my aid. Just when I was at my lowest ebb, worried about my injured leg and beginning to despair of finding accommodation, two schoolboys on a small Honda had stopped to cluck over the pouring blood and had taken me under their wing, guiding me through the bazaar and negotiating for me at the *muzzafir khanas*. None of them had a private room and it would have been most improper for me to sleep on a charpoy with all the men. Finally we had been directed out to the by-pass, where the boys had found me my dirty, but private, room. I had offered them a Coke for their trouble but they had declined. 'No. It is our duty to help.' The Muslim duty of hospitality to strangers was as scrupulously observed in Pakistan as it had been in Turkey and it made me ashamed of our 'Christian' indifference. As they left, one of the boys looked at me anxiously and said, 'Why don't you go to Lahore? Ahmadpur East is not a suitable place for a lady to come on her holidays.' I heartily agreed.

Next day, despite a painful leg, I reached Bahawalpur and a comfortable hotel where I had a blissful hot shower and felt very pleased with myself. I knew now that I could somehow manage, even in the most unpromising terrain.

The Jhelum river flows into the Chenab, which in turn flows into the Indus. I now turned north towards Multan to join the Chenab. The Punjab (Panj Nad – Land of Five Rivers) was more prosperous than Sind, but the colour had gone. The men were dressed in brown, beige or white; there were no more road-menders in glittering magenta caps and embroidered turquoise slippers. There were brown minah birds and hoopoes, pretty in their way but less spectacular than parrots and kingfishers. Even the sheep were brown. With their long, floppy ears and their curly wool right down to their toes, they looked like crosses between unclipped poodles and teddy bears. Their shepherds had transistor radios instead of plaintive pipes.

My progress was slow. The road surface was cracked and potholed and camel carts blocked the traffic, travelling in stately processions, each piled with a mountain of cotton and

each camel gliding along with an air of infinite disdain. The sun
was hot and the dust was suffocating but my chief problem was
tiredness; my diet was simply inadequate for such strenuous
physical exertion, day after day. I had never been a great lover
of curry and now I had to eat it at every meal. Sometimes it was
so fiery that I could scarcely push it down. Food was short in
country places, so that portions were small and the meat, if any,
was skin and bone. I started to eat eggs for breakfast, to get
some protein, but I could take them only on rest days; they
were fried in such heavy fat that it was impossible for me to
cycle afterwards, even though I had the digestion of an ostrich.
I had two days' rest in Multan and wrote to Heather, who was
joining me for Christmas, asking her to bring out a course of
vitamin pills.

The Aga Khan had just paid for the refurbishment of the
tombs in the Old Fort at Multan; the domed mausoleum of the
fourteenth-century Saint Rukni-i-Alam was a place of pilgrimage. I admired the beautiful glazed tiles, then slipped off my
shoes and joined the line of pilgrims. The sarcophagus was
covered with a golden cloth and the pilgrims were lifting it and
rubbing the edge of it against their faces. They kissed the
marble columns of the baldechino, hung with strands of
coloured foil and artificial flowers, and flung fresh blooms onto
the sarcophagus. Outside were groups of local musicians and
sellers of joss sticks and garlands.

Cricket-fever had seized Pakistan. The World Cup was over
and there was much commiseration because neither Pakistan
nor England had won; the Cup had gone to the outsiders,
Australia. Now there was the Test Series. Everyone who had a
transistor had it tuned in to the commentary. Near Kabirwala,
the attendants rushed out from their petrol station, waving
their arms. 'You English? Test Match! Test Match! See television!' They led me into a dark hut, where they sat me down on
a pile of sacks and plied me with tea and custard creams, while
we all watched the cricket together. I spent some time there,
then took the wrong turning out of town. Back on the right road
after a ten-mile detour, I crossed the Ravi river and pedalled
furiously along an embankment over desolate marshes with the
evening fast falling. The pie-dogs and bats were just coming out

when I saw the lights of Shorkot ahead. I was pursued by two growling, mangy curs who had become bold in the dusk.

There was a cluster of restaurants and a bus stop on the outskirts. I stopped at the stall in the forecourt. 'What can I do for you, sweetheart? You look all in,' said a Welsh accent. I cheered up immediately. 'First you can give me an ice-cold Pepsi. Then you can tell me where to find a hotel.' The stallholder had worked in Cardiff for four years. He was very keen that I should spend the night with his family but I was too weary for sociability. I fell into bed in the first hotel I saw, where I tossed and turned all night, my body still vibrating from 75 miles of rough road and my nerves still jangling after my race against the darkness and the dogs.

I met three charming businessmen in the hotel restaurant. They were appalled that I was going to spend the night in Shorkot and wanted to transport me forthwith to Faisalabad in their white Mercedes. The quietest of the three, who spoke the best English, was the only one who understood what I was doing. I said that to accept a lift to Faisalabad would be cheating and the others had no patience with that remark. 'But it would be so much easier for you,' they said, 'and nicer.' Younus replied on my behalf that it would obviously be much easier – and the easiest thing of all would be to stay at home and do nothing. But I had my project and he could quite see that I wanted to carry it through. I promised to stay with him when eventually I reached Faisalabad.

Just before Jhang I saw from my map that I had passed the confluence of the Jhelum and Chenab rivers but the road was so far away from the autumn course of the streams that I saw nothing. I had entered the territory where Alexander fought the Malli and where he received his near-fatal wound. It was flat land, with villages of sun-baked brick. I smiled at Arrian's account of Alexander's troops scaling mighty battlements. As mud was the only building material available, those fortified cities could have been scarcely more imposing than their modern village counterparts.

Faisalabad, formerly Lyallpur, was an eccentric piece of town-planning. The bazaar had been laid out by Mr Lyall at the turn of the century in the shape of the Union Jack. From the

Gothic/Doric clock tower in the centre radiated four broad St George's Cross roads, with four narrower St Andrew's Cross roads bisecting the angles.

It was an important industrial centre and Younus had a textile mill there. His house was a rambling two-storey building round two courtyards, where fifteen extended family members lived with three servants. I had coffee on arrival in his parents' flat, then I was taken to the men's quarters (in Pakistan I was an honorary man) to meet Younus' friends and watch the cricket. I had tea in his own apartment with his wife, Robina, and their four children. Robina was a lovely girl who had just enrolled as a medical student. Her English was excellent and I was disappointed when she stayed at home while Younus took me out to a men-only dinner with his best friend. That night, when I had just retired gratefully to bed, his parents appeared in my bedroom together with six other members of the family, and they all sat on and around my bed talking for over an hour. Privacy is not prized in the East and guests must be entertained at all times.

My bicycle pump had fallen off and been squashed by a lorry. Younus' youngest brother gave me his motorcycle footpump, cutting off the nozzle so that the rubber tube simply slipped over my cycle valve. It became one of my most valued possessions. He and his friend guided me to the road out of town on their motorcycles and asked for my autograph.

I passed the offices of a gas pipeline company and was invited in by the head of the audit department. At least 50 admiring men crowded round me in his office, where I was given a Coca Cola followed by tea and biscuits. They were keen to hear all about my trip and one of them called me 'azim', a great woman.

I was clutching two addresses, one of Younus' uncle in Sargodha and the other of his second cousin in Malikwal, my next two stops. The Sargodha uncle, aunt and seven children had little English between them but they were so thrilled to have me as their guest that they sent for a professional photographer to take pictures of the event. I was fed to bursting point, then invited to recline on the dining room divan under a beautifully embroidered quilt. Some sat with me on the couch, others on the floor and we all took tea together and smiled.

Then they got up, bade me goodnight and switched off the light. I was obviously expected to sleep just as I was, fully clothed, under the quilt. The reason for the lack of sheets in hotels suddenly came to me: Pakistanis must sleep in their day clothes, which are just like loose pyjamas anyway, then shower and change the next morning. We, on the other hand, complicate our lives with sheets, pillowcases and special outfits for sleeping. The simplicity of their system has much to recommend it.

I promised to explain that Sargodha was called 'The Eagle City' because of the outstanding bravery of its citizens during a war with India. It was a great citrus centre and I pedalled through miles of orange and lemon groves where the golden globes were ripening among the dark, glossy leaves. I passed a Government fish farm where the boys wanted me to stay for a fish kebab lunch, but I was pressed for time if I was to reach Malikwal by evening. The elderly official at the toll-booth opposite the farm gave me tea and pleaded to come to London as my servant. Then the countryside changed. The roads were in good repair, the dwellings were concentrated in neat brick-built villages and the land was well tended, more like English parkland than rural Pakistan. It was obviously a region of large, well-managed estates and had such a gracious air that I expected Chatsworth House or Longleat to appear through the trees at any moment.

In Bhawal I stopped to ask the way of an old man sitting with his friend outside a scrap-metal shop. He sent for the inevitable cups of tea and, as I was leaving, delved into the pocket of his *shalwar* and produced a handful of rupee notes. There were 21 of them – only about 60p in English money but worth a great deal in Pakistan. They would have paid for a night in a *muzzafir khana*.

'Here! Take these. You'll need a lot of cups of tea on your travels. These will help to pay for them.'

I protested. 'That's very kind. But I really can't take your money.'

'Of course you can. You *need* money. You're on a bicycle.'

His neighbours crowded round, urging me to take the money. No one believed that I had enough. Why was I riding a

bicycle if I had money? In the end, I decided that the only thing
to do was to accept it as graciously as it had been offered.

'Thank you very much. I shall think of you every time I buy
myself a cup of tea between here and Peshawar.'

His worried face creased into a smile of relief. I still think of
him to this day.

I was particularly grateful for the Malikwal introduction, as it
proved to be a one-bazaar town without so much as a *muzzafir
khana*. Younus' second cousin was the doctor there and his son
the pharmacist. Mrs Dastgeer was small, plump and vivacious.
She had no English but she rushed up, beaming, and flung her
arms round me – a welcome better than a million words. My
food was separately cooked and served in my bedroom, while all
the neighbours dropped in to see me. I was given bland soup,
followed by unseasoned boiled beef with boiled potatoes and
turnips. The Pakistani idea of English cuisine.

After Malikwal, I cycled along all day with a canal to my right
and the invisible Jhelum river somewhere to my left. It was not
as picturesque as I had hoped, for the land became arid as I
neared the Salt Range and there was no shade. I finally saw the
river, all four broad channels of it, as I crossed over the endless
bridge towards Jhelum City. There was a perfect Gothic spire
in the middle distance. I had arrived at Alexander's point of
embarkation and I had also reached the Grand Trunk Road
with its cities, traffic and rows of hotels. An easier route lay
ahead, but I doubted if I should love it as much as I had loved
the villages, deserts and people of the Lower Indus.

11

The North West Frontier

JHELUM – PESHAWAR – KHYBER PASS – CHARSADDA
– MARDAN – SHAHBAZ GHERI – CHANAKA DHERI –
JEHANGIRA

Nothing is so virtuous as a bicycle. You can't imagine a
bicyclist committing a crime, can you?

(Dorothy L. Sayers)

IN Jhelum I spent two days nursing yet another cold. Most of
the time I watched the First Test in the controversial
England *v.* Pakistan series, feeling embarrassed by the
behaviour of members of the English team both on and off the
pitch. Pakistanis are such strict Muslims that they never
uncover their arms and legs, and even their fast bowlers keep
their shirt-cuffs tightly buttoned. The sight of English players
relaxing round the pitch in shorts and T-shirts caused a sharp
intake of breath from the Pakistanis round me and I thought our
representatives might have shown a little more sensitivity. As
English and Urdu were joint official languages, the commentary alternated between the two. I became as addicted to cricket
as the Pakistanis and it provided a never-failing topic of
conversation.

Pakistani television helped me survive many evenings in
desolate places. There was the News in English, with a catchy
signature tune which became one of my more cheerful cycling
songs. The News was obviously Government-controlled and
there was little international coverage, but it gave me some idea
of what was going on in Pakistan. Then another two hours of
prime time were devoted to English-language programmes,
usually naive American soaps (undubbed) without sex or

violence: *Murder She Wrote* was a local favourite in every country across the East. I bought one of the English-language newspapers whenever I was in a town, to get a further insight into Pakistani politics and preoccupations; world news came from *Time* or *Newsweek*. After two months in Turkey, where I had understood so little, it was a great treat to have some contact with the outside world again.

I spent my mornings sipping tea in a stationer's shop owned by three brothers. One of them had worked for seven years on the buses in Rochdale and now had a corner shop there. He liked England, despite the yobs who occasionally put bricks through his windows, and after a month in Jhelum he was anxious to get back. In his broad Lancashire accent he said, 'The problem here is the food. I just can't stomach it. I'm looking forward to a nice chip butty.' Many of the men in Jhelum had worked in England and had saved up to start their own businesses back home, including the maker of the most delicious fudge in the world. Having seen the purdah in which their women lived and their own strictly Islamic life-style, I understood how bewildering – and unkind – they must find life in England, despite its material benefits. Perhaps the main weakness of Islam in the modern world is that its strict codes of practice make life in non-Muslim countries extremely difficult.

From Jhelum I took the train to Peshawar so that I could cycle back to Lahore in the 'right' direction; had I been able to cross Afghanistan, Peshawar would have been my first major city after entering Pakistan. A regiment was on the move from the large army barracks at Jhelum. Military guards travelled on the train and once we entered the sensitive North West Frontier Province there were troops positioned at all bridges, tunnels and junctions. Sabotage was not uncommon.

When the British took control of India, they left the native cities intact and built adjoining cantonments for their own barracks, offices and homes. It was an excellent system and nowhere can its success be better appreciated than in Peshawar. Its cantonment was green, shady and spacious, with lawns, a little patchy these days, and grand public buildings lining The Mall. There was the hollow sound of ball on bat as white-flannelled boys played cricket in the grounds of the Victorian public school and the Gothic spires of the churches soared above the treetops. I could have been in Cheltenham on a warm June afternoon. Old Peshawar was untouched – the stuff of legends, its maze of narrow alleys still surrounded by the ruins of its walls. The Balahisar, the mighty fort built in 1526 by Babur, the first Moghul Emperor, still dominated the northern approach and the Kabuli Gate still led to the Street of the Story Tellers, where plots were hatched and tales told over the hookahs. There were streets for the coppersmiths, swordmakers, shoemakers, jewellers and sellers of teas and spices, where merchants crouched together at the back of their little open-fronted wooden cubicles, haggling over prices. The smell of charcoal-grilled lamb was everywhere.

Peshawar was one of the world's great cross-roads where the caravan routes from Central Asia and the Indian subcontinent met, and it retained the swashbuckling air of a frontier town. The clothes of the tall, striding Pathans were khaki, brown or grey, camouflage for the dusty rocks of the Khyber. Violence was just below the surface. A bomb exploded in the crowded bazaar shortly after I left, killing twenty; and the cantonment echoed to more bombs in the evening. They were said to have been laid by Soviet agents trying to foment discord between the Pakistanis and the Afghan refugees. Even in the twentieth century, control of this crucial junction and listening-post was being fought over.

In the middle of it all, an oasis of beauty and calm, stood the great Mosque of Mahabat Khan (1670), the Governor of Peshawar under Shah Jehan. Its plastered interior was richly decorated with flowers and leaves – browns, creams and damask roses in full bloom, strangely reminiscent of Victorian wallpaper. There was a fountain in the courtyard and the old men of Peshawar sat in the cool of the arcades, chatting and passing a peaceful day.

Because of the war in Afghanistan, one of my major roads, the Khyber Pass, was closed to tourists. But my horoscope in *The Pakistan Times* read: 'You could use a break. If you can get out of town for the day, do it.' I could get out of town so I decided to try my luck and set off in the direction of the Khyber. Looking innocent, as if I had every right to be there, I

sailed past a police check-point and a road-block set up by the
narcotics squad and came to the gates of the main refugee camp,
where the army was on duty. I smiled and waved, and they
raised the barrier for me. I rode with such confidence that they
probably took me for a Red Cross nurse. Women can get away
with much more than men in tricky situations. We are less
threatening.

I was now on the main road to the Khyber Pass, which ran
through the centre of the camp. I was amazed by its size and its
air of permanency. The official number of Afghan refugees in
Pakistan was three million, but unofficially it was known to be
well over five. For Pakistan, a relatively poor country with a
total population of some 90 million, the burden of those
refugees was almost insupportable (about US$1 million a day),
yet the Pakistanis bore it willingly as their duty to their Muslim
neighbours. I felt that their sacrifice was insufficiently appreciated in the West.

The camp had the same houses of sun-baked brick and the
same roadside stalls as I had seen in every Pakistani village. It
even had a hotel and some substantially built shops and restaurants. Medical centres, clinics and welfare agencies were dotted
along the road. There were more turbans and beards, but the
same waves and greetings as elsewhere to a passing cyclist. For
the first time on my trip, I was stoned by small boys, but
otherwise my crossing of the camp was uneventful. Then the
houses finished and I was out in open, stony country. I pedalled
for twenty minutes through silent emptiness, rounded a corner
by some rocks and came to a really serious road-block. It was
manned by six Pathans, one of them armed to the teeth with a
machine-gun and bandolier of ammunition as well as the pistol
which they all carried. I greeted them with an innocent air:
'Wasallah allaikhum.' 'Allaikhum salaam,' they replied, their
eyes popping. A notice on the barrier stated that no one was
allowed beyond that point without a permit from the Khyber
Agency. Their officer emerged from the hut and asked me in
faultless English, 'How on earth did *you* get here?' 'Easily,' I
said. 'I just got on my bicycle in Peshawar and cycled here. I'm
a historian and I've come to see the Jamrud Fort.'

I knew that it was out of bounds beyond the road-block, but it was worth a try. Quite rightly, the officer refused to let me through but he took me to a small rise behind the hut from which the fort was just visible. The dip in the mountains behind it was the start of the Khyber Pass. I asked if they were Pakistan troops. As they were wearing the flat brown woollen cap of the Pathans with their khaki *shalwar kameez*, I got the answer I expected. The area was tribal territory, not under direct Pakistan control. They were Pathan tribesmen and they were in charge of the land surrounding the Khyber Pass. We rejoined his group, who asked the usual questions about my age and itinerary. We talked in the shadow of the hut and I took their photographs there; they refused to be photographed by their barrier, as it was too exposed to gunfire. I had in fact cycled into a danger zone and they were concerned for my safety. A Suzuki van was summoned with a driver and two armed guards but after much discussion they decided not to put me and my bicycle in the back of the van, as I should be a moving target. Instead, the officer gave instructions that I was to ride along the edge of the road while the van cruised beside me, covering my right side completely and at least making me less conspicuous from the left as we crossed the empty stretch. When we reached the centre of the refugee camp, my guards tooted their horn, smiled, waved, said, 'O.K. No problem,' and sped back to their post. I cycled back to Peshawar, well pleased with my morning.

I had still not quite finished with Alexander the Great. When he invaded Pakistan in the summer of 327, he sent Hephaestion, Perdiccas and a friendly rajah, Taxiles, through the Khyber Pass with all the baggage with instructions to build a bridge over the Indus and wait for him there. He himself took the older route through the Hindu Kush, through Laghman, Bajaur and Swat, fighting the local people all the way. He captured Peucelaotis, thought to be modern Charsadda, then fought his way down to the Indus at Hind, sixteen miles above Attock, where he crossed by Hephaestion's bridge. At Taxila, the capital of his Indian ally and the largest city between the Indus and Jhelum, he made sacrifices and held public games before marching into the Punjab.

Alexander had no time to consolidate his hold over Pakistan and Greek rule was consequently brief. By the end of the century the Mauryan Empire under Chandragupta had filled the vacuum; Buddhism entered the Peshawar valley during the reign of Chandragupta's grandson, the great Ashoka. But Graeco-Roman influence remained, fusing with Indian culture to produce the Buddhist Gandhara civilisation (first century BC to third century AD). The Victoria Memorial Museum in Peshawar had a superb Gandhara collection. In Buddhist convention, the Buddha is portrayed with a round face and a naked or half-naked torso. The Gandhara statues had narrow Western faces and Classical Greek draperies falling from both shoulders. There were friezes of acanthus leaves, vine scrolls, swags of fruit and flowers, nymphs and cupids. And it may have been imagination, but I thought I saw the occasional Greek face peering out from under a Pathan cap in the bazaar.

Determined to follow Alexander to the last, I postponed my ride down the relative comfort of the Grand Trunk Road and headed north-east out of Peshawar to join him at Charsadda. I knew that Peshawar meant 'the city of flowers' in Sanskrit and that the valley's fertility had been legendary from antiquity, but even so I was amazed at the luxuriance of the orchards, sugar cane and bananas. The leaves of the poplars and willows were just turning colour and the autumn sun cast a golden glow over this idyllic landscape.

Charsadda was crowded on market day and a bomb had just demolished a large building in the main street. People were scrabbling in the rubble with their bare hands, screaming and searching desperately for survivors. There was a police cordon, Frontier Guards, ambulances and the inevitable crowds. I managed to push my bicycle through.

Three teenage orange-sellers greeted me as I cycled by and I responded with a smile and a wave, so I was incensed to be struck on the back of the head a moment later by a flying orange. I jumped off my bicycle, determined to go back and give them a dressing-down in real headmistress style, but my move was anticipated. A man had already leapt across the pavement, turban-ends flying, and was shaking his fist at the boys and shouting loudly, while a disapproving circle of bystanders glared at them. The boys cowered behind their barrow. It was the last time they would ever aim an orange at a passing stranger. His harangue completed, the man raised a hand to his forehead. I returned his salute and cycled off. Boys in Pakistan could sometimes be quite objectionable, though their aggression usually amounted to nothing more than jeers and catcalls.

The atmosphere in the North West Frontier Province was electric. It was the day of the local elections, the first democratic elections to be held under General Zia. Political parties had been banned and candidates stood as independents, each with his voting symbol (Government-approved). There were umbrellas, lanterns, candles, lions, even bicycles. Men and women were queuing in the villages at their separate polling booths. A few districts, thinking to be liberal and progressive, had spoken out against sex discrimination and set up combined booths, a measure that effectively deprived many women of their vote, as they were not allowed by their families to enter the mixed booths. There were some complaints in the press that the Government had used bureaucratic procedures to foil the candidacy of known opponents, but on the whole the elections ran smoothly and seemed to be fairly conducted. The Pakistanis were to demonstrate their political maturity again in 1988, after the death of General Zia, when they held an orderly general election, their first since 1977.

The villages between Charsadda and Mardan might have been more of a challenge to Alexander than the mud-brick towns of the Indus valley. Their walls were built of local stone, solid and high enough to afford real protection. I sat in the shade of one, eating my lunch-time bananas, when two men got out of their lorry and offered to sell me marijuana. There were no hard feelings when I refused to buy and they joined me in the shade for a chat.

A political procession preceded me into Mardan, a sprawling, dusty town where I made for the 'best hotel', a kind of ramshackle caravanserai round a courtyard off the main street, Judge Bazaar. The manager was a charming young man, who did his best to please. I asked if there would be tea the next morning. 'Yes. Tea, cake, biscuits, whatever you like. Here *everything* is available.' The primitive accommodation made this claim seem unlikely but it was well meant. 'I am a literate

boy,' he confided. And so he was. He found it difficult to follow
my spoken English, but his own vocabulary was remarkably
wide, the result of assiduous reading of the best English prose.
He asked me what I thought of my room. It was the usual bare
concrete kennel but I had not the heart to be critical, so I said
that it was 'quite nice'. He thanked me, looked wistful and said,
'It's not *really* nice, is it?'

At 5.30 the shooting started, rounds of automatic gunfire.
The firing began in the distance but worked its way towards the
hotel, coming so near that I dived away from the window and
door and crouched in the corner of my room. I was interested,
in a detached sort of way, to note that I felt no fear. By seven
o'clock I was feeling very hungry and ventured down to the
courtyard, despite the continued shooting. The manager
explained it all: 'They fire their guns in happiness. They have
won the election. In the sky. No problem.' Feeling faintly
foolish, I went out into Judge Bazaar for my dinner – a delicious
chicken, chopped into bony chunks and fried with vegetables
on a pavement brazier. It was served, piping hot, in its cast-iron
pan with warm new bread.

Nights in the hills of the North West Frontier were cold and I
was glad of my down sleeping-bag to supplement the hotel
bedding. Nights were also long, so I went to bed early and rose
late. I was reluctant to buy winter clothes which I should need
for only about a fortnight and made do by wearing everything I
had.

When I set out from Mardan, it was cold and overcast. I
cycled first to Shahbaz Gheri to see the Rock Edicts, which the
warrior king Ashoka had had engraved after his conversion to
Buddhism, renouncing war and all its evils. I was keen to see
the original, as I had sometimes read from the translation in my
school assemblies. The inscription was carved on a massive
outcrop, separated from the main mountain range by what was
once the main road into the Indian subcontinent from the
Hindu Kush, the route Alexander had followed. I crossed a
field, attended by a gaggle of goatherds and schoolboys in navy
woollen berets, which they said were their 'blue-blacks', their
school caps. Without a qualm, I left my bicycle and all my
possessions under a tree while I climbed up to see the Edicts.

I was in the heartland of the Mauryan Buddhist Empire and the Gandhara Civilisation. An elderly man in a lilac *shalwar kameez* and a gold embroidered cap knew where the ruins of the Buddhist monastery at Chanaka Dheri were to be found and led me there on his bicycle. I could make little of the ruins and had the further embarrassment of not knowing whether to tip my guide. He made tea-drinking signs, which I interpreted as a hint. I got out my rupees, but it was a mistake. He was inviting me. He was delighted when I accepted and asked me to wait while he cut a heap of maize and tied it to the back of his bicycle. Then I followed this wheeled haystack back along the jagged path to his home.

We entered a crowded courtyard. My guide's wife and teen-age daughter were there, another woman with three small children and an old man. In addition, there were two buffalo, one pregnant and one with a tiny calf, a donkey, two hens and ten chickens. The women seized the maize and removed the corn cobs, tossing them onto a cloth-covered charpoy spread with corn grains which they had picked off ready for grinding. They gave the green stalks to the donkey and the buffalo. The daughter lit a fire and grilled one of the fresh corn cobs for me; without butter or salt it was hard to get down. Then they brought a dish of home-grown oranges and tangerines, sent out for a packet of expensive wafer biscuits and served me tea. The old neighbour asked if I would photograph the little boy and I said that I should like a picture of everyone. To my delight, the women lined up with the men to be photographed, a most unusual occurrence. The teenage daughter was about to cover herself but her mother told her not to, so I got a row of smiling women's faces.

My guide then invited me to take a tour and I quickly revised my ideas of 'the poor elderly man'. He had orange groves as far as the eye could see, two large fields and more fruit orchards in the distance, and a wood, which was his pride and joy. It contained examples of every kind of tree that would grow there, from banana palms to pines. As it was autumn, there was a dazzling display of reds, yellows, browns and greens.

I had clearly stumbled on the local *khan*. We exchanged addresses and he promised to visit me in London. He wheeled my bicycle to the road, we shook hands and he touched his forehead and his heart. The photographs came out well and I hope the copies I sent arrived safely. They were a charming family and I was once again astonished at the ease with which we established a friendly relationship when we had scarcely a dozen words in common.

I was aiming for Attock, where I knew there was a Government tourist bungalow, but the road was as bumpy as a choppy sea and my normally accurate German map seriously underrated the distance to Swabi: at Swabi I turned south-west to look for Hund, the place where Alexander crossed the Indus. Miles from anywhere the heavens opened. I stopped under a tree to put on my cagoule and waterproof trousers and realised that my back tyre was going flat. Fortunately it was a slow puncture and I had my very effective new foot-pump to keep me going, but the Indus was some distance from the road, night was falling, as was the rain, and my progress was halting, so I had to abandon my search for Hund. I just got over the Kabul river into Jehangira as darkness fell.

The Water Board officials told me there was nowhere I could possibly stay in Jehangira but I was taken in hand by a crowd of men and found shelter for the night in a *muzzafir khana*. The proprietor covered my charpoy with a magnificent crimson quilt embroidered in gold and silver thread, obviously a family heirloom. His friend, who had been in the navy and had once sailed into Liverpool, escorted me to the best restaurant, sat with me while I ate my dinner, then escorted me back to my hotel, checking that my door locked properly.

It was too dark in my room to read, so I started preparing for an early night. When I was half-undressed there was a frantic clatter of footsteps outside and an urgent banging on my door. I peered out to see my naval friend standing there as interpreter to the proprietor. They were both in an agitated state. They had just learned that the proprietor's son had charged me 25 rupees for the room, five more than the rightful price. The proprietor thrust the unlawfully gained rupees into my hand and both men touched their foreheads and their hearts and apologised. I had paid the 25 rupees willingly, only too relieved to find a safe, dry place for the night, and I was moved by their concern and their scrupulous honesty. They could so easily have pocketed the five rupees which were so little to a Westerner but which would pay for a good meal in Pakistan.

Next morning I reached rock bottom. I awoke to the rattle of rain on the roof, catarrh had given me such a severe sinus headache that I felt sick, and I had churning intestines. I thought of the unspeakable communal latrine and the lack of running water. What a place to be ill, after months of robust health. To crown it all, there was the puncture. I crawled downstairs for tea, clutching my packet of biscuits and my pain-killers, then crawled back upstairs and sat quietly on my charpoy in the dark, cocooned in my sleeping-bag. By ten o'clock I felt well enough to begin packing and by 10.30, after more tea and biscuits, I was positively cheerful. My headache cleared, my insides settled down, the sun came out and the shop opposite repaired my puncture – only my second in 4,834 miles. The long-awaited rain had settled the dust and wonderful fresh, clear air filled my lungs as I joined the Grand Trunk Road.

12

The Imperial Road

JEHANGIRA – ATTOCK – HASAN ABDAL – WAH –
TAXILA – RAWALPINDI – ISLAMABAD – JHELUM –
GUJRANWALA – LAHORE – DELHI – MATHURA –
AGRA

Heaven smiles, and faiths and empires gleam,
Like wrecks of a dissolving dream.
                              (Percy Bysshe Shelley)

THE early Moghuls* never really liked the Indian subcontinent. When they were sweltering in the dust and heat of Delhi, Agra or Sind, they pined for the mountains, streams and orchards of their homeland. Babur, the founder of the dynasty, complained in his memoirs about the lack of politeness, artistic achievement, amenities and decent food in his Indian domains and he laid out Persian gardens wherever he went. Having consolidated his kingdom in Kabul and Kandahar, his forces surged through the Khyber Pass into India only as a second best because they had failed to recapture Samarkand and the northern territories of Tamerlane.

The Moghuls were Turks. Formerly Mongols, they had embraced Islam and come under the civilising influence of Persia. Whereas Tamerlane had been a destroyer, razing Delhi to the ground in 1398, his descendant Babur arrived in India in 1517, five generations later, as a soldier-statesman, a man of letters, aesthetic sensibilities and humour. He laid the foundations of the Moghul Empire which was to stun Western travellers with its magnificence.

*The six great Moghul Emperors were Babur (1504–30); Humayun (1530–56); Akbar (1556–1605); Jehangir (1605–27); Shah Jehan (1627–58); Aurangzeb (1658–1707).

Babur himself wrote in Turki, but Persian became the official language of his empire; its descendants, Urdu and Hindustani, are today the languages of Pakistan and northern India. The Moghuls had a passion for building. Their architecture was originally Persian in style but it developed through the Indo-Persian of Akbar's day to achieve its own incomparable elegance in the buildings of Shah Jehan, the creator of the Taj Mahal. Persian mysticism, music, poetry, sport, their love of flowers, gardens and fountains, their rich, dainty decorative arts and their miniature painting were all developed by the Moghuls in their own unique fashion. They began by trying to establish a little Persia in India and it took the genius of Akbar, Babur's grandson, to see the intrinsic worth of Hindu culture and to incorporate it into the Central Asian framework. He forged a new civilisation, reconciling the Moghuls to India and making Moghul rule, with its Persian fashions, more acceptable to the Hindus. He united warring factions, consolidated the administration and introduced the Persian idea of the godhead of the Emperor – a concept which was to work in the favour of the British Queen, when Victoria was proclaimed Empress of India.

India was always a prey to invaders from Central Asia; they poured through a number of passes into the Peshawar valley to seize the rich soil of the Punjab. Babur used the Khyber Pass, the direct link with his home base of Kabul in modern Afghanistan, and followed the easy route down from Peshawar to Delhi, the route that later became the Grand Trunk Road of the Raj.

The original paved road was not in fact a Moghul creation. There was a hiatus after Babur's death, when his son Humayun was dethroned and went into exile at the Persian court. His deposer was a brilliant Afghan, Sher Shah Sur, one of Babur's aides who had established a power-base for himself in Bihar. In the five years before his death in action against the Rajputs, Sher Shah built on Babur's foundations and gave firm administrative shape to his empire. Like all good generals, he realised the importance of effective lines of communication and laid the well-engineered Shahi, or Imperial Road, from Kabul through to Delhi, then on to Bihar. A short stretch of it, with carefully laid cobbles still intact, can be seen south of Rawalpindi. Humayun, with the help of the Persian Shah Ismael, returned to reclaim his throne after the death of Shah Sur; and his son, Akbar, the greatest of the Moghul Emperors, improved the Imperial Road and the forts along it.

The Moghuls were uppermost in my mind as I bowled along the Imperial Road. As a follower of Akbar, I was more than reconciled to my surroundings. I delighted in the gleam of the Kabul river through the trees to my left and had no wish, on that bright morning, to be anywhere but in Pakistan. I stopped in a kind of Moghul tea-garden filled with roses and tropical flowers, and had a magnificent view of the merging of the Kabul and Indus rivers. The Kabul was browny-grey while the Indus, flowing down from the mountains of Kashmir, was the purest sky blue. The two streams flowed side by side for a while before their waters mingled. In the distance I could see Akbar's mighty Attock Fort guarding the strategic crossing just below the confluence.

I crossed the Indus, checked in at the Indus View Tourist Inn, then cycled off to see Akbar's fort. It was the headquarters of the Powindah Regiment and I discovered that visitors were not allowed inside without a permit from GCHQ in Rawalpindi. But the guards did their best for me, serving me tea while they made telephone calls on my behalf. Eventually, a young captain appeared. The commanding officer had given him permission to take me on a tour of the outside, provided I took no photographs. From a rocky height we could see inside the battlements, where there were lawns, gardens and the regimental swimming pool. Passengers on the train to Peshawar had told me that political prisoners were kept in Attock Fort, but I think this was popular rumour. There was no sign of prison activity in that calm, green enclosure. The captain described the underground rooms for Akbar and his family, warm in winter and as cool as air-conditioned apartments in the summer; there was also an escape tunnel for him under the Indus. Below the walls was the path of the old Imperial Road, on the opposite side of the fortress from the present main road.

After my tour I was entertained to lunch in the married quarters by my guide and his wife. They were first cousins from

Murree, where they always marry within the family because they 'like to know what they're getting'. The captain was very worried that I was travelling unarmed and wanted to take me out then and there to try to get me a revolver, which he would teach me to use. I explained my view that arms were a provocation to violence: if I produced a gun in a dangerous situation, I was bound to be shot first.

It was very still and eerie at the Indus View: a thick fog rolled over the river, the garden filled with howling pie-dogs and I was the only resident. I ate a large cooked breakfast next morning while I waited for the mist to clear, then set off in search of Hazro. I had failed to reach Alexander's embarkation point at Hund on the north bank of the Indus and I was equally unsuccessful with his point of disembarkation on the south bank. The Indus had changed course and no one in the little town of Hazro had a clue about Alexander. Perhaps it was the wrong Hazro? But it was a pleasant detour. A stranger was a rare event there and I was treated to innumerable cups of tea. As usual, they were most impressed that I was cycling at such an advanced age. 'In Pakistan ladies of fifty are old, but I think in England ladies are not old until seventy-eight.' I was pleased to have a specific age set for the start of my senility. One young man exclaimed (uncharacteristically for a Muslim), 'Jesus! What a beautiful state of health you have!'

I was accompanied back to the Imperial Road by three boys on bicycles. Their machines, like most in Pakistan, were wonders to behold. What they lacked in refinements such as gears, brakes and cycle oil they made up for in balls of multicoloured wool round the hubs, artificial flowers and joss sticks sprouting from the handlebars, mirrors, vivid plastic seat-covers with fringes and scalloped edges, fringed plastic crossbar covers, baskets swathed in brightly patterned material, and horns with bizarre moans. My sea-green Condor looked very plain by comparison. Two had the brand-name 'Reliagh' with an approximation to the Raleigh crest on the rear mudguard.

I stayed two nights in Hasan Abdal, where my simple hotel was clean, crowded with Pathan truck-drivers and cheerful, unlike the expensive Indus View. It had three gas fires in the restaurant – a great treat, as the nights and early mornings were

still cold. I dined on delicious charcoal-grilled Indus fish and
spent blissfully warm hours over my notes and correspondence
while the waiter fussed over me, moving a fire nearer as the night
grew colder and plying me with tea and sweets. I made a day-trip
from there to Taxila. The museum had some fine examples of
Gandhara art, including a famous Fasting Buddha. There was
Greek decoration on the pottery and some beautiful Hellenistic
sculpture. I particularly liked a sleeping musician, a boy who had
nodded off over his drum, and the little terracotta toys – horses,
bullocks and ducks on wheels. The sophistication of the jewellery, glassware and toilet articles was evidence of a high level of
civilisation. The excavations were less easy to read by a non-
archaeologist, spread out as they were over a number of mounds.
I did a quick tour on my bicycle, then sped with a light heart back
to the main road. I had finally finished with Alexander!

To concentrate my thoughts on the Moghuls, I spent an
afternoon of tranquil delight in the Wah Gardens, laid out by
Akbar to refresh the traveller on the Imperial Road. A spring
fed the streams which criss-crossed the rose gardens; there were
cypresses, much loved by both Persians and Moghuls; and
vistas opened from pavilion to pavilion through avenues of
mature trees. They were a bit run down, as the Pakistanis have
more treasures than they can afford to maintain, but I was
pleased to find the gardens well patronised by pensive strollers
like myself.

Between Hasan Abdal and Rawalpindi I climbed over the
Marghalla Pass. In his memoirs the Emperor Jehangir wrote
that Marghalla meant 'the place to plunder caravans'. It was an
apt description, as there was only just enough room for a narrow
road between the rocks; the train had to go through a tunnel.
The pass was dominated by an obelisk and a Classical temple in
memory of General John Nicholson who died in the aftermath
of the Indian Mutiny. As I was taking photographs of these
singularly inappropriate monuments, an old road-mender came
up, pointed to the sky and told me in sign language that there
was one god and we were all his children. I agreed and we
smiled and shook hands. Then he touched his forehead and his
heart, kissed my hand and returned to his digging.

After the pass it was downhill most of the way to Rawalpindi.

The Grand Trunk Road became The Mall where Gothic spires again soared over white-clad cricketers and the taxis were all Morris Minors. Some were so patched, beaten and re-beaten that the RIP on their number-plates seemed very appropriate. Rawalpindi was already lower and noticeably warmer than Peshawar and I found myself humming the most cheerful of all my cycling songs, 'The Teddy Bears' Picnic', as I cruised down into the city centre.

There was little to see. The Military Museum was closed for refurbishment and there were no Moghul mosques. It had been a busy cross-roads city long before an arm of the Silk Road had passed that way, then the British had established a major military cantonment there as a staging-post to the Khyber Pass during their wars with the Afghans. It was still a military town, the headquarters of the Pakistan Armed Forces, and a busy, sprawling commercial and industrial centre. In fact, it sprawled almost the whole way to Islamabad and half the population of Rawalpindi seemed to pile onto buses in the mornings to go to work in the new capital. The two cities would inevitably merge in the near future into one great metropolis, not unlike London, with diplomatic and commercial quarters. The proximity of Rawalpindi was the salvation of Islamabad, giving it the vitality lacked by other isolated new capitals.

True to their Moghul heritage, the Pakistanis had planted woods, trees, lawns and gardens as soon as they had started to build their new capital and it was already green and shady. I liked it immediately. My first objective in Islamabad was to try to persuade the Indian Embassy to amend my visa, which was stamped 'Entry/Exit by Air Only'. I naturally wanted to enter India by bicycle so that I could continue along the Imperial Road from Lahore to Delhi. I had no success. The Indian half of the Punjab was closed to visitors because of terrorist activity by the Sikh separatists. Three convoys a month were escorted through by armed troops but my bicycle was not an eligible vehicle. Sadly I pedalled round to the British Embassy, where the anxious Consul-General in Karachi had told me to report my safe arrival. There I was cheered up by the Consul for the North West Frontier, who whisked me home for a lunch of fish and chips, then invited me to stay.

I had a wonderful three days. Susanne drove me into Rawalpindi that afternoon to collect my luggage from the hotel and
installed me in a sparkling clean room, with a lavatory that
worked and a bath with good hot water. My clothes went
through the consular washing machine and I was fed on chicken
with mushrooms and pasta, petit pois, claret, apricot pie, coffee, chocolates and malt whisky. My liver had had a well-earned
rest in alcohol-free Pakistan and I had been surprised at the ease
with which I had endured those dry evenings. But it was good
to take a comforting drink and to be able to taste the flavour of
food without curry. We went to a party at the Dutch Ambassador's Residence; I wore my silk suit and black fishnet tights and
everyone expressed amazement that such an elegant person had
just stepped off a bicycle. I went to look at the Faisal Mosque,
designed by a Turk and financed by the Saudis to grace the new
capital, and loved the giant structure, like a tent frozen in
concrete. I had my safe gamma globulin injection at the
embassy clinic, caught up with the news in the diplomatic
copies of *The Times* and went out with Philip and Susanne in
their jeep, looking for a suitable place in the surrounding
countryside for Philip's staff Christmas picnic. Though pressed
to stay longer, I left after two nights, afraid that the ease of the
consular family and home might spoil me for the realities of life
on the road in Pakistan.

One of the realities of the road was the over-attentiveness of
some hotel staff. In a strict Muslim country where women were
never unescorted, a lone traveller was a great provocation. On
my first night out of Islamabad I met the most persistent of all
my admirers, a brisk young waiter. First he tried my door,
which was locked. Then he got out onto the balcony and tried
my window, which was bolted. He went away, to return to the
balcony in the small hours of the morning when everyone was
asleep, presumably with a chair or a step-ladder. There was a
small window near the ceiling above my bed and it had a hole in
the pane of glass. He climbed up and glued his mouth to the
hole, whispering, 'My love, my love, open this door.' I tried
ignoring him, then I told him to go away, both without effect.
Soon he began to pull out pieces of glass to widen the hole. As
the total frame was less than a foot across, my only worry was

the glass splinters. I pulled the hood of my sleeping-bag firmly over my head and pretended to sleep. His next ploy was to lower a length of rubber hose-pipe through the now empty window-frame and rattle it against my iron bedhead. At that point, I really lost my temper. I sat up in bed and shouted very loudly. 'Go away! If you don't go, I shall scream. I shall wake up the whole hotel.' He fled, never to return. I got some broken sleep at last, but the room was cold and the bed uncomfortable. At seven o'clock, there was a hammering on my door: 'Sweep. Sweep.' I had to leap out of bed, dress quickly and admit the sweeper with his twig brush. I had a feeling he had been sent early, just to spite me. The waiter wore a blank expression as he handed me my tea and chapattis. I left at 8.30, even though it was still cold and misty, relieved to be out on the road. Generally my admirers were not difficult to handle. Sometimes they were engaging in their simplicity and one, a black-haired, blue-eyed boy from the mountains of Gilgit, was quite the most beautiful creature I had ever seen in my life. But a day's toil on rough, dusty roads under a glaring sun was no fitting preparation for a night of passion.

I cycled across the Salt Range, whose strange, eroded shapes I had seen from the train. It was a barren, empty, forbidding landscape and I was pleased to cruise down into Jhelum, my northern diversion over. I was back in the flat, fertile Punjab. Three of its five rivers, the Jhelum (Hydaspes), the Chenab (Acesines) and the Ravi (Hydraotes), I crossed on three consecutive days, cycling over territory where Alexander had campaigned against Porus. The Jhelum was so wide it was difficult to see the further end of the bridge in the morning haze; the Chenab with its marshes and watermeadows seemed endless too; only the Ravi, on the outskirts of Lahore, was a modest stream. The landscape was featureless, just miles to get under the wheels. I lost the mountains of Kashmir to my left and gained only fields of vegetables, rows of factories making electric fans, and dusty, sprawling towns.

The villages of Pakistan were always brightened by their mosques. They were painted in delicate colours – pale green and white, pale blue and primrose, or dusky pink, terracotta and white – and had so many cupolas, towers, multifoil arches, pinnacles and scalloped edges that they looked more like fairy palaces than places of worship. On the Grand Trunk Road I discovered how they achieved these flights of fancy. There were builders' yards crammed with fibreglass domes, minarets, pinnacles and scalloped woodwork surrounds to nail over doors and windows. They stood in rows, in all the favourite pastel shades. The villagers obviously built a plain rectangular structure, painted it in their chosen colour combination, then went shopping at one of the yards for matching Moghul baubles, as many as they could afford. The results would win no prizes for architecture, but they were cheerful sights.

I needed cheering in the Punjab. I was unlucky with hotels, my cold still lingered on as catarrh and dust-inflamed sinuses, my left calf was still bruised and aching from the month-old injury of Ahmadpur East and, worst of all, I had some disconcerting little chest pains in Gujranwala and was sure I was on the verge of a heart-attack. I was relieved to reach Lahore, where the emergency contact I had from Zuhra happened to be a doctor. But my health problems disappeared without medical aid after a week in a good hotel on The Mall, watching the Third Test Match and admiring the Moghul sights. 'This Gatting will not be Captain again. You English are too gentlemen to allow,' said a fellow-guest, consoling me in my embarrassment. Admittedly the umpiring left something to be desired but my team's behaviour was shaming.

I collected my post at the American Express office. One of my correspondents remarked that my postcards were too cheerful, that I was not suffering appropriate angst or bouts of depression. The reason was simple. I could write postcards only in proper hotels where I had electric light and/or a window. When I managed to find such amenities, my spirits rose and my postcards were enthusiastic. On long, empty evenings in unlit kennels, writing was out of the question and I could only take my dejection and my anxieties early to bed.

My fights with bureaucracy over a flight-ticket to New Delhi occupied a number of mornings, but I was free in the afternoons for the beauties of Lahore. The Moghuls had developed it into a major cultural and intellectual centre and the British had retained its ethos, adding a Victorian Moghul university,

High Courts, schools and museums adjacent to the Old City. There was still an unhurried, intellectual air about the place.

I went first to Akbar's great fort. As with the fort in Agra, Akbar had been responsible for the outer walls, the functional end of the structure, while his successors had concentrated on embellishing the palaces within. Jehangir had added an elegant quadrangle but the loveliest buildings were Shah Jehan's. His favourite material was marble inlaid with semi-precious stones, pietra dura work. Poppies, carnations, honeysuckle, lotus, tulips and roses were linked together in swirling stalk and leaf designs, all worked in jasper, blood stones, cornelian, agate and malachite. As always, these Moghul buildings defied the camera. Their beauty lay in their symmetry and proportion, the balance of space between structure and courtyard, the vistas where trees continued the lines of the masonry, the detail of the craftsmanship, the play of the fountains and the tranquillity. Unfortunately, the fort had been damaged the previous week, when a dinner had been given there in honour of the Aga Khan. Walls had been gouged to install electric lights and a beautiful floor hacked to erect a dais. Ironically, the dinner was to thank him for the interest he took in Pakistan's historical buildings and the generosity of his contributions towards their restoration.

Two of the loveliest Moghul buildings were a cycle-ride out of Lahore, in the small village of Shaddara. They were the tombs of the Emperor Jehangir and his Empress Nur Jehan, Light of the World. Shah Jehan built his father's mausoleum in 1627, surrounding it with a high brick wall faced with red sandstone inlaid with marble. Inside the walls were lawns and gardens and a pathway led through an arch and an avenue of trees to the mausoleum itself, its white marble sarcophagus inlaid with pietra dura flowers and engraved with the 99 names of Allah. Across the railway-track the mausoleum of Nur Jehan was a lower structure in a smaller garden, but built of the same materials as that of her husband and memorable in its simplicity. This was a place to see the two faces of Pakistan. Well-dressed families and groups of friends strolled or picnicked in the gardens, taking photographs of their children against the Moghul background. Outside, the shanty-dwellers lived in tents of old sacking, their ragged, dirty children playing barefoot in the dust among the goats and bullocks. It was not an easy area to cycle through. As I sat in Nur Jehan's garden, making notes under a tree, one of the well-dressed young men came up with an English grammar in his hand. Would I kindly explain to him the meaning of 'on the horns of a dilemma' and 'a hand-to-mouth existence', with examples of usage?

As I passed the park on my way back to my hotel, the masseurs were hard at work, one of them marching up and down a customer's spine. It was another pavement profession to add to my list, along with palmistry, official form-filling, gluing sheets of newspaper to make bags, squashing the ends of twigs to make toothbrushes, stripping, chopping and bagging sugar-cane and painting billboards by hand.

I spent my last morning in Lahore in the Shalimar Gardens, laid out by Shah Jehan as an outdoor palace where his family could camp in the summer. As well as the obvious pleasures of lawns, pools and pavilions, I loved the red brickwork paths laid out in intricate patterns of squares, hexagons and octagons. Decorative brickwork was a well-developed Moghul minor art, still practised today; the hard shoulders of modern highways are often paved with neatly laid narrow bricks. In the afternoon I visited the excellent museum in The Mall, where Kipling's father was once curator, took my last look at Kim's gun, Zam-zana, and finished my tour of the city's mosques.

Predictably, the hotel staff were horrified that I was taking my bicycle into India. 'In Pakistan we are honest. You can leave your cykel anywhere. But in India they are very poor. They steal.' I promised to watch my possessions and my own safety at all times and pedalled out to the airport. I was leaving my seventh country after cycling 5,207 miles from London. An hour later I was in New Delhi.

Early next morning I cycled through the icy mist from my modest airport hotel to Delhi International Airport to meet Heather's flight from London; she was coming out to spend Christmas and the New Year with me. I had been alone for a long time now. I couldn't wait to see her friendly face and I stood with the crowds in the reception area, clutching my bicycle handlebars and scanning the arrivals. I was wearing all my layers of cycling gear that chill December dawn and they were all well past their best. My once canary yellow cagoule was black with a hint of greyish gold, my cotton cycling trousers were thin, patched and frayed at the edges, my trainers were scuffed and filthy and I wore a faded Turkish headscarf against the dripping, freezing fog. Heather appeared. Tall, graceful, elegant from the top of her coiffure down to the tips of her Ferragamo shoes, she swept through the hall with her retinue of attendants and her four suitcases, looking as groomed as if she had just that minute set out from home, not spent the night on an intercontinental jumbo. My former world, the world of influential headmistresses, had come out to India to find me and there I stood in my scruffy clothes, blinking in surprise. In a dream, I forked out more on tips to porters than I normally spent in a day, then, with my bicycle and my recent past dumped unceremoniously into the boot, I drifted with Heather into the waiting limousine to be driven by the liveried chauffeur to Delhi's most costly hotel.

I had asked Heather to bring me a tablet of expensive soap: if water was short and facilities basic, I could at least boost my morale with the best of *something*, no matter how small. It would be my one luxury through the rigours of the next leg of my trip. We sat in our unbelievably sumptuous quarters – you have to spend nights in *muzzafir khanas* to have a real appreciation of luxury – and Heather emptied her cornucopia. Soaps, bath oils, skin creams, books, English newspapers, vitamin pills, films, stationery – everything I had asked for and more besides came pouring out of my Christmas stocking. There were even extra clothes for me to wear, which Heather had thoughtfully brought out on loan, as she knew quite well the limitations of my wardrobe. I soaked in my first hot bath for months and savoured my first Glenmorangie. And we talked all day.

We toured northern India and Rajasthan for two weeks, staying in former Maharajahs' palaces and international hotels. I shall never forget the Lake Palace in Udaipur, with the moonlight gleaming on its white marble terraces as we crossed in the launch from the city. We had a wonderful time, punctuating our avid sightseeing with memorable food and drink. When the duty-free Glenmorangie ran out, we resorted to IMFL (Indian Manufactured Foreign Liquor). The holiday came at just the right time to restore our strength and spirits – Heather's for the next school term, mine for the rest of India.

My share of the tour had been paid for in London, so that my budget was unaffected by the expense of the fortnight. Considered in English terms, it was an expensive holiday, but not outrageously so. What worried me – and it was a constant niggle which I had to crush with resolution – was the outrageousness of our expenditure when viewed in Indian terms. Our young graduate guide in Agra, who considered himself to be quite well paid, would have had to work for more than three months to pay for one night without breakfast in our hotel. International hotels throughout the world charge too much for too many facilities, but their prices and their very existence become an obscenity when they are utterly and forever beyond the reach of their own countrypeople. I had lived among the poor of Pakistan, eaten their food, slept in their *muzzafir khanas* and been humbled by their generosity. I realised, as I lay in my golden bed in the palace of the Maharajah of Jaipur, that I was fundamentally changed. I could never feel entirely easy in such surroundings again. Which is as well, because I can no longer afford them.

We both had some Indian clothes made in Udaipur. Mine were a *shalwar kameez* in shocking pink silk and a pair of baggy green cotton Punjabi trousers which tied at the waist and ankles. They became my fourth pair of cycling pants, replacing the well worn Turkish pair which were now too delicate even to hold their patches in place. The pink silk *kameez* was not a success but the *shalwar* trousers were magnificent; their colour was exactly the shocking pink which lurked among the dark jewel colours of my tried and trusted silk suit, so they made a spectacular new ensemble with the suit jacket. I wore it on Heather's last night in India, when we went to supper with the British High Commissioner in Delhi.

By the time Heather left, I had already spent ten weeks in Pakistan and northern India and was keen to be on my way again. Despite their religious and political differences, the two countries shared the same history and cultural background and the similarities between them were greater than the differences. I guessed that there would be the same food and the same standards of accommodation between Delhi and Calcutta as I had met between Karachi and Lahore and I was growing weary of scratching along in country places at subsistence level. The sooner I finished my crossing of the Indian subcontinent the better, but before I could pick up speed I had work to do.

The Moghuls were still very much with me; many of their finest buildings were in Delhi and Agra. But in Delhi I was also at the hub of British power in India. As usual, the British had left the ancient cities on the site intact and had laid out their own capitals beside them. At the great Delhi Durbar in 1911, graced by the newly crowned King George V and Queen Mary, the transfer of the capital of India from Calcutta to Delhi was announced and a major building programme instituted. The Raj Path, the great ceremonial avenue, was laid from the India Gate up to the red sandstone Rashtrapati Bhavan (built for the Viceroy and now the official residence of the Indian President) and the Sansad Bhavan, the Parliament Buildings. This monumental complex, designed by Sir Edwin Lutyens and Herbert Baker, was completed in 1929 and the new capital inaugurated in 1931, symbolising the might of the British Raj for only sixteen years before it was handed over to independent India in 1947. From New Delhi, the Grand Trunk Road ran north-west to the Khyber Pass and south-east to Calcutta, the original home of the East India Company and the first capital of British India. For the Raj, as for Sher Shah Suri and the Moghuls, it was the vital link between the far ends of their empire.

Like the British, Shah Jehan had wanted to move his capital to Delhi, to a newly constructed Shahjehanabad. The Red Fort on the Yamuna river in Delhi was his construction, as was immediately evident from the scalloped edges of the crenellations, fancier than Akbar's stern battlements, though just as effective. The inside was a depressing sight. The white marble in the Hall of Private Audience (the Diwan-i-Khas) was chipped and the pietra dura had lost most of its semi-precious stones. The Peacock Throne had long ago been taken to Teheran. The mirrors in the Shish Mahal were broken, water no longer flowed in the Canal of Paradise and Shah Jehan's own marble apartments were under scaffolding and closed to the public because of the *son et lumière*. Aurangzeb's tiny, fairy-tale Pearl Mosque (the Moti Masjid), totally enclosed and worked throughout in fine marble relief, had fared better. Opposite the fort was Shah Jehan's final extravagance, the Jami Masjid, the largest mosque in India with a capacity of 25,000 worshippers. It took fourteen years to build but Shah Jehan never rode there in state on his elephant across from his Red Fort. In 1658, the year of its completion, he was deposed by his son Aurangzeb and kept prisoner in the fort at Agra. Aurangzeb was the first and only Moghul Emperor to rule from the new capital. For the Moghuls, as for the British, the transfer to Delhi was the beginning of the end.

My bicycle was invaluable in Delhi; it meant I could cover great distances in my sightseeing tours in freedom and independence. Just outside the city centre I visited the tomb of the second emperor, Humayun, who died in a manner eminently suited to a cultivated Moghul; he stumbled down his library steps. His wife, Haji Begum, commissioned a Persian architect to design his mausoleum. It was a simple building of red sandstone with marble inlay, set in an ornamental garden, but it was important because it introduced the Moghul double dome. The two skins allowed a lofty, imposing exterior dome without destroying the intimacy and balance of the interior. In style it foreshadowed the elegant Moghul tombs of later years and their culmination in Shah Jehan's Taj Mahal.

I had transferred to the Marina Hotel in Connaught Place, the shopping centre of the modern city: later I learnt that it was in the Marina that Mahatma Gandhi's assassins had stayed. I tried to take photographs but Delhi is the photographer's nightmare. It was foggy every morning and in the afternoon the sun shone low and red through the haze of woodsmoke. The view down the Raj Path to the India Gate was always lost in mist. I photographed a sacred cow chewing peacefully on the lawn in front of the Parliament Buildings, then was rushed off the Raj Path for 'panj mint' (five minutes) while Rajiv Gandhi's caval-cade screamed by. I had seen Prime Minister Junejo and his cavalcade in Lahore. Both Premiers had sped along the cleared streets with police sirens blaring. The one difference seemed to be that Rajiv Gandhi had no ambulance in attendance.

I always tried to leave capital cities on Sundays to avoid the heaviest traffic. On the second Sunday in January I waited for the worst of the morning mist to clear but it was still cold and clammy as I set out and I needed all my layers of clothing. I was happy to be on the road again. I bowled merrily down the Raj Path to the India Gate, took two wrong turns and a lengthy detour, then spotted Humayun's tomb through the mist and found my road at last. The pavements of the outskirts and the grass round the Lodi tombs were crowded with families who lived there. I passed pavement-dwellers huddled up in their quilts on that cold morning, with their poor bits of possessions lined up beside them. The green parrots nesting in the tombs were the only cheerful sight. Agra was not signposted for twelve miles and then it appeared in Hindi. But I was delighted to see a street sign, 'Sher Shah Suri Marg'. That was the preferred official name for National Highway 2 between Delhi and Calcutta, though the Indians I met still called it 'The G.T. Road'. Their attachment to the old imperial names often caused problems. Street maps would print Mahatma Gandhi Marg or Jawaharlal Nehru Marg in city centres and no one would be able to direct me there. Suddenly, understanding would dawn. I wanted to go to The Mall or to Queen Victoria Street!

Acrid smog persisted all the way to Agra, making my eyes smart, and cycling seemed rather hard work after my long break. Some 30 miles from the Marina Hotel the factories, industrial wasteland and poor roadside shacks began to give way to fields of mustard, winter corn and newly planted orange groves. A road sign said 'Weak Bridge Ahead. Drive Slow'; lorries and motorcycle rickshaws bore such instructions as 'Horn Please', 'Long Vickle', the enigmatic 'Wait for Side' and 'OK. Ta Ta'. They were less colourful than those in Pakistan, but their slogans were more varied.

The state of Haryana is one of the best equipped in India to cope with the travelling public. A chain of clean and pleasant tourist complexes, each named after an Indian bird, stood at intervals along the Grand Trunk Road. After 60 miles I booked into a bungalow at The Dabchick. Mine was the only white face there and everyone came up to chat, admire my bicycle and offer me tea or sweets. I was back to my familiar life-style. Next morning I watched an amusing scene as I ate my breakfast. The Dabchick had an elephant, a camel and a pony to give rides, a dancing bear and a snake charmer. The men and their beasts lounged on the grass, smoking, chatting and grazing till a coachful of tourists appeared. It was as if someone had flicked a switch. There was an instant flurry of activity. The bear began to dance, the elephant, pony and camel paraded up and down and the snake charmer began to play furiously on his pipe. Fifteen minutes later the coach left and lethargy once more descended on the garden.

Between The Dabchick and Mathura I got a puncture, only the third of my trip. The back tyre had finally given up after 5,300 miles, splitting along six inches or so of its circumference. I was on a long flat, empty stretch of road, miles from the nearest town, but I need not have worried. I pushed my bicycle along and in less than ten minutes a little boy of about six rushed out into the road from a thatched wayside tea-stall, rattling his repair kit in a biscuit tin and shouting 'Puncture! Puncture!' Then his father appeared, which gave me more confidence, and I was soon seated over a cup of tea while the inner tube was patched and my spare tyre substituted. It took a long time, as my kind of bicycle wheel was unfamiliar, so I doubled the payment, giving the father ten rupees instead of the modest five he had asked for (22 rupees = £1). The usual crowd had gathered. I said 'Ram, Ram' and put my hands together in the *namaste* sign. Everyone beamed and said 'Ram, Ram' in reply. They were heartbreakingly poor, barefoot and in rags, but they still refused payment for the tea so I handed my biros and my packet of biscuits to the children. My bicycle had carried me back through the plate-glass window which separates the tourist from the realities of life in India.

Mathura was the birthplace of Lord Krishna and a centre of pilgrimage for Hindus. As I was concentrating on the Moghuls, I was able to miss Vrindaban, where Krishna had sported with the milkmaids, his cradle at Mahaban, and Goverdhan, where he had lifted the hilltops on his fingertips to keep off the rain. I ventured into the chaotic town from my new hotel on the Grand Trunk Road only to visit the Jami Masjid, the mosque built by Aurangzeb in 1661. Aurangzeb was an iconoclast, a devout Muslim who lacked the respect of his predecessors for the Hindu religion. In Mathura, he pulled down one of the Hindus' holiest shrines, the Kesava Deo Temple, built on the spot where Krishna is said to have been born, and erected a mosque in its place. The mosque stood in a squalid street beside a market of rotting vegetables and was in a sadly neglected state. I spent half the afternoon searching for it and got thoroughly lost, as there were no road signs in English, no one could understand me and no one seemed to care. The lack of concern and initiative extended even to the tangerine-sellers, who refused me half a kilo: it was a kilo or nothing. When I finally found my hotel again late in the evening, I switched on the welcome fan-heater to warm my bedroom while I took a shower and it burst into flames. Fortunately, I smelt burning rubber from the bathroom and just managed to smother the fire with my bath towel before it caught the bedroom curtains. The hotel staff were quite unconcerned. They just sent up a porter with a replacement fan.

In Agra I fared even worse. I was cycling into the city over a footbridge, crowded as only India can be crowded with bicycles, cycle rickshaws, bullock carts and seas of pedestrians. Halfway across the bridge, a cycle rickshaw collided with my right pannier and tore it off, snapping both the clips. The rickshaw man and his two women passengers laughed. I stood in the middle of the swirling traffic, trying to manage my unbalanced bicycle and the detached pannier. No one came to help and I was plagued by two jeering little boys on bicycles. Finally I persuaded one of them to wheel my pannier off the bridge on his rear carrier for two rupees. Down on the road, I found that I could push the bicycle along slowly with the pannier balanced on my handlebars. I was hot, tired and dusty, in no mood to enjoy the peals of laughter on all sides. I was saved by a Sikh on a motor-scooter who went off to find a cycle rickshaw and helped me load all my luggage inside it; I could then cycle comfortably behind it to my hotel. Agra was an unkind city. I had my compass stolen by the attendant I had paid to look after my bicycle at a Moghul tomb, and the new pannier clips I had made there were a disaster. I had asked for steel but I discovered later that the work had been done in a soft metal alloy which worked loose on rough roads. Another pair had to be made in Calcutta. The unfriendliness of Agra's people, possibly spoilt by the crowds of tourists, was in marked contrast to the kindness and ready assistance I had received in other countries and I hoped that India would improve as I got further away from the capital.

But no personal or practical difficulties could rob Agra of its splendour. It was my third visit there yet I still had a busy schedule, particularly as my bicycle had extended the range of my sightseeing. Agra was the first Moghul capital. Babur laid out gardens; Akbar built the fort; and Shah Jehan embellished the palaces inside it. Akbar's tomb, with its interesting mixture of Hindu and Persian architecture, stood in its ornamental gardens at Sikandra, just outside the city on the Grand Trunk Road. And at Fatehpur Sikri, 25 miles west of Agra, was Akbar's magnificent empty capital, abandoned in 1586 after only sixteen years, because the water is said to have run out. There he had developed his new religion, comprising elements of Islam, Hinduism and Christianity. He had even married a wife of each faith in an attempt to forge a strongly united empire.

In Agra itself I made a tour of the marble palaces and the tombs of jasper, watching the strength of Akbar's syncretic style develop into the stunning elegance of later Moghul architecture. My last afternoon was devoted to the Taj Mahal. Although I had seen it four or five times before, time had dulled the image and I was bowled over again by its perfection. No pictorial representation can do it justice. It is simply the most beautiful building in the world, as wonderful in the precision and grace of its detail as in its overall conception. Shah Jehan spent twelve years building it for his favourite wife, Mumtaz Mahal, who died after bearing their fourteenth child in seventeen years. He is said to have planned a replica in black marble for himself, but he was deposed by Aurangzeb before he could begin its construction. As a prisoner in a palace within Agra Fort, he spent his declining years gazing out over the Yamuna river at the Taj Mahal, where he was eventually buried beside his Mumtaz. The guides tell it as one of the world's great love stories but there seems to me to be a considerable amount of selfishness and self-indulgence in Shah Jehan's devotion. His obsession must have been a trial to Aurangzeb, who was probably right to lock his father away before he emptied the Moghul treasury. But the obsession produced an architectural miracle. I gazed at its white marble beauty reflected in the pools, climbed the white marble steps for a closer look at the intricate carving and the pietra dura work, then walked round the gardens, catching the gleam of the dome through elegant vistas. Most wonderful of all, I cycled back in the evening and stood spellbound in the moonlight.

13

The Grand Trunk Road

AGRA – SHIKOHABAD – ETAWAH – KANPUR –
LUCKNOW – FATEHPUR – ALLAHABAD – VARANASI –
SASARAM – AURANGABAD – BODHGAYA – KULTI –
DURGAPUR – BURDWAN – CHINSURAH – CALCUTTA

Down to Gehenna or up to the Throne,
He travels the fastest who travels alone.
(Rudyard Kipling)

AGRA may have represented the pinnacle of Moghul achievement, but for comfort and pleasantness it ranked so low that I set off in a chill drizzle to avoid spending another night there. I was determined now to get up steam. As the weather was cool there was no reason why I should not manage my average of 50 miles a day, five days a week, and cover the 1,000 miles to Calcutta in a month. That would mean pedalling across the flat immensity of the state of Uttar Pradesh, with its 90 million inhabitants, for over two weeks until the never-ending fields of sugar cane and mustard turned into the paddy fields of Bihar. Uttar Pradesh and Bihar were the two poorest states in India and I knew the journey would be difficult. How difficult I was yet to discover.

There were three major cities on my route – Kanpur, Alla-habad and Varanasi (Benares) – where I knew that I should find proper tourist facilities. Those cities would be my targets and I would sprint as fast as possible across the intervening country. On my first day out of Agra I was apprehensive about accom-modation and relieved to find a small hotel in Shikohabad. It had one wash-basin in the upstairs lobby, where my toilette was of great public interest; but my room was clean and the hotel was one of the two buildings in town which had electric lighting. The tailors in the bazaar, even the 'New Yark Tailor', worked by the light of hurricane lamps, shops had candles and policemen with *lathis* patrolled the dark streets. My enquiries about hotels at first met with blank stares until I realised that hotels in small towns were generally called 'guest houses'.

The state of the roads in Uttar Pradesh ranged from bad to appalling. Fortunately there was little traffic, so that I was able to weave my way along, sometimes swooping and dipping like a graceful seabird on my light, responsive bicycle, but more often picking my way round the potholes like a frenzied hen. Bridges were a particular trial as the sections were not neatly joined and the regular bumping loosened my pliable pannier-clips. The bridge at Dehri-on-Son was the longest in India, just short of three miles, and I lost my right pannier eight times on the crossing.

What traffic there was seemed to move much more slowly than in Pakistan and it was a few days before the reason dawned. I had lost the neat little donkeys which had trotted so briskly beside me all the way from southern Italy to Lahore. The donkey is unclean to the Hindus and market-day traffic moves at the pace of the bullock-cart.

But worse than the lumbering carts and the ruined asphalt were the gangs of cycling youths, who darted round me, poking me, grabbing my luggage, laughing, jeering and squawking like flocks of highly strung cockatoos. If I pulled up by the roadside to let them go ahead, they stopped and waited. If I showed annoyance, they mocked me. They were over-excited and I was one to their six, seven, eight or more, so I felt I had to be very careful. I had one terrifying moment when I had the misfortune to cycle past a high school just as the boys were all pouring out for lunch. There were hundreds of them and I was mobbed. They shot out into the road, screaming with excitement at the sight of a white woman on a bicycle, and started to grab at my handlebars, my panniers, my arms, the back of my shirt and even my hair. They were not malevolent, they were certainly not intending to attack me, but Indian crowds are very excitable and I sensed that their near-hysteria could easily tip over into violence. Two men on bicycles dismounted to watch. I cast a mute look of appeal in their direction but they did nothing to quell the mob, just standing there with blank stares. I started to panic but I knew instinctively that there was danger in appearing to be a victim. Somehow I had to take control of the situation. My years as a headmistress saved me. I glared around with a steely eye and, controlling the pitch of my voice with great effort, said slowly and authoritatively, 'Will you kindly step back and let me pass through.' It worked like a charm. Whether or not they understood what I said, they recognised the magisterial tone. They quietened instantly and stepped back. 'Thank you,' I said coolly, pushing my bicycle forward and pedalling off with a confident air. I had acted my little scene well but my legs had turned to jelly with fright and I had to get off at a safe distance and lean against a tree until the trembling stopped. I was then pursued by a gang of little boys with sticks.

Sometimes I was accompanied by one or two boys on bicycles who asked me innumerable questions in English, then failed to understand my answers. They were wearisome companions but at least they were courteous and they kept the mobs at bay. Beyond Kanpur, I had fewer difficulties. The people were so poor that they simply sat by the roadside and stared. Poverty had eaten into their souls and they lacked the energy to mock.

In Pakistan I had lunched on tangerines and bananas which I bought from village stalls. The villagers of Uttar Pradesh were too poor to afford fruit except the hard, pippy local guavas, so I existed on tea, biscuits and the occasional purchase of sickly confectionery. Sometimes I had a plain chapatti but on the whole I avoided the fly-ridden restaurants with their curries. Quite apart from considerations of hygiene, one curry a day in the evening was as much as I could face.

A quarter of the world's cattle live in India. The herds I saw were so grievously emaciated that their sharp bones seemed to be poking through their hides. They kicked up the dust as they wandered; there was no grazing in sight. The soil between the irrigated fields was barren sand. The stray, useless sacred cattle which crowded city streets and village lanes alike, nosing through the refuse and stealing from market stalls, seemed in much better condition than the herds in the countryside, as did the destructive goats. Women sat outside their houses making pats of cattle manure to dry in the sun for fuel and the sick and old lay on their charpoys by the roadside. Children scavenged for twigs, dead leaves, live branches, anything for firewood or fodder. Placards by the roadside were evidence of a Government campaign to preserve India's dwindling trees and stop erosion: 'Trees are water. Water is life.' But tell that to a family without fuel to warm themselves or cook their meagre dinner. The children had no toys; their dolls were their younger siblings, whom little boys and girls carried round on their hips. Hair was uncombed, bright saris were covered in dust and there was a general air of hopelessness and neglect. I passed a group of women squatting by the roadside to rest and realised that the object on the ground beside them was a child's bier, the small body covered with a thin red cloth. In one village, a lorry had leaked diesel fuel onto the road and three men in ragged *dhotis* and shawls were crouching round the puddle, mopping up the fuel with rags and wringing them into tins. I was ashamed of our wanton, throwaway society and depressed that human misery could still, at the end of the twentieth century, plumb such depths.

I was fortunate enough to find simple hotels in Shikohabad and Etawah, but on my third night from Agra I ran into difficulties. I arrived at Bhagnipur quite late, having cycled 69 miles over poor roads to find a very dingy little town with a muddy main street where cattle and pigs wandered about among the rickshaws and barefoot inhabitants. I was directed to a guest house, but it looked like an ordinary grain shop in an arcade. The proprietor brought out two chairs and we sat by the roadside surrounded by at least 50 people. I kept asking to see my room but my request was ignored. I was offered betel nut to chew, which I declined, and still we sat. At the end of half an hour, a boy in the crowd who spoke some English volunteered the information that there was no room available. He and a friend offered to take me to another guest house. It was another shop-front. They spoke to the owner, were turned away and led me on to a third. Marching ahead of me, they gave no explanations and I toiled wearily behind, pushing my bicycle through the mud. When the third proprietor turned us away, I asked if there was a problem. 'No locks,' they replied. I told

them that I always carried a padlock, so we went back to the first
guest house and all was well.

The accommodation lay behind the shop, round an enclosed
courtyard with a communal tap and latrine. My room had a
red-tiled floor, bright green walls and a wooden bed consisting
of three planks on four short legs. There was no bedding and no
other furniture but I was grateful to have found a hutch for the
night. Half the town followed me, crowding into the courtyard
and even squeezing into my bedroom to watch. I had difficulty
in shooing them out; even after I had locked the door, they still
peered through the window. Fortunately, an electric light came
on at sunset and I was able to close my shutters. It was a
dharamsala, accommodation for pilgrims attached to the
temple, where chanting and bell-ringing went on all night. One
man chanted a line and a chorus responded. The responses
thinned out in the early hours of the morning when only a few
really keen worshippers were left, but by dawn everyone was
back in the temple chanting vigorously and I had the communal
tap to myself.

I dined in a lean-to with a thatched roof, earthen floor and
hurricane lamp. When I asked for a lemonade to wash down the
fiery vegetable curry I was told that none was available; my
extraordinary request was repeated round the restaurant, to the
great amusement of the clientele. As I left I noticed a soft drinks
stall almost opposite and marvelled once more at the Indians'
lack of initiative.

I was relieved to reach Kanpur, formerly Cawnpore, a major
cotton city on the Ganges. The approach road stretched out for
ever, lined with the squalid shacks of migrant workers and
seething with humanity, traffic, sacred cows, dogs and pigs. I
made for the spaciousness of the Civil Lines and found accommodation in The Attic. It was the largest house in Kanpur and
two wings of it had been converted into hotel rooms. It was
owned by an engaging family who invited me to dine with them
and treated me as their guest.

The lady of the house, Santosh, was a woman of parts, a
prominent member of the All Indian Women's Conference, a
writer on political topics and an energetic organiser of voluntary
services in Kanpur. Her father had been a Chief Justice and an

Ambassador, an Oxford man who had shared a flat in London with Nehru when they were both reading for the Bar. I gained a tremendous insight into Indian society from my conversations with her and from the useful reading list she prepared for me. She took the view that no one could know India without knowing the villages, where 75 per cent of Indians lived, and she was most enthusiastic about my cycle ride and the unique opportunities it afforded. Whenever she visited a village herself, they goggled at her like frogs in a well and refused to believe that she was Indian because she drove a car. Despite language difficulties, it was probably easier for me to make contact because I was on a bicycle.

Santosh and her daughter-in-law, a successful furniture designer, took me to a wedding in the grounds of what is still called 'The Cawnpore Club'. As usual on interesting occasions, I had left my camera behind. The bride and groom were both from wealthy Jain families so the bride wore a yellow and gold sari instead of the usual wedding scarlet. The *shamiana* (wedding marquee) was a vast palace of white and peach pleated silk, with crystal chandeliers, carpets, an elaborate dais and tables groaning with food. The hire of the *shamiana* alone would have cost over £1,000. The bridegroom's party arrived carrying lighted *pièces montées* – huge green neon lights in the shape of fans or fronds, with little red fairy lights jumping about among the green like pin-table lighting. We left after the exchange of garlands of marigolds by the bridal pair but not before Santosh had extracted the promise of a large charitable donation from one of the families. We toured the Club, which was sadly neglected. Santosh remembered it from the glittering heyday of the Raj and was depressed by the dust and disorder.

I left my bicycle in The Attic and took a shared taxi to Lucknow, a very Italianate city with cream, terracotta and pink plasterwork, Classical shopping arcades, palm trees and broad avenues. It put me so much in mind of Palermo that I felt suddenly homesick for Europe, for Italian food, wine, the laughter of friends, telephones that worked and conversation I could understand. It was the first time I had consciously wondered what on earth I was doing, alone and so far from home.

'Lucknow, the Capital of Uttar Pradesh', read the Tourist

Office pamphlet, 'is a storehouse of visceral memories.' Unfortunately there was no official tour of the city and the rickshaw drivers were quite unaware of their visceral heritage. I had to try five of them before I found one who had heard of The Residency.

The British inhabitants of Lucknow had taken refuge in The Residency compound at the outbreak of the Indian Mutiny (now called the War of Independence) and had held out for 87 days under the command of Sir Henry Lawrence. When Sir Henry Havelock's small force had finally broken through to the starving residents, it too had been trapped inside. The final relief by Sir Colin Campbell had come 22 days later. The cemetery of the ruined church held the graves of 2,000 men, women and children who had died of wounds, starvation or disease. The Residency buildings had been left exactly as they were in 1857, roofless and scarred with cannon shot. The ladies' quarters were still intact and housed a model of the positions during the siege, a sad, neglected object in a dusty showcase. I spent the afternoon wandering through the poignant ruins set in tropical gardens and well-kept lawns. It was the first time on my trip that I had visited a ruin so close to our own times and I felt emotionally involved. It was the Indian Mutiny which had decided the British Government to take direct control of India, instead of administering it through the East India Company. The Union Jack had flown day and night over The Residency until 1947, when it was lowered for the first and last time at independence.

In Fatehpur, Santosh arranged for me to stay with friends of hers, a retired Gurkha brigadier and his wife, Pushpi, who had converted part of their huge mansion into a nursery school for 300 pupils. Like Santosh, they had inherited a building and a colony of servants for whom they needed to find employment. The hotel and the school were two different, but equally successful, answers.

The brigadier went shooting and fishing, bred labradors, wore a Harris tweed jacket, drank whisky and was very keen on 'standards'. 'Would you believe it! Today of all days the blasted boiler's conked out!' he exclaimed as he greeted me. If he had been dropped down in Camberley he would have been quite indistinguishable from his British counterparts, except for his paler skin. Indians keep out of the sun.

Their *bhawan* was large enough to house three separate establishments, each with its own kitchen and team of servants. The brigadier managed the beautiful gardens and the farmland round the *bhawan*, while his bachelor brother managed the orchards; his widowed sister-in-law and her family had the third home. A manservant waited at the brigadier's table. He wore a tweed jacket and grey flannel trousers short in the arms and legs because he was taller than his employer, from whom he had obviously inherited the outfit. His feet were bare but his head and neck were swathed in a thick woollen scarf. He needed considerable guidance from Pushpi and was obviously not at all keen on his duties as butler, but the brigadier said he was excellent at shooting grouse and flying kites. He was the sixth generation to work for the family; he had been born in the compound and he and his dependents had always lived there, hence the need for the nursery school to provide extra work. As the brigadier explained, it was impossible in those circumstances to say, 'Sorry, old chap. Times have changed and we don't really need so many servants. Here's a month's notice and a bonus. Take your family away and find yourself another job.'

We discussed the apathy of the Indians, which the brigadier attributed to the negative nature of the Freedom Movement. Passive resistance, fasting, strikes, sit-ins, days of silence, had been the weapons of the Congress Party, so that when their leaders came to power in 1947 they had had no experience of positive action or forward planning. I felt the apathy went deeper, that it was the result of the Hindu's acceptance of his fate and his station in life. If the welfare of his soul was the only thing that really mattered, there was no point in striving to improve his own or his neighbours' circumstances and he had no responsibilities towards others. Virtue lay in being good, not in doing good, and would lead in the next incarnation to promotion within the caste system. *The Times of India* had recently carried a strong leader on the topic (the press in India is free and never hesitates to criticise), chastising the Hindus for watching in silence while people were murdered, forced to commit *sati* and, horror of horrors, while a man beheaded his seven-year-old son to propitiate Kali, the Goddess of Destruction. In that context, the failure of two bystanders to come to my assistance when I was mobbed by schoolboys was easy to understand.

Pushpi arranged a permit for me to stay in the Public Works Department bungalow at Kharga, as Allahabad was too far for comfort in one day and there was no other accommodation on the road. She packed me a picnic which I ate by candlelight during a three-hour blackout. After another long day pushing miles under the wheels over flat, featureless arable land, I reached the city of Allahabad in my target time of two weeks, well pleased with my progress to date.

I cheered up in Allahabad because I began to relax and accept the Indians on their own terms. I had been frustrated and angry at times because I had judged them by Western standards instead of seeing them as their own carefree, chaotic and slightly mad selves. As I pushed my bicycle wearily towards my hotel, I was pursued by three street-vendors, one with clockwork peacocks, one with men's underpants and the third with dancing plastic dogs – the last things I should have wanted to buy even in the best of circumstances. In Allahabad's best restaurant, where the table linen was crisp and sparkling white, mice scurried everywhere in the gloom and no one seemed to notice. In my hotel corridor, where they were painting the ceiling, it occurred to no one to cover the floor-tiles and varnished doors. The decorators splashed their paint with gay abandon and next day squadrons of sweepers were on their knees, trying to scrub the tiles clean and removing most of the varnish along with the paint splashes from the doors. It was all engagingly ridiculous.

Their productivity, again according to *The Times of India*, was the lowest of any country in the world, developed or developing, and I could see no prospect of improvement. The four main estates of Vedic scripture had splintered into some 5,000 castes and sub-castes, each with its own exclusive role in society. It was closed-shop trade unionism carried to the very heights of inefficiency, yet beyond reform, as it had divine authority. Below the castes were the outcastes, the Untouchables, who performed defiling tasks such as lavatory cleaning and scuttled along the ground in a crouching position with their little twig brushes, because they were not allowed to stand in the presence of a caste Hindu. The system had been designed by the Aryan invaders to keep India's dark, indigenous Dravidians in their place, but it had developed into a cruel straitjacket, encouraging resignation at all levels and stifling initiative. No doubt the painters in the hotel were hired to paint the ceiling and the damage they might do in the process was someone else's problem; and the waiters in the restaurant would feel no more responsibility for the mice than they would for the cleanliness of the lavatories. Indians had a remarkable capacity for failing to notice.

Yet their lack of social mobility had its brighter side. Their narrow responsibilities left them carefree and made them tolerant of others. In part, this accounted for the contrast between their own personal cleanliness and the public squalor around them. A religion in which every creature, every stone, every river could be a manifestation of one of the three main gods, who in their turn were the three aspects of the one Creator, could provide for every kind of religious experience, from intellectual monotheism to primitive tree-worship. Hinduism was syncretic, absorbing new gods rather than denouncing them, so that the Buddha had been accepted as the tenth incarnation of Vishnu and Hindus had cheerfully added Buddhist Sarnath and Bodhgaya to their places of pilgrimage.

Allahabad was one of the holy cities of the Hindus and I arrived there in time for the Basant Panchami, the Spring Festival. Pilgrims had converged in their millions to bathe at the Sangam, the confluence of the Ganges, the Yamuna and the invisible, mystical Saraswati river. The devout were camping in the water meadows for a month, in a huge city of official khaki tents, washing away their sins and listening to discourses. I hired a cycle rickshaw to take me to the Sangam and joined the pilgrim hordes making their way towards the rivers. Motor vehicles were not allowed. The affluent were riding in twos, threes or fours in rickshaws; horse-drawn tongas carried twenty or thirty; and farm-carts were crammed with as many as sixty people. In addition, there were two or three thousand on foot, naked and half-naked *sadhus* mingling with families in their brightest and best clothes. I never reached the Sangam but to see such a mass of humanity was an experience in itself. I saw the throngs of bathers next day when I cycled out of the city over the Ganges Bridge, having first inspected the outside of Akbar's fort at the strategic confluence.

From Allahabad it was two days' ride to Varanasi. I was cycling steadily south-east and the day-time temperature was rising, though the nights were still cold. I put on a short-sleeved blouse for the first time since Turkey but hesitated over my Italian cycling cap, afraid that it might provoke even more jeers and derision than usual. Instead it had the opposite effect. From the distance, in my cap, trousers and baggy shirt, I was taken for a man and treated with greater caution. 'Sahib! Sahib! One tea!' shouted a teacher from his outdoor school. When I went over to accept the offer, he peered at me in some surprise, then said, 'Oh! A *mem* sahib.'

His school was a dusty yard, shaded by a tree, where his class of little boys sat cross-legged or knelt over their slates with a look of desperate eagerness. There were no resources whatsoever, nothing but a passion for teaching and learning so intense as to be almost palpable. In England we have buildings, books and hardware, yet teaching is a struggle. I wondered where we had gone wrong. The schoolmaster and I talked shop over cups of tea, then the school stood up and clapped me on my way.

I was crossing a region famous for its carpets; sheep added variety to the landscape and huge skeins of coloured wools were on sale in the village markets. Children with white rags on the end of long bamboo poles were driving flocks of plump, speckled birds, which looked like quail, though they may have been small guinea fowl. The only town of any size between the two holy cities was Gopiganj, where the one *dharamsala* had three black, windowless cells without even a plank bed on the concrete floor. The local pharmacist directed me to Gyanpur, four miles off my road, where the Vishnu Temple had a *dharamsala* with better accommodation. The vast temple complex, with its huge tank, occupied almost the whole village. As well as the Vishnu shrine, Hindu eclecticism had erected altars to Durga,

Ram, Hanuman with one head and Hanuman with five heads. Upstairs I was shown another temple and the administrative offices of Brahmaji, a guru of some renown in America. I was installed in one of the cells for pilgrims beside the tank and gratefully spread out my mat on the plank bed. I even had a chair and a window for my five rupees.

I was befriended by the caretaker, Mr Gupta, who had a stall by the main entrance selling joss sticks, toiletries, buttons, sweets and even a few boxes of underwear labelled 'Master Queen Beauty Bra'. He offered me tea and it arrived from the tea-stall in the small earthenware cups which are smashed after use so that Hindus of a higher caste may not be defiled by drinking after members of a lower one. Then he invited me to dinner at nine o'clock, asking me to bang on the shutters when I arrived. The stall was the usual Indian wooden box on short legs, about ten feet long by three feet deep, and Mr Gupta sat cross-legged on the floor with his wares arranged on a low counter in front and shelves behind. I had assumed that we would go to his house but when the shutters were opened to me that evening I realised that the tiny shop *was* his house. Inside were Mrs Gupta, who had put on her red wedding sari in my honour, Mr Gupta, their eight-year-old son, Mr Gupta's mother and his uncle from Jodhpur. We sat on mats on the floor, covering our legs with quilts against the cold, while Mrs Gupta crouched in the yard behind the stall, cooking dinner. They were proud to be able to switch on Episode 11 of *Great Expectations* and I was relieved to watch their small, crackling black-and-white television, as Mr Gupta's English was little better than my Hindustani and conversation was halting. Dinner consisted of one spoonful each of curried potatoes and peas, a small dish of *dahl* and some chapattis. In England it would scarcely have constituted a starter and I could see why the family were all so painfully thin. Had I not eaten two fried eggs at a market-stall in the early evening, I should have been too hungry to sleep.

The night was filled with the ringing of bells, the beat of drums and the chanting of my fellow-pilgrims. At breakfast-time, Mr Gupta sent his son to buy 'a slice', a small packet of sliced white bread which was obviously the height of luxury in that poor household. We dipped the slices into our tea and I was given a leaf of vegetable curry in addition, the one spoonful remaining from last night's meal. The shutters were open and the village flocked to watch me eat my breakfast. Mr Gupta kept telling me that I was 'a good man' and I understood enough to know that he was praising me to his neighbours for not smoking, drinking or eating meat. He asked for my home address so that he could write to my husband. He wanted to tell him that I was safe and well and that I was a very good man. After my adventure with Ünal the florist I had never again confessed to being a widow; it sent out the wrong signals. It was safer to have a husband in the background. I told everyone, in perfect truth, that my husband was a lawyer who had stayed behind in London and was not interested in cycling. In India the small deception was even more valuable, as widows are considered unlucky.

After our exchange of addresses, we had a photo-session. I hope the Guptas received the copies I sent, because they would take no payment for their hospitality. When they were waving me off, Granny joked that she wanted to come with me round the world, sitting on the back of my bicycle. She was such a frail little thing that I think I could have carried her without noticing it. The warmth and generosity of that poor family is one of my most abiding memories of India.

My hotel in the Varanasi Cantonment had a garden and a Chinese restaurant, where I revelled in my first non-curried dinner for five weeks. Although I had visited the city with Heather at Christmas, I still spent four nights there to finish my sightseeing, enjoy a little comfort and get up my energy for the last 500 miles of India.

There were sometimes more cats than mice in the holy city. Crowds of tourists went out in boats at sunrise to watch the handful of Hindus at their ritual bathing in the Ganges and the funeral *ghats* were thronged with spectators, though I saw no cremation on either of my visits. The broad avenues of the cantonment were a world away from the Chowk and the fetid, narrow lanes winding down to the *ghats*. Gurus sat under large umbrellas teaching their disciples. Bells, drums, gongs and even jazzed-up electronic Bach resounded in the temples, and more sacred cows clattered over the cobbles than I had seen in the whole of the rest of India. Crowds watched reverently as a guru drove by in a van, seated beside his white cow. He was preceded by a double-decker bus clad in carved wood to make it resemble a green elephant; its interior was packed with model temples in an exotic toy landscape.

I visited Aurangzeb's mosque, which stood on the elaborate foundations of the great Hindu temple he had destroyed. Soldiers were on guard there to ward off attacks by Hindu fanatics, but their job was not onerous. One was anointing his bare legs with oil while the other two stretched out on quilts under an awning. The Moghul colonnade had become a family picnic spot, overlooked by a giant garlanded statue of the Nandi bull, Shiva's vehicle. The *swami* in charge blessed me and put a red spot on my forehead, and a seller of garlands gave me a lotus flower and a garland of marigolds. As I picked my way cautiously through the excrement and refuse down to the Ganges, a canny sacred cow poked a horn in my ribs, then seized and devoured my garland.

I went to the Tourist Office to enquire about hotels between Varanasi and Calcutta to be told that there was none: I should go to the District Magistrate's Office to get a permit for accommodation in Public Works Department bungalows. The DMO was 1820 neo-Classical, as were the adjacent Civil Courts. The gardens were like a fairground; stalls for tea, *pan*, sugar cane juice, fruit and every kind of cooked snack imaginable jostled for space with Xerox machines, stationery stalls, incense, medicines and jewellery. Litigants of all social classes were milling round in their hundreds. Letter-writers and official form-fillers were hard at work, banging away on their ancient typewriters while the lawyers strutted proudly by, black gowns flying. A few wore suits, but many were in grubby shirts and knitted pullovers with their starched white barristers' tabs pinned to their polo necks or open collars. The buildings themselves looked as if they had seen neither brush nor duster since 1947 and the glass-fronted bookcases, mahogany tables and leather chairs of the Bar Association Room had lost their well-polished respectability.

I was directed upstairs and given the name of the official who dealt with permits, a fat man in an unbecoming pale blue jumper with a yellow zig-zag pattern round the waist and sleeves. He was one of many clerks at a huge table piled high with briefs, some at least a foot thick, with dog-eared documents bursting out of the restraining red tape. He kept me standing there while he pushed documents about the table with great officiousness, to show how busy he was and how important. When he finally deigned to pay attention to my request, he informed me that PWD permits were issued by the Tourist Office, not by the District Magistrate's Office. I gave up. I had served myself as a magistrate in Suffolk and my husband had spent his life at the Revenue Bar, so I thought I knew quite a lot about law courts and lawyers. But the courts of Varanasi were a revelation.

Next morning, with no PWD permit to reassure me, I cycled away across the Ganges and looked down on a human anthill. Barges laden with gravel were moored along the east bank and literally thousands of men and women with small baskets were streaming down to them, filling their baskets, then taking the gravel up the bank on their heads to empty it onto large heaps. There was no mechanical equipment of any kind. The long bridge had nasty gaps between the sections and the outskirts of the city were one vast lorry-park. Between Mughalsarai and Mohania I finally came to the end of Uttar Pradesh and entered Bihar. As I crossed over, I remembered with amusement the warning given to me by Santosh's son: 'You'll be all right in Uttar Pradesh, but take great care when you get to Bihar. It's full of *dacoits*. They'll rob you, they'll steal your bicycle . . .'

When I reached Sasaram, a largish town at the junction with the Patna Road, I found that the four guest houses and the tourist lodge were all full. As night was falling I made my way to the railway station to enquire about retiring rooms, but it was a small station with only one retiring room and that was already taken. I stood in the station master's office looking so weary, helpless and forlorn that he eventually took pity on me and offered me the exclusive use of the First Class Ladies' Waiting Room. The floor was alive with mice, cockroaches and other unidentifiable beetles, but I laid out my mat and sleeping-bag on the solid Victorian mahogany table and left them all to scamper merrily below. Dinner was two boiled eggs from one market-stall and a *masala dhosa* (a kind of pancake with curry filling) from another. The station buffet was open at breakfast time. As the trains roared by, as angry passengers tried to force their way into the waiting-room and a myriad tiny feet pattered below me, I thought longingly of my own comfortable bed at home and my clean, warm duvet. But at least I had a roof over my head and was more fortunate than the hundreds of people sleeping out on the platforms, wrapped in sacking and flimsy cotton garments.

Despite its discomforts Sasaram provided one of the highlights of my journey – the tomb of Sher Shah Suri, the Afghan Emperor of India who laid the Grand Trunk Road, standing in barbaric pride on the island in the middle of its lake. Built of warm golden sandstone with traces of blue faïence remaining, its finials had red sandstone inlays, and decorated pillars rather like Elizabethan chimneys sprouted round its roof and over its gateway. A heavy dome crouched above the octagonal chamber and the four entrances had niches engraved with the names of Allah. It was not elegant but it was an overwhelming statement of power, one of the most surprising and exciting buildings I had ever seen.

I travelled uneven distances, sometimes covering 80 miles, sometimes stopping after 30, depending on the size of towns and the likelihood of accommodation. A short ride to a clean, new Muslim-run hotel in Aurangabad was followed by a long haul to the Buddhist pilgrim centre of Bodhgaya, a twenty-mile detour from the Grand Trunk Road into the north wind. When I arrived there, I was at a low physical and mental ebb, so exhausted that I easily slept through the nocturnal chanting from the Hindu temple next door to my Government Tourist Lodge. I awoke only at dawn when an electronic organ, much amplified, added its weight to the bells and drums.

But Bodhgaya, where the Buddha sat under a *bodhi* tree and received enlightenment, soon restored my spirits. I spent the next day wandering through the tranquil gardens of the temples and monasteries, mingling with the monks and nuns in their claret and saffron robes. My ticket to the great Mahabodhi Temple, originally built by Ashoka, read 'May all beings be happy'; even the hordes of beggars and children selling goldfish in plastic bags failed to detract from the peace and contentment of the place. Prayer flags flew, prayer wheels turned, rosary beads were counted, monks prayed on a platform to the blowing of horns, women with Mongol features circled Ashoka's pillar, keeping their backs in contact with it, and Europeans in Buddhist robes did meditation exercises. There were pilgrims from all over the East. The monasteries for Thailand, Bhutan, Tibet and China were painted in brilliant colours and built in their national styles. The Japanese had built their temple, a severe, elegant building, in pre-stressed concrete with a flight of polished marble steps leading up to the gleaming grey marble floor. Adjacent was the site of the colossal Daijokyo Buddha, still under construction. The stonemasons had got up only as far as the folded hands but already, with Japanese attention to detail, the avenue of saplings leading up to the statue had been planted. In the crowded streets, well-fed monks in rickshaws and ten-year-old novices sucking iced lollies jostled for space with Hindu pilgrims. An old man in orange rags with a miniature gold stupa on his head and a trident in his hand stalked barefoot down the main road and paused by a tree which sheltered an image of the Buddha complete with Shiva's phallic symbol, the lingam, and a cobra. Bodhgaya was a multi-cultural religious fair, where worshippers of all races could choose from any stall they fancied. Yet it retained its dignity and the serenity of the Buddhist philosophy was all-pervading.

I was happy in Bodhgaya and bought a tiny green soapstone box with a carved lotus-blossom lid, one of the few mementos of my travels. When I left my hotel, all the staff lined up to see me off and the manager presented me with a red rose and made a little speech, telling me how they all admired my courage. They hoped the rest of my journey would be happy and that I should reach my home in safety.

I had parted company with the Ganges at Varanasi and now, after weeks of flat, featureless landscape, I reached wooded hills. I passed two men carrying a dead wild boar between them on a pole, but otherwise the forest was deserted and I began to think of the *dacoits* for whom Bihar really does have a bad reputation. But the only disturbances I met were in the towns and villages where Sikhs were parading, calling for their own independent homeland, Khalistan. I circled the Tilaiya Reservoir, a beautiful lake surrounded by wooded hills, to find my next night's hotel in Jhumritilaya, sixteen miles off the Grand Trunk Road. I was moving into more prosperous country where there was more varied work for the people. I enjoyed watching them making furniture, huge clay storage jars like those at Knossos, and clay cylinders, which they sliced down the middle to make roof tiles. The roads were in better condition and the gentle warmth of the sun brought smiles and relaxation. The women wore bright saris and the men white singlets with sarongs of green- or blue-checked cotton.

Accommodation, always a worry, had by now become the obsession which ruled my days. I looked with envy at the lorry-drivers who simply laid down their bedding on filling-station charpoys and passed sociable nights under the stars. The compensation for my worry came in the warmth of welcome I received in small places where they had never seen a tourist. In Dumri I became the most popular person in town. I was standing in the main street looking through the railing of Hanuman's shrine at the statue of the dancing monkey god when the shop-keeper next door came out and gave me a piece of coconut. By this time a silent crowd had gathered, all watching me intently. I realised that I was supposed to make an offering but I had no idea how to go about it and was nervous of giving offence. After some hesitation I performed a kind of Cenotaph ceremony, moving forward towards the god in stately fashion, laying the coconut on the ground before him, putting my hands together in the *namaste* sign, then bowing and stepping backwards. Beams of delight all round showed that I had passed the test and I was swept off to the tea-stall by the approving multitudes. Later I slept fitfully in the local *dak* bungalow; the unshaded electric light was centrally controlled and blazed all night above my bed.

Next day I began my crossing of the most industrialised part of India. The pollution was on a scale unimaginable in Europe, even in the grimmest days of the industrial revolution. I choked my way through a belt of coal mines and refractories plants, where chimneys belched out black smoke, rivers ran black and trees were smothered in coal dust. The ponds in the villages, where the women were doing their washing, were covered in black scum. Filthy animals and filthy, half-naked children wandered through the grimy refuse. The squalor was appalling. I passed only one hotel, a new one obviously intended for businessmen. It was complete and fully furnished, but not yet officially open. Unlike the Greeks of Pheres, the Indians of Kumardhubi turned me away and I pedalled on into the evening, crossing the black-flowing Baraker river into West Bengal and still finding nowhere to stay.

It was nearly dark when I stopped at Kulti for tea and enquired in desperation about guest houses. An eager group of men took me to a nearby temple and showed me a straw-covered verandah where I could sleep with the pilgrims among a flock of goats. I demanded a charpoy. After some discussion, they led me up the road to a boys' club: when the basketball finished at seven o'clock I could have the gymnasium to myself. One end was without a wall, so that my night's sojourn would have been a very public affair, but there was a gate with a padlock and it was cleaner than the temple. I was rescued by Sanjoy, one of the basketball players, an A-Level Maths and Science student at the Asansol de la Salle College, who insisted on taking me to his home for the night. His mother had won national prizes for classical Indian singing and was persuaded to give a performance, accompanying herself on a small keyboard with bellows. Neighbours dropped in all evening to greet me; Sanjoy's friends left late at night and reappeared at dawn to talk to me again and go for short spins on my bicycle. I was the first foreigner they had ever seen in Kulti.

Bengal was noticeably different. Bengalis were smaller and darker, with bright eyes, quick wits and a good command of English. The intellectuals of India, they had their own language and a highly developed, sophisticated literary tradition, and bitterly resented the fact that Nehru, born in Allahabad, had picked his local Hindi out of the fifteen languages and over 600 dialects of India to be the nation's official language. Children who spoke Bengali at home had to do their elementary schoolwork in Hindi before proceeding to English for their advanced studies. Early school-leavers were consequently deprived of the opportunity to learn the international language that would open the doors to employment. The additional hurdle of Hindi compounded the problem of illiteracy in a country where the population was expanding so fast that the proportion of illiterates continued to grow despite the significant increase in the actual number of literates. The same grievance led to unrest among the Tamils of the south and other major linguistic groups, but nowhere was it felt so deeply as in Bengal. There they used Hindi as little as possible, writing their signs in English, speaking English on public occasions and conducting their business in English. Readers of the Calcutta *Statesman* even did *The Times* crossword, which appeared daily by special arrangement with London. I had struggled to acquire some basic Urdu in Pakistan and had been relieved to find that spoken Hindustani was virtually the same, though written in a different script. Now I was even more relieved to find that English would carry me comfortably through West Bengal.

Durgapur was a major steel town, where I really needed the hot water of my good hotel to wash off the day's grime. The hotel restaurant was obviously the smart place in town and I there noticed another way in which Bengal was different – there were as many women dining out as men and they were participating actively in the conversation. I was tempted to rest there for an extra day but the ghastliness of Durgapur outweighed the comforts of its best hotel. I pressed on across a surprisingly rural stretch with paddy fields, banana plantations, palm trees and huts of thatch. It was hot and steamy. I had crossed the Tropic of Cancer.

'Is this cykel your fellow-countryman?' asked a young man in Burdwan. His friendliness cheered up an otherwise depressing town and a dirty hotel. He took my hand and held it in his. 'You are an Englishman. I am Indian. The relationship between our two countries is like this, friendly and sweet. May God keep you safe on your journey.' God kept me safe but not in a good humour, as I fought a headwind, diesel fumes and the dust of roadworks. I made a detour down to the Hooghly river, to the former Dutch colony of Chinsurah where there was said to be a guest house. Laughing crowds mocked me as I cycled in but I

tracked down the hotel by the bus station and collapsed on the
bed under mosquito netting and an electric fan. When I was
reading in bed at 10.30, the young manager appeared with six of
his friends. They had come for a social chat.

Calcutta! The end of cycling in India. Its outskirts stretched for
fifteen seething, smoggy, grimy miles, then the Grand Trunk
Road entered the city through its worst slums where hordes of
its nine million inhabitants live, sleep, eat, reproduce, defecate
and die on the streets or in sacking and cardboard shacks. Past
Howrah Station I crossed the teeming Howrah Bridge, the
congestion on the road such that I dared not cycle. Trams,
buses, bicycles, bullock-carts, a few cars, and rickshaws pulled
by barefoot, running coolies fought for every available inch of
space. I picked my way along the pavement, harried by vendors
and beggars, to reach the equally crowded but slightly less
sordid east bank of the Hooghly. Then I cycled south to
Chowringee and my haven in a clean hotel. I was exactly on target. I had covered the 1,100 miles of rough road between
Delhi and Calcutta in four weeks, two days.

I spent almost two weeks in Calcutta, exploring its two sides.
The dark side was to be found at Kali Ghat, the village on the
Hooghly which had given Calcutta its name. Kali, the terrible
goddess with the black face, protruding tongue and the necklace
of skulls, the Goddess of Destruction, had her ancient temple
there. I was glad to have the protection of a temple brahmin as we
pushed through the pilgrims, beggars and sacrificial goats.
Incense burned, flies swarmed round the fresh blood of the
victims and an aura of horror and blood-lust pervaded the site.
The brahmin assured me that the temple's work was charitable,
that the goats offered up to Kali were later cooked and distributed to the poor. In my anxiety to escape from the hideous
shrine I gave him what I considered to be a generous 50 rupee
donation towards this good work. He glowered and told me that
it would buy only one quarter of a sackful of rice and he was
expecting at least a thousand rupees from a rich woman like me.
Violence and bloodshed were so near to the surface that I almost
ran out of the temple and only felt safe again when I reached the
normality of the modern Metro Station.

The other side of the city was presided over by the splendid white marble rotunda of the Victoria Memorial, the museum tracing the history of the British in India. Opened by the Prince of Wales in 1921, it rose dreamlike from the morning mist of the Maidan, symbol of the might and authority of the British Raj on the eve of its decline. The severe, elderly Queen Empress herself guarded its approach, while a statue of her younger, gayer self graced its interior. The Marxist Government of West Bengal had recently become reconciled to this embodiment of their former subjection and, carefully refurbished, it gleamed through the Calcutta night in floodlit radiance.

The huge bulk of the East India Company Writers' Building, from which British India had been administered until 1931, occupied the whole northern end of Dalhousie Square. It was now the headquarters of the Government of West Bengal and the square had been renamed B.B.D. Bag. The nearby Raj Bhavan, modelled on Lord Curzon's Kedlestone Hall, was now the residence of the West Bengal Governor.

These alien buildings were the tangible remains of an involvement in India which had begun as a trading venture in 1599, become increasingly political as the merchants strove to safeguard their expanding trade and had ended as direct rule of the entire subcontinent after the 1857 Mutiny. As with the Moghuls, so with the British, India had originally been their second choice: unable to break the Dutch monopoly of the East Indies spice trade, they had turned their attention to India and created of that second-best trading-post the Jewel in their Crown.

Strangely enough, the empire which had started almost by accident, through indignation at a rise in the price of pepper, began to move towards its end because of a handful of salt. In 1930 Gandhi had challenged the British rulers by leading his followers across India to the sea and gathering up its salt, in defiance of the Government monopoly. His action had been the start of an intensified struggle for independence and in that struggle none had been more vociferous than the clever, politically active Bengalis.

Their city of Calcutta, the largest in the Commonwealth, still had the vibrancy of a capital. It had lost its former status and,

more importantly, it had lost at Partition the hinterland which
had grown the jute for its factories and port. Separation from
Bangladesh had brought industrial decline as well as hordes of
refugees to swell the already teeming slums. But its wit and
vitality were unsinkable. Volatile Bengalis still protested about
everything, marching up and down with banners, staging sit-
ins and lock-outs and sabotaging the electricity supply. Politics
was their lifeblood. Their radicalism and determination to be
different, if not downright shocking, had produced a Marxist
government. They had delighted in provoking the Americans
during the Vietnam War by renaming the street where their
Consulate stood Ho Chi Minh Marg. The city was culturally
alive, too. Bombay might be Bollywood, churning out
thousands of lurid films for mass consumption, but Calcutta
had Satyajit Ray and a small film industry of international
repute. There was a Russian Film Festival in progress, a
Russian Ballet, exhibitions of paintings and scores of excellent
bookshops. Even the street vendors sold books, magazines and
pictures. It was one of the world's most lively, exciting cities.

I obtained my Thai visa then left my bicycle in Calcutta while
I took a pleasant holiday, touring the cleaner, more prosperous
south of India by train and bus – Madras, Mahabalipuram,
Thrikalkundram, Kanchipuram, Bangalore, Mysore and
Hyderabad. On my return to Calcutta, an incident occurred
which seemed to encapsulate the squalor and ludicrousness of
that fascinating, beautiful, exasperating country which somehow remained a democracy against all the odds – 'a functioning
anarchy', to quote J. K. Galbraith.

With my heavy luggage, I had no choice but to take one of the
degrading human rickshaws from Howrah Station. As the cool-
ie dragged his springless vehicle over the potholes of filthy,
teeming backstreets where the odour of urine drying in the sun
was overpowering, I experienced the ultimate, mediaeval disaster of Calcutta: someone emptied a bucket from an upstairs
window and drenched me from head to foot. Fortunately, it was
nothing worse than greasy washing-up water. With that rare
Indian gift for the inappropriate, a market porter chose that
very moment to come in hot pursuit, exhorting me to go
shopping with him in the market; and a fortune-teller waved in

my streaming face a card which his parrot had just selected for me with his beak, and invited me to step out of the rickshaw to have my fortune told. The hotel receptionist failed to notice that I was creating puddles on the smart vestibule carpet and went through the registration procedure as if I was a normal, dry client.

Then Indian bureaucracy had its final fling at Dum Dum Airport. The clerk at the check-in desk refused to accept my bicycle. An argument ensued after which he said he would have to consult his supervisor. He left me standing in a corner for twenty minutes while he busily issued boarding cards to all the other passengers. I was just about to make another scene when a simpler solution appeared in the shape of a diminutive porter in a woolly hat. He came over and gazed lovingly at my bicycle. 'Very good cykel,' he said. With sudden inspiration I announced, 'Cykel flying Bangkok.' 'Bangkok flying?' said he. Then he pointed out that the cykel had no Bangkok label. He darted over to the check-in counter, seized the correct tag from under the nose of my enemy, attached it to the handlebars and began to wheel the bicycle towards the exit. 'No problem. I am taking care,' he said to me, ignoring the angry shouts of the ticket clerk. No one was going to prevent him from riding that glorious machine across the tarmac.

Cycling across India had been an experience I would not have missed for the world, but all the same I was enormously relieved when my flight was called and I followed Condor onto the Bangkok plane. I had had enough for the time being.

14

Interlude in Thailand

BANGKOK – PHETCHABURI – HUA HIN – PRACHUAP
KHIRI KHAN – CHUMPHON – LANGSUAM – SURAT
THANI – SICHON – NAKHON SI THAMMARAT –
SONGKLA – SADAO

Fremd bin ich eingezogen,   (A stranger I arrived,
Fremd zieh ich wieder aus.   A stranger I leave.)
                                          (Wilhelm Müller)

MY next road should have been the Burma Road, but travelling along it was out of the question. The Burmese issued visas for one week only and even after months of practice I could not have cycled the length of Burma in that time. So I flew over Burma into Thailand, my ninth country.

In Bangkok International Airport my spirits rose: I had forgotten that public buildings could be so clean and well organised. As the airport was 25 miles from the city centre and my brakes had been damaged during the flight from India, the girls at the tourist desk suggested the Golden Dragon in an outer suburb for me as a stopover, drawing a neat, accurate map with the street names in both English and Thai characters. The multi-lane highway into town could have been a nightmare but lane discipline was good. My brakes presented no problem en route. People in cars waved and smiled at me and train passengers at a level-crossing gave me the 'V for Victory' sign. The Golden Dragon was immaculate and my Chinese dinner was packed with all the delicious fresh vegetables I had so missed in India. After months of struggling to find life's bare necessities, I had reached a country where certain standards of comfort and efficiency were taken for granted.

I began my stay in Thailand with three weeks' holiday.

Priscilla flew out to join me again, this time without her bicycle, and I was thrilled to see her. Ten months' solitude really makes you value your friends and I realised how lucky I was to have people who cared enough about me to travel halfway across the world to keep me company. She brought out my second spare tyre, another inner tube and £200 sterling. Thailand was new to us both. As I would later be cycling south from Bangkok, we decided to take the train up north to Chiang Mai. From there we trekked into the Golden Triangle in the hills of the Thailand/Burma/Laos border, where the opium poppy is the richest crop. We stayed with the hill tribes in their wooden huts on stilts, rode Burmese climbing elephants into the jungle and one day made a trip by boat down the Pai river into Burma, my tenth country. The one pipe of opium I tried tasted of tainted meat. No danger of my becoming an addict.

I had made contact in Bangkok with a fellow-Girtonian whom I had not met since our graduation, many years ago. Helen was Greek, with a Classical profile straight from an Attic vase. She could have been an opera singer but had gone instead into international relief work and was now with UNICEF in Bangkok, with special responsibility for Malaysia. When Priscilla and I returned from the north, Helen invited us to stay in her flat and came round to our hotel to pick us up. I was a bit apprehensive, wondering if I should recognise her after such a long time, but the years had been kind to her. Her hair was as black and sleek as ever and she rushed across the coffee shop in her slim black linen dress, talking with tremendous animation, as she always did. I would have recognised the profile anywhere. She had a lovely flat, cool and spacious – the perfect setting for her exquisite pictures and artefacts, collected with discrimination throughout her years in the Far East. We were lucky to be staying with her, not least because Priscilla suffered a violent reaction to her malaria tablets and ran a temperature of 104°. Helen knew exactly how to deal with the emergency and which hospital to go to. Had we been alone in a Bangkok hotel, I have no idea how we should have coped.

Bangkok was an exhausting city. March was the start of the hot season and the air was already humid. It was also suffocatingly polluted. The old *khlongs* (canals) had been covered over to make eight- or ten-lane highways along which the traffic crawled nose-to-tail. A ride in a *tuk-tuk*, a scooter-taxi, through the Bangkok rush hour left us blackened with exhaust fumes and gasping for breath. It was a relief to escape into the air-conditioned cleanliness of the international hotels, shopping malls and cinemas which made Bangkok such an impressive modern city.

We toured the Grand Palace and a few of the 400 or so Buddhist temples, the familiar *wats* with their extravagant, overlapping roofs and curved gables, each one ending in the flourish of a *garuda*, the man-bird vehicle of Vishnu. They were guarded by sinuous dragons, which undulated down both sides of the entrance steps to face the visitor in a multiplicity of hectic, hideous heads, tongues and gleaming fangs. The buildings were overwhelming in their colour and glitter. Paint-box primary reds and yellows were encrusted with plain glass to represent diamonds, and coloured glass for sapphires, emeralds and rubies. Figured Chinese porcelain was laid on floors and columns, and painted murals, mostly of the Hindu *Ramayana* epic, covered every inch of the interior walls. But the main decorative material was pure gold. Pillars were gilded, doors were gilded, finials were gilded, stupas were gilded, sometimes entire temples were gilded. The Buddhas themselves, with the distinctive Thai flame rising from the crown of their heads, were often of solid gold. It was all so rich and so exotic that I found it difficult to make any connection. I felt an excluded alien, gazing at objects and rituals quite outside my frame of reference.

As the Foreign Office in London had advised, I checked in with the British Consul before setting out on my bicycle. The Thai Embassy in London had warned me of dangers in the south, where the influence of Malay/Indonesian culture was strong and the Thai Government had difficulty in keeping control. There was a Muslim separatist movement and brigands, both political and non-political, attacked trains and buses. But the British Consul was reassuring: there was no threat to foreigners, provided they kept out of local politics.

My journey south through Thailand to Malaysia gave me a rest from history. Thailand was the one country in that part of

Asia which had retained its independence from Western colonisers. Surrounded by the British in Burma and Malaya and the French in Indo-China, the Siamese had steered a careful course, exploiting their role as a useful buffer state. Although the kings of the present Chakri dynasty had undertaken a steady programme of modernisation from the middle of the nineteenth century, moving towards the British model of constitutional monarchy and giving their legions of royal princes an English education, they had exercised judicious selectivity and managed to retain the integrity and individuality of the Thai nation. It was not a country which had absorbed the culture of Western invaders, nor did it have a famous road. I was free to travel through it as the fancy took me.

By the time I set out from Bangkok, I was a truly international traveller. I wore English trainers, Turkish socks, Italian underwear, Indian trousers, a Thai shirt and an Italian cycling cap. As always, I returned to cycling with great enthusiasm, sailing past the snarled-up traffic of central Bangkok free of responsibilities and delighting in the fact that everything I had and needed was packed away in two bags on the back of the world's simplest and most energy-efficient form of transportation. Life could be so uncomplicated. My earlier regrets at giving up my house and possessions had dwindled and finally died. Why on earth did I need those four bedrooms, three bathrooms and four reception rooms full of clutter? I felt a freedom I had never enjoyed before. I had not quite achieved the perfection of the Afghans, who carry all they possess in their waistcoat pockets and stride through the world unencumbered, the blanket which serves as their bedding and overcoat slung elegantly over one shoulder – but I was getting there. I cruised past the costly hotels on the banks of the Chaophya river, finding them most unappealing, crossed a bridge and made for the start of Highway 35. It was good to be on my way again.

Bangkok and Chiang Mai had been geared to tourists, with hotels of every class from international luxury to backpackers' hostels. In Samut Sakhon I discovered what small provincial towns could provide. There was one hotel, run by a Chinese-Thai family, where I was booked in by an old Chinaman with a

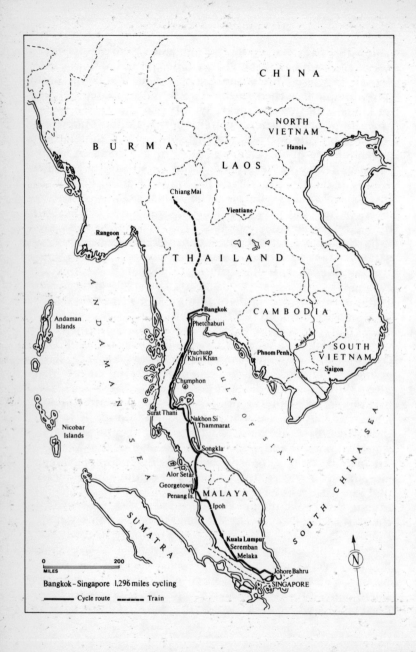

CHINA

NORTH
VIETNAM

Hanoi.

BURMA

LAOS

Chiang Mai

Vientiane

Rangoon

THAILAND

Andaman
Islands

Bangkok

CAMBODIA

Phetchaburi

Prachuap
Khiri Khan

Phnom Penh

SOUTH
VIETNAM

Saigon

A
N
D
A
M
A
N

S
E
A

Chumphon

Surat Thani

Nakhon Si
Thammarat

Songkla

G
U
L
F

O
F

S
I
A
M

Nicobar
Islands

Alor Setar
Georgetown
Penang Is.

MALAYA

Ipoh

S
O
U
T
H

C
H
I
N
A

S
E
A

SUMATRA

Kuala Lumpur
Seremban
Melaka

Johore Bahru
SINGAPORE

0   200
MILES

Bangkok – Singapore 1,296 miles cycling

——— Cycle route   ----- Train

N

wispy white beard, navy blue shorts and white vest. I was to find that most of the local hotels in Thailand and Malaysia were owned by Chinese. My room was a simple concrete box but it had a shower, a window with effective mosquito-netting (not full of holes, as in India) and a ceiling fan, a welcome change from the ice-cold air-conditioning of Bangkok. Condor was accommodated in the downstairs lobby which doubled as a storeroom, under the eye of reception.

I strolled down to the ferry across the estuary and gazed at the brightly painted fishing boats over a pot of weak China tea. There was a covered market nearby and the pavements were crowded with stalls as well as shops. Everywhere in Thailand, buying and selling were the main occupations. Everyone traded in something. Samut Sakhon was not at all prosperous. Children scavenged on rubbish tips, an old man slept on the market floor and mangy dogs limped about the streets. Yet even the poorest people were reasonably clean and well fed. The poverty of Thailand was in a different league from that of the Indian subcontinent.

I could see that food was still going to be a problem. The Pakistanis and Indians had eaten curry at every meal. The Thais ate rice and noodles – rice and noodles for breakfast, rice and noodles for snacks, rice and noodles with everything. Even an omelette would appear on a bed of shrimp-fried rice; it was inconceivable that anyone should wish to eat eggs on their own. My first breakfast consisted of Pepsi Cola and cake, as I was unable to find a café serving coffee or tea. I later discovered where to look. Hot drinks were sold in general stores or at noodle stalls. It was the practice to pay for a cup of Nescafé, then a pot of China tea was given free. I would take in my own cake or biscuits to avoid a noodle breakfast.

Next day I almost gave up my travels. The land between Samut Sakhon and Samut Songkhran was one vast salt flat, where coolies in shorts, vests and wide straw hats were sifting and piling the crystals. Even in sunglasses, I was almost blinded by the reflected glare. It was overcast but the invisible sun was so torrid that my hands and arms turned scarlet and my back burned through my shirt. But worst of all was the wind. With typical cyclist's luck, I had embarked on my journey south

in the season of the trade winds, which were sweeping up the
Gulf of Thailand against me. The days began with a gentle,
refreshing dawn breeze which stiffened throughout the morning. By noon it was a strong, gusting wind, so hot that it seemed
to come in blasts from an oven door. The road was well surfaced
but narrow, and I was often forced off the carriageway by
passing lorries. Just before Samut Songkhran, I bumped down
too fast onto the stony hard shoulder and got my fourth
puncture. I reached Phetchaburi at 4.30, utterly exhausted
after 54 miles of heat, dust and searing wind.

The day had only been made bearable by the kindness of the
Thais. Police at a road-block had flagged me down, told me I
was 'Number One' and given me fresh lychees and a glass of
iced water. A girl on a moped had blown a kiss. And a red
Nissan pick-up truck had pulled into the side moments after my
puncture, its occupants two young teachers with their little girl.
They had taken me and my bicycle on board, driven me to the
nearest cycle-repairer and waited with me while the patched
inner tube from Thessaloniki was replaced by one of my own
spares. The repairer in his wooden outhouse had at first refused
payment, but I had eventually got him to accept ten bahts (45
bahts = £1) to buy sweets for his children.

I spent two days in Phetchaburi, strolling under the bougain-
villaea and revising my cycling schedule and my philosophy.
Thailand was a beautiful country with charming people and I
might never pass through it again. So why not linger on the
way, instead of struggling to the brink of exhaustion? I reduced
my daily target from 50–60 miles to 30–40 and resolved to enjoy
Thailand, with its tropical climate. I made leisurely starts to my
Phetchaburi days, marvelling at the graffiti on the wall beside
my bed. The head is sacred to the Thais and should never be
touched; even a pat on a child's head is regarded as sacrilege.
This reverence for the head had clearly influenced someone's
erotic art, as the sexual gymnasts on the wall were all portrayed
from the neck down. Not a single one had a head.

On a rocky outcrop near my hotel stood one of the palaces of
King Mongkut (1851–68), the king who engaged Anna Leon-
owens as governess to his children. I climbed the hill, which
swarmed with fat, greedy monkeys, and roamed through the

courtyards and the palace apartments stuffed with heavy
nineteenth-century furniture. King Mongkut had lived for
years as a Buddhist monk before ascending the throne and his
devotion and scholarship were reflected in the temples and the
observatory. I was the only European among the crowds of
Thais. They smiled and giggled and three families asked me to
pose for photographs with their children. I felt large and
clumsy beside the neat, small-boned Thais and I sensed that for
all their courtesy and surface charm, they found me a slightly
comic figure. They were pleased and proud to be Thais, not a
lumbering, gawky *farang* like me.

After a long siesta, I went on a tour of the *wats* under a
fabulous evening sky: the palest, most delicate possible blue
with wisps of pink cloud shading to mauve as the twilight
deepened. The cicadas in the trees were deafening, almost
drowning the gentle voice of the vocalist in the restaurant. Thai
pop music was distinctive – a soft voice-line over the most
modern synchronisers and electronic instruments. As in so
many other fields, Western ingredients and the latest technology had been blended with Thai traditions. Their culture
borrowed from the West but stamped everything it touched
with its own instantly recognisable Thai identity.

My days began to fall into an idyllic routine. I set out in the
cool of the dawn and pedalled hard to complete half my day's
distance before taking a rest over breakfast. Then I cycled more
slowly, stopping at filling stations and cafés for soft drinks and
refills of my water bottle. I wore long sleeves, gloves and long
socks to protect my skin from the burning sun, while a scarf
flowed down over the back of my neck from under my cycling
cap. At eleven o'clock the lotus-eating began. If I came to a city,
I would check into one of the best hotels, which would be well
within my budget. There I would spend the afternoon eating
fresh pineapple and dozing in the shade by the swimming pool.
In smaller places I often had to make do with a traditional Thai
guest house, a wooden building on stilts, where the breeze
cooled the rooms through the wide gaps between the slats.
They were basic buildings but wonderfully adapted to the
climate. I would sit outside under the palm trees, then walk
across a beach of the purest white, fine sand to bathe in the

sparkling sea. In the evenings, I feasted at rickety outdoor
tables on delicious seafood, freshly caught and cooked to speci-
fication. The local Singha beer was more expensive than the
food, but on those steamy tropical nights the ice-cold glasses
were worth every *baht*.

I travelled down the east coast all the way to Songkla, with
the craggy mountains of the peninsula to my right. Their slopes
were lush with vegetation but for the first few days the countryside bordering the road was disappointingly scrubby. There
were few trees to offer shade. Instead, there were little roadside
shelters like miniature Thai temples, furnished with benches
and an earthenware jar of water. They stood at regular intervals
and provided a welcome respite for the passing traveller.

South of Hua Hin the road itself became hilly, which
added to the rigours of cycling. One terrible day, despite my
resolution to limit my distances, I had to toil for ten hours
across sparsely populated mountain terrain before finding a
bed for the night in Bang Saphan, nine miles off the
highway. At the cross-roads leading to the village I staggered
into a shop so weary and dehydrated I was scarcely able to
walk. I gulped down two glasses of water and two bottles of
Pepsi Cola without pausing for breath, enduring a catechism
meanwhile from the most insensitive man. 'Where you go?
Where you from? You go Bangkok? You go Phuket? You
travel round world? You alone? What your name?' I was too
exhausted to reply and when I finally summoned the strength
to ask my own vital question, 'Is there a hotel in Bang
Saphan?' he was unable to understand.

There was in fact a wooden guest house on the beach there,
run by a man who spoke good English; he told me he had
learned it as a small boy from British prisoners-of-war. He was
born in Kanchanaburi on the River Kwai and he used to slip
into the camp to take oranges, papaya and sugar to the prisoners
working on the notorious Japanese railway. Two particular
officers had befriended him and taught him English in return
for his fruit. He was a member of Lions International and kept
up his English by reading their magazine from cover to cover.
He told me that my name should be Margaret, as I was 'stlong'
like Mrs Thatcher. Even so, he and his great friend, the local

policeman, were worried about the next stage of my journey.
I had only just survived the 57 miles from Prachuap Khiri
Khan to Bang Saphan. Chumphon was over 70 miles away,
across much more mountainous country with no villages and
few filling stations. They feared that the highway patrol
would be picking me up and rushing me to hospital if I tried
to ride to Chumphon in the burning heat of summer on a
laden bicycle. It was the only occasion on my journey round
the world when I listened to that kind of advice. I knew the
ride would be beyond my physical resources and reluctantly
settled for the train.

Next morning I lay on my bed and watched the sun, a
fiery red ball, rise up from the Gulf of Thailand. I had the
leisure to enjoy it, as the Chumphon train left at 9.20. I
relaxed over Donsong's European breakfast of bread fried in
eggs, a pot of coffee and fruit, then cycled to the station.
Buying the ticket was no problem, as Donsong had given me
a note for the station master, but getting onto the train was
an ordeal. It stopped on a distant track, far away from the
platform, and the luggage van was chin-high. The immaculate khaki-clad station officials stood around like elegant statues and I should not have managed to carry my
bicycle over the tracks and stow it in the van without the help
of a cheerful young woman and her mother. As the train ran
down the narrow strip of land between the sea and the
Burmese border, I gazed from my carriage window at the
desolate Bilauktaung Mountains and was pleased to be riding
in comfort for once.

Cycling became easier after Chumphon. Perhaps I was
adapting to the climate and pacing myself more skilfully. I
loved the early morning hours, when the mountains rose
from the mist like imitations of Chinese paintings and the
monks were out with their alms bowls. At first I was amazed
at the number and age-range of these saffron-clad figures.
Then I learned that all Thai men become monks for a period
in their lives, normally between education and work, but
sometimes in the months of mourning after the death of a
close relative or at times of uncertainty. It seemed a very
civilised system and I had no doubt that it contributed to the

tranquillity and spiritual wholeness of the Thais. The Buddhist
Eightfold Path was for everyone, not just for a group of professional clerics.

As I travelled further south, I became more of a rarity. Adults
pointed out the *farang* to their children, the usual crowds
gathered to stare when I stopped at a village stall and one old
market woman came up and squeezed my arm, presumably to
see if I was real. Fortunately, television has made Western looks
familiar, even in the remotest villages of the East. They may
never have seen us in the flesh before, but they know who we
are. Unlike the travellers of former days, I was no god, no
supernatural creature, no foreign devil to be pelted with stones.
I represented the glittering world of *Dallas* – or I would have
done, had I not been a poor person, who rode a bicycle as the
Thais did. I was a bit of a puzzle to them, but obviously
harmless, and they peered at me with benign, slightly amused,
curiosity.

Children the world over wave and shout to a passing cyclist,
but in Thailand all the adults joined in, shouting, waving,
blowing kisses, so that cycling through a village became a royal
progress. Even the monks waved. One junior monk was so
overcome with excitement that he quite forgot his dignity and
rushed down the road with me, hitching up his saffron robes to
free his spindly, little boy's legs. But Buddhism is a kindly faith
and his superiors smiled indulgently. I met only three other
cyclists: a flying Dutchman, who rocketed past me one morning, and a young Austrian couple, whom I met in the guest
house in Chaiya. They had bought their bicycles in Singapore
and were heading for Bangkok. As we were doing the same
journey in opposite directions, we were able to exchange up-to-
date practical information about places to stay.

Between the eighth and tenth centuries AD Chaiya had been
the regional capital of the Srivajaya Empire, based in Sumatra.
Wat Phra Mahathat and Wat Kaew were said to show Javanese
influence, but my inexpert eye failed to identify the distin-
guishing features. Many of the southern *wats* were simpler than
those further north, with whitewashed walls and pink stucco
work round the doors and windows. Some village *wats* were

little more than thatched huts. But I found *wats* in general so hard to read. It seemed as if the Thais had decided on the perfect form of the *wat* sometime in the twelfth or thirteenth century and from that time onwards had constructed all their major *wats* on the same model. I found them impossible to date and the regional variations mentioned in the guide books were so subtle that they eluded me. Despite a lifetime of dedicated culture-seeking, I had to admit defeat. Without years of further study, a *wat* would remain a *wat* – a weird, incomprehensible building. I decided in Chaiya to give up *wats* and concentrate on beaches.

I also spent a lot of time in Thailand concentrating on myself. With no one to talk to in the evenings and only the briefest of chance encounters in the day-time, my thoughts inevitably turned inwards. I found myself reviewing my life – family, friends, loves, professional career – sometimes reliving small triumphs and moments of happiness but more often suffering again the humiliations and the failures. I dwelt with regret and remorse on situations I might have handled better, people I might have treated more kindly, opportunities I might have taken. In the long hours of solitary cycling, I took out my failures one by one and scrutinised them. Unable to escape in the flurry of workaday busy-ness, I was forced to look my inadequacies in the face and try to come to terms with them, a journey into myself I would have been more comfortable avoiding, but reconciliation with the past seemed necessary in order to clear the way for the future. The opportunity to travel this inner road had been one of my motives for the physical journey. I made many resolutions, some of which I have managed to keep.

I spent most of Easter Sunday by the swimming pool in Surat Thani. Some built-in time-clock at Christmas had started me off on Christmas carols, but Easter had no such effect. My Thai songs were 'Mad dogs and Englishmen' when the cycling was brisk and Schubert's 'Winterreise' when the going was hard and I felt an outsider. Passing a Chinese cemetery, I discovered that Easter coincided with the eve of Cheng Meng Day, the Chinese All Souls. Families were swarming round the tombs, decorating them with flowers, paper streamers, lanterns and food and letting off fire-crackers in honour of their ancestors. Chinese cemeteries were always on hillsides, where the dead would be protected from wind and weather and could also keep an eye on their descendants in the valley. Their tombs were low, horseshoe-shaped enclosures which seemed to embrace the dead, and the festivals in their honour were invariably cheerful.

Near Surat Thani I lost the international trucks; they took the direct inland route to the Malaysian border while I continued along the coast. The vegetation was now lushly tropical and I cycled along in the shade of banana and coconut palms. Fishing boats lined the beaches and fish were spread out on racks to dry in the sun. The village shops were full of kites, elaborate creations in the shapes of fish, birds, boxes, men and rampant animals. My enemy, the Trade Wind, was called *lom wao* (kite wind) and March and April were the traditional kite-flying months. I began to see village mosques. Many of the women now had their heads covered, like good Muslims, but they rode motorcycles and sat in the cafés drinking coffee and chatting in much greater freedom than their Muslim sisters elsewhere.

The cultural variety of the south became most evident in Nakhon Si Thammarat. There were three Hindu temples in the city, as well as mosques and Chinese Buddhist temples. A bomb had just been found under the statue of a Thai Buddha and the police were looking for political agitators; Muslims were not suspected, as Muslims and Buddhists always showed respect for each other's shrines. The Thai National Anthem usually blared out over loudspeakers in small towns at 8 a.m. and 6 p.m., when traffic would come to a halt and everyone would stand to attention. Nakhon Si Thammarat was the first major city on my journey where this occurred. Presumably, it was part of the Government's effort to forge one nation out of the divergent elements in the south.

There was rain on the way to Songkla but it was at body temperature and did nothing to cool the air. I still wrote my notes with a wad of paper tissues under my hand to absorb the perspiration and my back and arms still got burnt through my rain-soaked shirt. I woke in Ranot to a tropical downpour. My hotel there was my only really bad one in Thailand. I disturbed a huge cockroach in my shoe and surprised a rat on the landing. Clouds of flies infested the shop next door where I took my breakfast coffee, and the floor was deep in refuse. I had to set out, whatever the weather: another night in Ranot was not to be contemplated. I stood for a while in the hotel porch, hoping the rain would abate. Two men sheltered with me, one in a large panama hat with elastic under the chin and the other in a puce-coloured crochet bonnet with scalloped edges, a sarong and nothing else. Two small children came to the shop to collect the family's morning tea in a plastic bag. They stamped their bare feet in the puddles and giggled together under a big umbrella. By 7.15 the storm was over and I set out cheerfully but I was to regret my late start. The rain had swept the sky clean and the sun shone remorselessly down from the clear, brilliant blue. I just had to grit my teeth and concentrate on keeping the pedals turning, cycling into the stiffening wind through a ribbon development of shabby houses, where the domestic rubbish was left to rot by the roadside. The south of Thailand was much less tidy than the north.

Women enjoyed considerable respect in Thai society. They were outgoing and well dressed. They drove their own cars and motorcycles and were commercially active, both as employees and as owners or partners in their own businesses. Little girls were loved and cosseted. All this made an agreeable change after India and the wholly Muslim countries, where the position of women ranged from low to abject. But the oddity in Thailand was the shortage of female animals. I passed bullocks, but no cows; backyards were full of cockerels, but few hens; dogs were invariably male; and on the outskirts of Songkla I saw a huge, glossy, pampered boar reclining on the family porch.

After six consecutive days' cycling, the last two over 50 to 60 miles in hot, windy, rainy weather, I was ready for my break in the best hotel in Songkla. Cleanliness, air conditioning and good food can only really be appreciated after a spell of cycling in the rural tropics. Crossing the threshold into the cool marble foyer was an instant restorative to body and spirit. Everything was of luxury standard, including the hotel Spirit House.

The Spirit House is one of the unique features of Thailand.

Every home has to have one, to ensure that the family ghosts have attractive accommodation. The Spirit House usually stands in the garden, looking like a brightly coloured, temple-style bird-box on a pole. It has to occupy the most favourable position on the site, so its location is included in the planning stages of the building; and if the family home is extended or improved, the Spirit House must receive similar treatment otherwise the family ghosts might prefer the main house and move in to haunt their descendants. Offerings of food are made daily and incense is burned. Hotels and public buildings also need their Spirit Houses, which must be of matching impor-tance. My luxury hotel in Songkla had a magnificent Spirit House in the shadiest corner of the terrace restaurant. When the tables were laid for the guests, a table was also laid before the Spirit House and a delicious selection of food and drink spread out for the spirits on a crisp white table cloth.

I met a group of Scots in the hotel. They were waiting to start work on an off-shore oil-rig and were spending leisurely days reading paperbacks by the swimming pool. They passed on a Frederick Forsyth to me, which was a great treat as I had had nothing to read since Bangkok. The hotel pool was far too busy for my taste, crowded with Thais in goggles, flashing up and down the marked lanes at great speed. Thais have no need to sunbathe and take their swimming as serious exercise. I wandered down to the beach and joined the fishermen in the shallows. We were all fully clothed, as the sun was far too strong for naked skin.

From Songkla I turned inland, heading with relief for the slightly cooler air of the central hills, cycling through forests of tall, leafy trees. When I saw the little cups attached to the trunks, I realised I had reached rubber country. I had planned to stop at Khlong Ngae, on the way to the Malaysian border, but there was no hotel. By the time I reached Sadao, the main border town, it was noon, searingly hot and there was still no hotel. The police directed me to Padang Basar, another small border town seven miles off my road, and there I struggled gratefully into my last guest house in Thailand. I felt particularly weary; I had planned to cycle only 30 miles and had sailed into Khlong Ngae thinking I had reached journey's end. Disappointed, I had set out to cover a further fifteen miles uphill, only to find that yet another seven miles lay before me in the heat of midday. Fifty-two miles in fits and starts are much more wearing than 52 miles carefully planned and timed to suit the climate.

Padang Basar was a gastronomic disaster. The only restaurants were outdoor noodle stalls at the border-crossing. I went along there for a late lunch and selected what I thought was chicken casserole. It turned out to be curried heart. I ate the accompanying noodles. At dinner-time even the noodle stalls were closed, so I had to make do with four packets of crisps, a bar of chocolate and a bottle of beer from the general store. I pedalled back to Sadao early next morning and managed to find a restaurant, but all the tables were occupied by a huge party who were treating eight monks to a sumptuous breakfast before they all piled into coaches together. I squeezed into a corner on a stool and watched the party, eating my slice of dry cake without relish, but fancying their mountains of noodles even less.

I felt a stranger in Thailand. The Thais always smiled at me and showed unfailing courtesy, yet they somehow kept themselves carefully hidden away. I moved among them, I watched them, I exchanged greetings and smiles with them, but I never seemed to make any real contact. Their traditions were alien and I had no point of reference from which to judge or appreciate their culture. I was always on the outside, looking in. The greatest barrier was undoubtedly their difficult language. Donsong in his Bang Saphan guest house was the only Thai with whom I managed to have a meaningful conversation. My attempts to speak Thai were always greeted with pleasure but rarely understood; Thai is a tonal language and the same syllable can have as many as five different meanings, depending on the pitch. Thais in their turn found English pronunciation quite beyond them and I often had the embarrassment of failing to understand them, even when they were speaking confidently in my own language. Standing in the passport queue at Sadao, 7,035 cycling miles from London, I realised that I was a lonely stranger. I was eager to cross into Malaysia, with its shades of the Raj, Conrad and Somerset Maugham.

15

Highway One, Malaysia

ALOR SETAR — SUNGAI PETANI — BUTTERWORTH —
PENANG — TAIPING — KUALA KANGSAR — IPOH —
TAPAH — SLIM RIVER — RAWANG — KUALA LUMPUR —
SEREMBAN — TAMPIN — MELAKA — MUAR — BATU
PAHAT — AYER HITAM — KULAI — JOHORE BAHRU —
SINGAPORE

> All I seek, the heaven above
> And the road below me.
> *(R. L. Stevenson)*

MALAYSIA was a delight from start to finish – a tropical paradise, vibrant and exciting in the diversity of its peoples and cultures. I cycled across No Man's Land, where posters with pictures of nooses warned me in a number of languages that I should be executed if I was caught carrying drugs into Malaysia. But a middle-aged lady cyclist is never suspected of trafficking and is never searched. Malaysia was no exception. I was greeted with a cheerful 'Welcome to Malaysia!' by the customs officers, who wanted to hear all about my trip. The passport control waved me off with a 'Mind how you go, now!' and I cycled out into the Malaysian morning, feeling like an astronaut home from the moon. The Malaysians were every bit as friendly as the Thais, but they were friendly in idiomatic English. I had bandied jokes for the first time since Calcutta.

I was back on the trail I had left in Calcutta. When Francis Light landed on Penang Island in 1786, he acquired it as a trading station for the East India Company. Penang was soon joined by Malacca, which was received from the Dutch in 1824 in exchange for the British settlement of Bencoolen on Sumatra. Penang and Malacca formed the Straits Settlements of the British East India Company and were administered from Calcutta. Sir Stamford Raffles' deal with the Sultan of Johore

Bahru added Singapore Island and in 1867 those three key ports and their hinterlands down the west coast of the Malay Peninsula became a British Crown Colony linked together by Highway 1, my next historical road.

And what a good road it was. The smooth dual carriageway had silken hard shoulders, even stretches of cycle path, while the central reservation was aflame with cannas, hibiscus and oleanders. As I cruised down from the central heights towards Alor Setar, my only problem that Sunday morning was lack of cash. There were no exchange facilities at the border and I had not a single Malaysian cent. Fortunately, Malaysia is a Muslim country where Friday is the holy day, so I was able to cash a traveller's cheque in a bank in Jitra and rush gasping into the café next door for a long overdue cold drink. It was a sight to delight my eyes – a clean, bright, modern snack bar with a wonderful selection of breads, buns and patisserie. I made a pig of myself on Danish pastries and a large pot of real coffee. I was going to enjoy Malaysia.

I pedalled into Alor Setar through green suburbs. Little wooden bridges led over roadside canals to neatly kept houses, shaded from the sun and screened from the traffic by magnificent trees, their gardens lovingly tended. Had they not been lush with tropical vegetation, I could have imagined myself in Wimbledon or the outskirts of Esher. I passed the Royal Kedah Club. Its white paintwork gleamed, its brasses glittered in the sun and its lawn was perfect. The Malaysians might not have enjoyed their colonial experience but they had the imagination and breadth of spirit to appreciate its heritage. The buildings and utilities of the Raj were as immaculate and well run as ever. They had been accepted totally and were cherished as an integral part of the country's history and richly varied culture.

At my beautiful hotel in Alor Setar, I had kebabs flambés for dinner. For the first time in months, I took a knife to chunks of tender, recognisable meat. There was a complimentary English-language newspaper in my room and my television had in-house films and three channels with programmes in English, Chinese and Tamil as well as Bahasa Malaysia. I was back in touch with the world again. Significantly, people in Malaysia usually asked me if I was cycling round the world; everywhere else, they had assumed that I was simply cycling across their own country. The Malaysians saw themselves in an international framework.

There was a lot to see in Alor Setar. My hotel window looked out over the Padang, the open space in the heart of the city surrounded by what must be the most whimsical collection of buildings in the world. There was the Balai Nobat, an octagonal neo-Classical tower with pilasters and mouldings picked out in ochre on a cream ground, all surmounted by a golden onion dome. It housed the State ceremonial percussion band. Next to it was the Balai Besar, the Great Hall, built in 1898 and still used by the Sultan of Kedah on ceremonial occasions. Two sweeping balustraded staircases led up from one open-sided auditorium to another and forests of columns supported the first floor and the roof, which was pitched in Thai style with garuda finials. Behind stood a terrace of red-roofed neo-Georgian administrative offices. Across the road, the Zadir Mosque, one of the largest in Malaysia, had its own gigantic car park. My feet sank to the ankles in its sumptuous green fitted carpet, then were cooled on the marble floor of the columned hall beside it, open to the four winds. Finally, there was the clock tower, Romanesque in style, yellow ochre and cream in colour, with a bright yellow half-onion dome. This whole wonderfully idiosyncratic complex was drawn together by paved walkways and embellished with fountains and lawns.

I went out after my siesta to take photographs in the evening sunlight and the heavens suddenly opened. Rain came down in tropical torrents and a fierce wind sprang up from the north. It was all over in an hour. It rained every day at the same time, which made the west coast of Malaysia slightly cooler than the east coast of Thailand, but even more humid. My hair, which was bleached blonde by the sun, was always damp and amazingly curly. I scarcely recognised myself in the mirror.

Cycling in Malaysia was comfortable. To begin with, the hour had changed at the Thai border. I still rose at dawn, but in Malaysia it was called 7 a.m., not 6 a.m., so that hotel coffee shops and local cafés were open for breakfast before I set out. Then every clump of trees seemed to shade a stall with a few tables and chairs, where motorists relaxed over their refreshments. Hotels were never a problem. The roads were shady; Bahasa Malaysia was written in the Roman alphabet, so that I could read road signs without difficulty; and a motorway syphoned off most of the heavy traffic. With no worries, I had the tranquillity to dream and the enthusiasm for travel to plan future trips. I was very content. I could think of nothing I would rather be doing.

From Butterworth I took the ferry over to Penang Island, paying 50 cents for my Basikal ticket. A ferry-boat docked and I watched in astonishment as hundreds of motorcycles, scooters and pedal cycles rushed to disembark. There were two cycle-rickshaws, each complete with passengers and piles of luggage, and only ten cars.

I loved Penang and its capital, Georgetown, from the moment I landed. As I had stayed in international standard hotels in Alor Setar and Sungai Petani, I needed to balance my budget, so I cycled up and down Lebuh Chulia, Georgetown's main street, and selected a modest Chinese hotel. A ceiling fan wafted a breeze through the louvred doors and windows and an endless supply of free China tea came with the room. The proprietor was pleased to have a tourist. He admired my bicycle and told me that British products were always the best, but unfortunately they were expensive and no one these days was prepared to pay for quality. 'So now the Japanese rule the world,' he concluded ruefully. On my first evening I took a nostalgic iced coffee on the terrace of the old E. & O. Hotel, looking out over the Straits at Somerset Maugham's view. He had used the hotel as the setting for some of his stories and I felt his ghost would still have recognised its manicured lawns and discreet, white-coated waiters. Only the package tourists would be different.

Sometimes I cycled round Georgetown and sometimes I treated myself to a cycle-rickshaw. In India I had found them depressing vehicles. Sitting on the hard, narrow seat of the unsprung trailer, I had watched the ragged, barefoot cyclist with pity and a feeling of shame. How could a heavy, able-bodied woman allow herself to be dragged round by such a weary, emaciated creature? Yet I hired him because I knew he desperately needed the money. In Georgetown I had no such mixed feelings. I rode in front, under a parasol, in a wide and extremely comfortable conveyance, carrying on a cheerful conversation with my cyclist, who was adequately fed, well shod and tidy. I felt like a pampered, overgrown baby, out for a ride in its pushchair.

Georgetown showed me Malaysia's cultural mix at its most exotic. The indigenous Malays (called *bumiputra* – sons of the soil) had, strangely enough, been converted to Islam by the Chinese under Admiral Cheng Ho, who had arrived in Malacca in 1409. Later waves of Chinese settlers had been Buddhist, while the indentured labourers subsequently brought across from southern India by the British to work their rubber plantations had been Hindu or Muslim. The Portuguese, Dutch and British had made a few converts to Christianity, so Georgetown had mosques, Chinese temples, Thai Buddhist shrines, Hindu temples of southern Indian style with elaborate, brightly painted gopuras and St George's Church, the oldest Anglican foundation in south-east Asia, consecrated by the Bishop of Calcutta in 1818. Every time I turned a corner I came upon a different place of worship in a different style with different rites. The most amazing was the red, green and gold temple to Kuan Yin, the Goddess of Mercy, where crowds of Chinese queued up in the forecourt to burn money in large iron furnaces on wheels.

With my great interest in food, I spent happy evenings sampling Malaysia's variety. There was everything the jaded palate could wish for: Malay, Sumatra and Java dishes; specialities from Peking, Canton and Hainan; and curries transformed by the excellent ingredients which were hard to find in India. Faint-hearted Westerners were catered for with porridge, toast and marmalade, Vegemite, sausages, roast beef and a bland array of international dishes. And when a cooling snack was required, skewers of pineapple, mango, papaya, jackfruit, starfruit and rambutan were on sale at every street corner.

Even more astonishing was the range of drinks. In addition to the world-wide Cokes, Sprites and Seven-Ups, they had every variety of coffee, tea and fresh fruit juice, Ovaltine, Horlicks, Milo, chrysanthemum tea, soyabean drink, 100 Plus

Isotonic, ice cream soda, root beer, ginger beer, sarsaparilla, orange, red, purple and livid green Fanta and even Li'l Abner's favourite, Kickapoo Joy Juice. Every known brand of beer and spirit was on sale: Guinness was particularly popular with the health-conscious Chinese, who took the slogan 'Guinness is Good for You' very seriously. Elderly Chinese would drink Guinness or hot, milky Horlicks with their fried rice and noodles. The only drink not readily available was fresh milk. This was available condensed, out of imported tins. I looked at the amazingly lush green grass. Perhaps Malaysians were so prosperous that they could afford to waste their natural resources – or perhaps they thought the world had too much milk anyway.

As Georgetown's population was predominantly Chinese, clothes were wildly casual. Shorts and vests, jeans, baggy Chinese pants, T-shirts, baseball caps, even solar topees, mingled with the more graceful Indian saris and the long skirts, headscarves and lace skull-caps of the orthodox Muslims. It was a city where even the Westerners in their sun-tops and dungarees looked reasonably in place, despite their long, lumbering limbs and lobster complexions. As in Europe, weedy, hollow-chested young men with long hair were being towed around by neat, well-organised girls. It was a world-wide phenomenon. I chatted to them occasionally in the modest local restaurants where we all ate, but it was too much like being back at school. They were so eager and receptive, so compassionate, but so uninformed. The naïveté of their solutions to the world's problems put me in mind of marking General Studies essays or giving mock university interviews. I had to exercise great restraint. But they were kind and I liked them. The old tourists I met in the smart hotel bars were in fact harder to take, with their heaps of purchases and their boasts about beating down some poor struggling market-trader over the price of a gimcrack article. As a middle-aged vagrant, living simply, I fitted into neither group. I found the Malaysians much more congenial and always happy to talk.

I wandered for hours round the streets, watching craftsmen making the rattan furniture for which Malaysia is famous, and gazing into the shops. The Chinese chemists were my

favourites, with their sections for antibiotics and all the latest
Western drugs competing for shelf-space with traditional
Chinese remedies – dried snakes and sea horses, herbs, barks
and tonic teas made of deer's tail and pilose antler. Sign-writers
were triply busy, as every sign had to be painted in three
languages. 'Beware of the Dog' in English had Bahasa Malaysia
above, Chinese ideograms below and a picture of a fierce
Alsatian, teeth bared, for those who could read no language at
all. Money-changers and book-sellers were usually Indian,
their little enclaves in the city immediately recognisable by the
pavements stained with red betel-juice, the smell of spices in
their corner shops and the frenetic, high-pitched squeal of their
popular singers, sounding like hysterical ten-year-old girls.

Malaysians had not always lived in harmony. One of the main
exhibits in the Penang Museum was the bullet-riddled Rolls-
Royce in which Sir Henry Gurney, British High Commissioner
for the Federation of Malaya, was ambushed and murdered by
Communist terrorists in October 1951, during the Emergency.
Another section was devoted to the history of the Chinese Clans
and the warfare between them in 1867.

I had time to visit only one of the great Penang Clan Houses,
the Khoo Kongsi, its sumptuousness reflecting the wealth and
influence of its members. The amazing collection of buildings
formed a square – temples, shrines for 'soul tablets', administrative offices, even a puppet theatre. The craftsmanship of the
lavish stonework was breathtaking, with dragons, fish and
foliage covering every inch of the temple walls and columns,
some figures in such high relief as to be totally separated from
their supporting masonry. Furniture was inlaid with mother-
of-pearl, floors were of marble and the whole complex, being
Chinese, was painted in glowing reds, greens and gold. Today
the Clans are charitable trusts and the walls of the administrative offices were lined with the photographs of successful
students who had been awarded bursaries.

I took an afternoon trip up to the top of Penang Hill in the
creaky old Swiss funicular railway and another day I visited
Kek Lok Si, the largest Buddhist temple in Malaysia, where a
giant statue of Kuan Yin, the Chinese Goddess of Mercy,
looked down over a hillside packed with vivid red, green and

gold buildings like an Oriental Disneyland. Then I had to move on. The rest of the city and island would have to wait for my next visit.

My next day's cycling took me to Taiping, the wettest place in Malaysia. It certainly lived up to its reputation. The rain came down in buckets, the surrounding mountains were completely hidden in cloud and all the other cyclists pedalled along under umbrellas. The vegetation was so thick that creepers and plants of every kind grew up the trunks of trees, trailing down from their branches. Only the trees in the rubber plantations were kept free.

It was a rich, tin-mining town. The name Taiping, 'town of everlasting peace', was given to it by the British when they took it over in 1874 and ended the violent feuds between the Chinese Clans. The Chinese were more peaceable in 1988 but they were still very rich and they still ran the tin-mining. Entire families came out to Sunday dinner at the best hotel, all generations in groups of 30 or 40, bringing their bottles of Black Label and Armagnac with them and taking family snaps with their expensive cameras. The menu was exclusively Chinese, which was a disappointment as I had gone there from my more modest Chinese hotel, hoping for some variety.

Next morning the sun shone and Taiping was transformed. It lay at the foot of Maxwell Hill, the oldest hill station in Malaysia. The old opencast tin mines had been landscaped into a beautiful Lake Garden. Chinese women in smart Western outfits were playing a morning round of golf, Chinese of both sexes were out jogging and I was greeted by Chinese fellow-cyclists whirling round the park. The other racial groups were content to sit and gaze at the mountains and the ducks on the lake. I passed the King Edward VII School and some elegant colonial buildings standing among the modern offices, then I was off on a fabulous ride over a high mountain pass, unbelievably rich in vegetation. The well-trimmed grass verges and the clean-swept tarmac gave the mountains a park-like air, almost as tidy as the formal gardens in Taiping.

Kuala Kangsar, the capital of Perak State, was celebrating the sultan's birthday and the 'Birthday Honours' appeared in the local newspapers. Malaysia is a federation of thirteen states

and their sultans elect one from among their number to be
Supreme Head of the Federation for a period of five years. The
Sultan of Perak had been chosen to take office from 1989. I was
pleased to see that he was a graduate of Nottingham University,
my own home town, and Lincoln's Inn. He had met and
married a Malaysian student schoolteacher in England and the
royal pair worked energetically for their state. Their capital was
one of the loveliest cities I had ever seen. A corniche, dominated by the palace and the Government Rest House, ran along
between the hills and the Perak river towards the eccentric State
Mosque, whose golden domes and four minarets were squashed
together to give a foreshortened effect. For once, I could get a
whole mosque into my camera viewfinder. The rich greens and
vibrant reds of the tropical vegetation contrasted with the
delicate primrose and white façade of the palace. It was in
Kuala Kangsar, at the agricultural station, that rubber trees
were first grown in Malaysia.

I stayed in the Perak Rest House. These rest houses, built in
the days of the Raj to house travelling officials, were a feature of
Pakistan, India and Malaysia. In the subcontinent, the Dak
Bungalows, as they were called there, had been taken over by
government departments and I had needed a permit to stay in
them. In Malaysia they had been leased out to private entre-
preneurs who ran them as normal hotels. My quarters in Perak
were gigantic. I had a spacious sitting room, a bathroom and a
bedroom with fitted cupboards large enough to take the entire
ceremonial wardrobe of a visiting High Commissioner. A green
arrow, suspended from the ceiling, with KIBLAT in Roman
and Arabic script, showed me the direction of Mecca.

The restaurant was a covered terrace with a view of the Perak
river and the misty mountains. My stay in Kuala Kangsar
coincided with the start of Ramadan, the month-long fast when
Muslims are forbidden to eat or drink during daylight hours.
There were suggestions in letters to the press that restaurateurs
should be fined if they sold lunch to Muslims, but Malaysia is a
free country and the decision was left to the individual Muslim's
own conscience. All through the afternoon, street vendors piled
their stalls high with delicacies and tempting little snacks. At
sunset a siren sounded for the Puasa, the end of fasting, and the

passers-by, who had been eyeing the stalls for the past hour or two, fell on them like a swarm of locusts. Hotels advertised special family buffet suppers, with cabarets to celebrate the end of each day's hardship. I tried the special supper one night later on in Seremban, but the quantity of food utterly defeated me, even after a hard day's cycling and a swim in the hotel pool. More money was spent on food during that month than at any other time of year, according to *The New Straits Times*, which chastised the Faithful for their self-indulgence. Ramadan ended with the feast of Hari Raya, when gifts were exchanged, and Malaysians of all religions thronged the stores and markets to do their Hari Raya shopping. 'Only twenty shopping days to Hari Raya.'

Ipoh is Sin City to the Malaysians. A wealthy tin-mining town, its grandiose public buildings jostle for space between the 'Gold Finger Massage Parlour', 'Booze City' and rows of 'Pubs'. Trendy Chinese teenage boys in baggy black trousers with tightly belted waists and long, slicked-back hair added to the city's macho air. As the restaurant near my hotel was unlocking its doors to start breakfast, the madam opposite was bolting her shutters at the end of a night's trade. I cycled out of Ipoh past a commercial college called 'The Goon Institution', reckoning that I had only about twelve cycling days left to Singapore.

Much as I loved Malaysia, I was beginning to look forward to the end of the East. The heat from mid-morning was so wearing that I reached each day's destination in a state of exhaustion. The humidity had given me athlete's foot, which itched with maddening persistence as I cycled. And my daily malaria tablet invariably stuck in my throat and gave me indigestion, no matter how carefully I swallowed it. The tablets annoyed me most of all, as the Malay Peninsula was non-malarial and I was simply finishing my Thailand course. But even as I grumbled, I registered how fortunate I was to have crossed Asia with nothing worse than an itchy left foot. I would throw away my disgusting wrecks of trainers in Singapore and have a real blitz on my feet in the dry climate of California.

I was now cycling the foothills of the Cameron Highlands. Most of the traffic took the motorway so I had the excellent surface of Highway 1 and its spectacular scenery almost to myself. Ranges of jagged mountains, sometimes as many as eight piled up behind one another, looked down on me like spectators at a show. The nearest were dark green, those behind pale green merging to grey; a bank of dark grey cloud towered behind them all, like the darkest, highest of the ranges. A livid yellowish sunlight spread upwards from behind the clouds and I sped along, hoping that the sun would remain well hidden until I had finished my day's journey. The gloom was kind to the traveller and the landscape was such a feast for the eyes that I even forgot to notice the kilometre stones. My friends from India, the mina birds, enlivened the grass verges and I saw giant lizards, alive and dead, and one squashed snake at least five feet long.

I stayed in Tapah, a stronghold of southern Indian Muslims, where my evening beer was hard to find, and at Slim river, where the retreating British had made their last stand against the Japanese. I enquired at the police station there for the rest house and was given a motorcycle escort.

I looked forward to the afternoons and a respite from the heat. I would retire to bed under the ceiling fan, using my large cotton square as a draught-excluder: even in the simplest hotels, the bottom sheet and pillowcase were fresh, but the quilt was unbearably hot, so the square became my top sheet. *The New Straits Times* occupied the afternoons and my diary kept me busy in the early evenings. Over dinner I would do one of my large supply of *Times* crosswords, which I had managed to spin out, supplemented by further batches sent by friends and two books of *Guardian* crosswords found in Calcutta. I went to bed soon after dinner, as there was rarely anything else to do. Evening is the loneliest time of day for the solitary traveller, so I made it as short as possible, rising early to enjoy the coolness and sociability of the morning hours.

In Rawang, only twelve miles from Kuala Lumpur, I found a delightful, inexpensive Chinese hotel; there was even hot water in the shower, a rare treat. The hotel was beside the bus station and a regular service ran to the centre of the capital, a ride of little over half an hour. I decided to base myself in Rawang, making bus-trips into Kuala Lumpur for sightseeing. One look at the capital and I knew I had done the right thing. Kuala

Lumpur is not a city for the cyclist or pedestrian. It was designed to suit the internal combustion engine. Flyovers, ramps and six-lane highways kept the cars moving swiftly, but pedestrians crossing the road diced with death. Pavements were bare and shadeless, there were no shop-windows to gaze in, as the shops were in multi-storey complexes with lifts and escalators up from the car parks, and the poor pedestrians had to toil up flights of steps from street level. China Town, with its covered arcades in front of crowded shops, was the only lively section; and it became even livelier at dusk, when its streets were closed to traffic and the stalls of the night market did a brisk trade.

I spent a frustrating morning and a fortune in taxi-fares trying to collect my mail from American Express. The address given turned out to be a bus station, miles from the city centre. When my taxi finally found it, I was told that letters arrived at the bus station office but had to be picked up from an office in the city centre. So back I went in another taxi. Then I walked in the heat for over an hour, searching for the Tourist Office, only to find it closed. Even cafés, ubiquitous elsewhere in Malaysia, were difficult to find in Kuala Lumpur and I was nearly dropping by the time I spotted a dreary little snack-bar in an arcade.

To restore my tranquillity I visited the Great Mosque, an elegant complex of spaces with marble floors, three halls of columns and no walls. It was certainly tranquil. The floors were covered with sleeping men, though two particularly energetic Malays had found the strength to read their newspapers, propped up in semi-recumbent postures against pillars.

Although it was only nine o'clock when I had finished my day's sightseeing, had dinner and returned to my Rawang hotel, the place was locked and shuttered. A violent tropical storm had cut off the town's electricity supply and I stood in the dark and the pouring rain, hammering frantically at the shutters on the verge of panic. But the *patron* greeted me with candle and matches, beaming with relief at my safe return.

On Sunday morning I took advantage of the quieter roads to cycle into Kuala Lumpur, intending to spend the night in a modern hotel there before continuing south. The city did

nothing to redeem itself; all the hotels I tried were most
unhelpful about my bicycle. They were busy enough with their
smarter clients without having to trouble with the likes of me
and my humble machine. I left the centre and pedalled despond-
dently along in the direction of my exit route for Seremban, not
quite knowing what to do. Opposite a park and surrounded by
its own gardens stood the YWCA, where my bicycle was welcomed and cherished and I had a beautiful room with breakfast
for less than a quarter of the price of the unfriendly hotels.
Since I was making a forced economy over accommodation, I
decided to treat myself to a really splendid Sunday lunch. I
showered, changed into my silk suit and went to one of the best
hotels, my mouth watering in anticipation. They had a special
set lunch that day – curried fish heads. Chinese families were
flocking in to savour this delight. I crept into the gloomy little
hotel next door for a faint-hearted omelette and chips. My
afternoon was spent in the cool of the white Moorish fantasy of
the railway station, drinking chilled root beer in the buffet and
reading in the newspaper about a ring of 'old women' who had
been used to smuggle drugs from Thailand. They had been
apprehended in their minibus. Their ages ranged from 30 to 54.

The clientele of the YWCA was surprisingly elegant. I
chatted over breakfast with two young housewives from the east
coast of Malaysia. They were sophisticated, widely travelled
and were driving a very smart car so I was surprised to find
them in a hostel. All became clear when they explained that
they had come to Kuala Lumpur for a one-week baking course
at the Shangri-La Hotel but were not allowed by their husbands
to be resident there on their own: they could come to Kuala
Lumpur only if they stayed in the secure respectability of the
ladies-only YWCA. They were very excited to be having a week
in the capital and told me that Malaysia was a wonderful
country to live in 'except for the politics'. They were Muslims of
Tamil descent.

I was often taken aside by Indians and Chinese to listen to
their grievances. Charles was a Chinese fellow-guest at one of
the rest houses. A former mathematics teacher, he had gone
into the firewood business with a friend who used to be a
mechanical engineer. They had both given up their professions

because promotion was blocked by positive discrimination in favour of the Malay *bumiputra*. Charles told me that 70 per cent of university places were reserved for Malays, so that the children of other racial groups had to be brilliant to qualify for one of the remaining 30 per cent. Families often pooled their resources and ruined themselves financially in order to send their young people abroad to study, out of the system. Charles was applying to emigrate to Australia where his wife, a journalist, already had the offer of a sub-editor's job and where he could return to his career in teaching and his two daughters could be sure of a university place. He was sad about the waste of human resources: Malaysia had oil, rubber and tin and could be a leading Eastern economy. Another Chinaman, a café proprietor who had worked as a chef in the United States and Singapore, regretted the departure of the British. They had known how to administer, unlike 'this lot', and had left the business community free to get on with its commercial activities. In those satisfactory days, 95 per cent of business was in non-Malay hands. Now the Government was redressing the balance by setting up the *bumiputra* in business. 'They get Government money and immediately go out and buy a big car – for the company, of course. Then they get a colour TV and a fridge and they do no work. The business fails and the taxpayer picks up the tab.' The Chinese and Indians still ran a good 80 per cent of the country's businesses, but they were bitter about the discrimination against them.

Malays form the majority of the population, but only just. It was a relief to them when Singapore left the Federation in 1965, two years after Independence, as the island's 75 per cent Chinese majority was in danger of tipping the balance for Malaysia as a whole. Country people in origin, the Malays are still the agricultural workers, and their interests clearly have to be safeguarded against the shrewd, industrious Chinese city-dwellers, with their centuries of commercial experience. Malaysians of Chinese and Indian origin complain, yet at heart they know they have a very good life. I met two Indian cousins running a café and general store. They told me that their grandfathers had come over from southern India as indentured labourers on the rubber plantations, served out their contracts and saved their money. Now the two families owned the shop, ran cars and wanted for nothing. The previous year they had taken a trip to India in search of their roots and had been appalled at the poverty and the rural squalor of their native village. 'Thank goodness our grandfathers showed a bit of initiative and got out,' they said. 'Imagine living in a dump like that!'

Kuala Lumpur, Seremban, Tampin, then Malacca – Portuguese, Dutch, British and finally Malaysian Melaka, its quays and wharves still bustling, though the barges were piled with charcoal and Coca Cola, not the silks and spices of the Orient. Jalan Hang Jebat (formerly Jonker Street) was lined with old houses elaborately carved and shuttered or faced with pretty ceramic tiles. There was a Dutch Stadthuys and a Dutch Protestant Christ Church built of pink brick from Zeeland; the romantic ruin of the Portuguese Church of Our Lady of the Hill, where St Francis Xavier's body had rested on its return voyage home from Goa, looked out over the Straits; mosques had roofs and minarets like pagodas, Sumatran-style; and there was British neo-Classical, spruce and freshly painted. Melaka was another city to wander in and enjoy. From there I booked my Singapore to Los Angeles flight with the help of two young Indian travel agents, who called me 'Auntie'. And I sent a telegram to Dorothy in Malibu, requesting an emergency dental appointment. I had lost the filling and most of the enamel from a much-excavated molar on my first evening in Melaka. Again, fortune had smiled on me, as the accident had happened just a few days away from American dental care. I could have been toothless in far worse places.

South of Melaka lay the least prosperous part of Malaysia. Cocoa, rubber, palm oil and pineapples grew between the poor villages. The country people were very Malay and very Muslim, so that roadside refreshments were difficult to find in Ramadan. The people sat under the palm trees outside their wooden houses, waving and smiling at me as I cycled past. It was more like southern Thailand than northern Malaysia.

In Muar I saw my only Georgian mosque – an astonishing neo-Classical construction in cream and white stucco, more like Heveningham Hall than a Muslim place of worship. Mosquewatching had become my favourite pastime in Malaysia. The

Turks had been so spellbound by Sinan that all their mosques were pale imitations of the Süleymaniye, while Pakistani style had been firmly rooted in the Moghul. The Malaysians had no such constraints and their rich cultural mix provided free flight for fantasy. Their minarets ranged from Romanesque towers through pagodas to Cape Canaveral rockets. The mosques themselves had 'domes' in the shape of pyramids, hexagonal lanterns and even a silver eighteen-point star, while their inner spaces were either forests of columns with no walls or huge areas, like sports halls, with no supporting columns at all, lit by dancing light from intricate filigree panels or vivid stained glass. No two were ever alike.

Batu Pahat was memorable for the Fairyland Hotel – unfortunately not magic enough to tempt me to stay there – and a jolly Chinese funeral. I was walking back to my hotel after dinner when I heard the sound of drums and strings. Under an awning outside a shop, casually dressed Chinese families were sitting round café tables, chatting, eating nuts and crisps and drinking fruit juice while their children rushed round playing noisy games. 'Come in, Auntie! Come and join us!' The Chinese love to have visitors at their ceremonies and I was soon bustled inside, given a carton of iced chrysanthemum tea and seated with a group of students. Adults of both sexes, dressed in white robes and hoods and looking not unlike the Ku Klux Klan, were circling before an altar. Many of the children were dressed in royal-blue cotton trouser suits with a royal-blue triangle of cloth on their heads. A few teenagers, who seemed to be stewards, wore pea-green shirts or sashes. Everyone was smiling and feet were tapping in time to the drum-beat. The band soon moved to another alcove, where there was a magnificent house made of bamboo and coloured paper, piles of fruit and a profusion of flowers and candles. At nine o'clock, when the percussion band reached its deafening climax, everyone queued up to file past the paper house to wish the dead man happiness and all good things in his new life. It was a cheerful, friendly occasion, full of hope.

My last two cycling days were rainy; breakfast in the drizzle was followed by breezy, overcast mornings with sudden, heavy showers. Cycling in tropical rain without waterproofs was as refreshing as going for a swim and much more interesting. I sped in my cool, wet clothes past cloudy, wooded hills under spectacular blue-black skies, covering 58 miles in a day. I was pleased to find that I could still cycle that sort of distance, given favourable conditions, after the indolence of the past month.

When I reached the end of Malaysia I still had five nights in hand before my flight to Los Angeles. I knew that Singapore would be more expensive, so I economised by resting for three nights in Johore Bahru, cycling and dreaming beside the Johore Strait and reading in air-conditioned cafés. *The New Straits Times* carried an article on a national drive to improve the status of women of Indian origin in Malaysia and when I looked up from my paper, I saw the necessity. Malay and Chinese couples were walking along the street together, deep in conversation, husbands helping to carry the children and the shopping; young Chinese couples were even holding hands. The Indian women were plodding behind their husbands, just as they had in the villages of Uttar Pradesh, and they were doing all the carrying.

I had enjoyed Malaysia and reflected that it would be the ideal country for Westerners to get their first taste of the East. The peninsula was non-malarial, tap water in the cities was safe to drink, there was food to suit every palate and pocket, hotels were clean, there was no tipping to worry about, roads were excellent and the beaches and scenery were stunning. Life for the visitor was relaxed and problem-free. Above all, the people were friendly, kind and full of initiative. And they spoke English.

In the mist of dawn I crossed over the Causeway to Singapore Island, my twelfth country. The immigration officer was so impressed when he heard of my travels that he came out from his kiosk to shake hands with me. I had no idea of the size of the island and was surprised to find that I had to cycle seventeen miles to reach the city centre. Parks and high-rise blocks lined the immaculate, totally litter-free highway, where squadrons of men and women were trimming the verges and picking up every tiny scrap of paper. Most looked like southern Malays who had come across the Causeway to do the menial jobs beneath the dignity of the wealthy Singaporeans.

It seemed a pity to be in Singapore and not to stay at the legendary Raffles Hotel so I pushed the boat out and treated myself to a suite, furnished with rattan and delicate floral chintz, looking out over tropical gardens. There were orchids on my dressing table and Condor was carried up to my suite with such brimming admiration that I half-expected him to be tucked up lovingly in the other twin bed. I looked at the permanent exhibition of photographs and letters from Conrad, Somerset Maugham, Noel Coward and all the kings and luminaries who had graced Raffles' Palm Court, but was unable to sample the famous Singapore Sling, as gin makes me sick.

I had an introduction to the English managing director of a Singapore-based firm. Don was a grass widower, as his wife was on holiday in England, so he was as pleased as I was to have a dinner companion. Guessing that I had reached saturation point with curry, noodles and fried rice, he took me out to smoked salmon, roast beef and Burgundy on the revolving top floor of the Mandarin Hotel, where we saw the lights of Indonesia twinkling across the Straits. Next day, the eve of my departure, he drove me out to Changi International Airport to deposit my bicycle in the left luggage: thanks to Don, I learned in time that the only road out to Changi was a motorway, on which cycles were prohibited. After another day among the skyscrapers and glittering shops of that opulent port, and a steak and Burgundy dinner with Don at the Inter-Continental, I took a dawn taxi out to Changi and flew across the Date Line to the western coast of America. I had cycled 7,658 miles from London and was disappointed not to have reached the Equator. Singapore was 1°N.

The California Trail

Roads go on
While we forget, and are
Forgotten like a star
That shoots and is gone.

They are lonely
While we sleep, lonelier
For lack of the traveller
Who is now a dream
    only.

(Edward Thomas)

DOROTHY had rightly identified the 'Tomb Blackly Airport' of my Melaka travel agents with Los Angeles' Tom Bradley International and was there to greet me at 12.30 with a hug and a 'Get your skates on. Your dental appointment's at two.' After six months in the East I was back in a country where things happened, and happened fast. My cavity was briskly plugged and in no time we were winding up through the canyons of West Mulholland Highway to the familiar house on the mountain-top over Malibu. I was settled into my usual booklined studio, where no rat or cockroach would ever dare set foot, plied with tea and, before I got too comfortable, informed by Ed that I was entered for a five kilometre road race on Saturday. Dorothy and Ed have both taken up running in their semi-retirement and represent the USA in Veterans' Olympics. They were soon to add to their imposing collections of gold medals; even I managed to avoid disgrace, finishing fourth after three regular runners in my age-group. Cycling had done wonders for my stamina. For once, I was almost as slim and fit as Dorothy and Ed. At dusk, Ed wheeled his powerful telescope out onto the terrace and showed me Venus. I was amazed to see a crescent, like a small, distant moon. The evening was still, the crickets chirped and it was good to be with old friends.

Having struggled across Asia to get there I relaxed a little, but not too much, afraid that if I really let go I should never find the energy and determination to start again. As the USA was my last major foreign country, I felt in some ways that my journey was almost over. Yet I still had 4,000 miles to cycle, about one-third of my total mileage. America was, after all, a continent. It was so gigantic I found it difficult to grasp and was uncertain how to come to terms with it. As my plane had flown over San Francisco, then turned south to follow the Pacific Coast down to Los Angeles, I had looked inland on that clear morning and seen California, with the snow-capped mountains of the Sierra Nevada stretching out to the horizon, stark, empty hills behind crowded beaches. And that was only one state. Had I really committed myself to cycling such a vast distance? I had not even worked out my route.

After two days' idleness, I forced myself back to work. I wanted to retrace the pioneer trails which had brought the settlers and gold prospectors out to the West. As it was already May and getting hot, I had to follow the northern routes rather than the southern Santa Fe Trail. An American geologist on secondment to Peshawar University had told me about Bike Centennial, the ride across the USA by thousands of young cyclists to celebrate the bicentenary of Independence. He thought they had followed the Oregon Trail and the Lincoln Highway. A map of their route would have been a good start but I was unable to find one. Surprisingly, it was the American Automobile Association of Southern California which came up with most of the answers.

We were told that Norty Stewart specialised in cycle routes and drove to see him, having phoned in advance to give him an idea of my requirements. We found him deep in a history of the Oregon Trail. An hour later we left his office laden with maps and handbooks. My route from San Francisco to New York was marked on a map of the USA, then traced in detail across fifteen other maps of individual states and cities. Norty knew the pioneer trails and the traffic regulations. He knew which roads

allowed cycles and, most importantly, how to cross rivers.
Sometimes he seemed to be tracing an unnecessary detour, then
we realised that he was guiding me to the one bridge in the area
with bicycle access. His knowledge of routes was encyclo-
paedic. He would choose the best scenery, avoid the highest
mountains, skirt the city centres and take me through the nicest
towns with the budget-priced hotels – and all the wrong way
up: the maps were spread out facing Dorothy and me, while
Norty leaned over from the other side of the counter, whisking
his orange felt-tip along the upturned roads at phenomenal
speed. He knew the United States of America both inside-out
and upside-down.

Back in Malibu I worked out my cycling schedule. The
eastern states would present no problems but I soon saw that I
had no prospect at all of dividing the West into comfortable
50-mile runs. Tracts of mountain and desert stretched for
hundreds of empty miles. Then there might be a tiny
settlement marked, but would it have accommodation? Most of
the towns I ringed on my maps as possible overnight stops were
not mentioned in the AAA handbooks and if they were, the
listed motels were far beyond my budget. I copied out the
names, addresses and phone numbers of all the AAA hotels on
my route under $30 – a task soon completed – then abandoned
the handbooks. As usual I reduced the pile of maps by cutting
out strips of my route with 100 miles or so on either side of the
road to give me meaningful information at junctions. By the
end of the second day I was waist-high in discarded paper and
had calculated that my crossing would take 70 cycling days.

The traffic on the Los Angeles freeways is notorious. It took us
two and a half hours to reach Union Station, too late to book in
Condor on the same train, as he had to have his pedals removed.
I left Dorothy to deal with all that and jumped aboard for San
Francisco. 'We do thank you for choosing Amtrak as your mode
of transportation,' announced the loudspeaker.

It was a spectacular ride. The track ran along beside
Highway 101, the old Spanish Camino Reale, with the Pacific
Ocean on my left and the mountains to my right. I noted with
satisfaction that a strong wind was blowing – from the west.

Towards San Luis Obispo the train climbed steeply on three engines, snaking up between the round, grassy hills to form a horseshoe on two levels, the lower arm visible from the upper. There had been 30 Spanish missions along that coast, each 30 miles away from the next, a day's ride on horseback. San Miguel was typical: a campanile, a church and a few small sheds within a surrounding wall. I was cheered by the sight of motels in small towns; perhaps I should find beds after all. I passed through 'The Artichoke Capital of the World' and 'Gilroy, The Garlic Capital of the World'. At sunset, flocks of wild geese screamed over the salt flats and I saw the tiniest, thinnest sliver of moon rise over the Pacific. My enthusiasm for cycling came flooding back. I couldn't wait to be out there, to become a part of that magnificent landscape. Meanwhile I was lionised by a woman from Albuquerque, who asked for my autograph and took photos of me, and by a crowd in the lounge car where I went for a tuna sandwich. An old man in a cowboy hat was playing the violin, Western style, and his fellow-passengers were clapping and singing. It was all a bit too gregarious and I hid my nose in my maps or pressed it against the window to escape.

It was my first visit to San Francisco. I liked what I saw but I was not in the mood for it: I would save the San Francisco experience for another visit when I had a different budget, different clothes and different objectives. Amtrak had removed my front wheel as well as my pedals and I had to take the bicycle to an expert to get the wheel properly aligned. I left it for a thorough service and made a token tour of the city.

My hotel was in Oakland and I was the only white passenger on the bus across the bay to downtown San Francisco. 'Porcelana Face Cream for Faded Southern Beauties'. Perms to 'relax your hair'. We all want to be other than we are. Whites buy sun-tan lotion and have curly perms; blacks use Porcelana Face Cream and have their hair permanently straightened. In downtown San Francisco, two gays were having a violent, passionate row on a street corner, junkies slept round the Settlers' Memorial and elderly derelicts in baseball caps wove their supermarket trolleys full of one cent bottles for the bottle bank in and out of the crisp, striding, unisex executives in their business suits. The shops glittered.

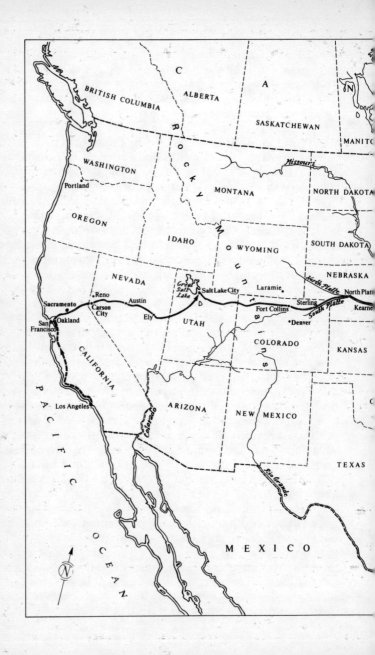

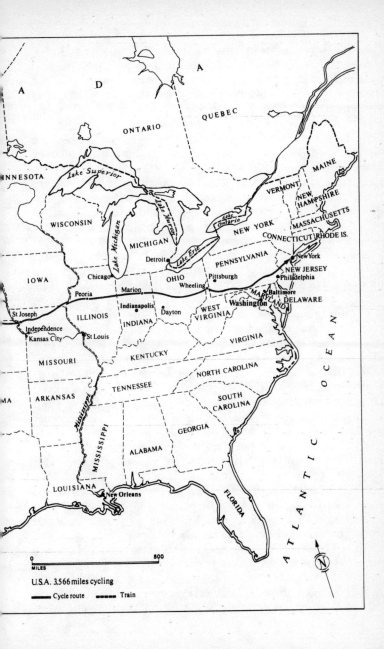

QUEBEC

ONTARIO

Lake Superior

MINNESOTA

WISCONSIN

Lake Michigan

Lake Huron

MICHIGAN

Lake Ontario

Lake Erie

MAINE

VERMONT

NEW HAMPSHIRE

NEW YORK

MASSACHUSETTS

CONNECTICUT RHODE IS.

Detroit

PENNSYLVANIA

New York

NEW JERSEY

IOWA

Chicago

OHIO

Pittsburgh

Philadelphia

Peoria

Marion

Wheeling

MARYLAND Baltimore

DELAWARE

St Joseph

Indianapolis

Dayton

WEST VIRGINIA

Washington

Independence

ILLINOIS

INDIANA

Kansas City

St Louis

VIRGINIA

MISSOURI

KENTUCKY

ARKANSAS

TENNESSEE

NORTH CAROLINA

Mississippi

SOUTH CAROLINA

MISSISSIPPI

GEORGIA

ALABAMA

LOUISIANA

New Orleans

FLORIDA

ATLANTIC OCEAN

0   500
MILES

U.S.A. 3,566 miles cycling

━━━ Cycle route   ▪▪▪▪ Train

N

You are never left out in America. At a bus stop I was automatically included in a conversation between a pale, unemployed girl of eighteen or so and a buxom, buoyant black nutritionist. The girl told us proudly that she was going to get married next year. 'You got somebody picked out then?' asked the nutritionist. 'I guess *he* picked *me* out.' 'Yeah, my last two picked me. But next time, I tell you, *A'hm* goin' to be doin' the pickin'.' The girl got onto the next bus, disaster written all over her face. She was one of life's inadequates, destined for disappointment and social welfare. The nutritionist travelled on my bus. She had just been to a conference in Liverpool and had been astonished at the number of 'poor whites' in the city.

On Friday, 20 May, I set off up San Pablo Avenue to follow the bay round to the Sacramento river. It was not to be my day. I was not very happy with my derailleur and just beyond Berkeley my chain snapped – so much for the expensive San Francisco service. I was directed to a local hardware shop. The proprietor had no new chains and no tools to repair my own but he was a kind man, keen on the great outdoors. He heaved the bicycle, panniers and all, into his pickup truck and drove me to a cycle shop in El Sobrante. The mechanic there was a girl, who told me what a good career it was for a woman: most of the work was delicate and far less dirty than repairing cars. She suspended my bicycle from a hook to fix the chain and the derailleur and it was then that we spotted a potential disaster. There was a crack in the main frame, running right round the vertical bar, just below the saddle. It had not been visible before, as my weight had kept the two parts tightly joined together. Brazing was not possible so she fitted an excellent clamp, which held all the way back to London. I had no idea how or when the damage had occurred, whether through wear and tear on bumpy Asian roads or a bad knock on a train or plane.

I had had a lucky escape and I celebrated with a pancake breakfast before cycling down another Appian Way to rejoin San Pablo Avenue. It was a Classical part of the world: Pomona Grocery, Hercules Avenue, Olympian Hills. There were wild olives, orchards and the heady smell of cypresses in the hot sun; even the oil refineries and tankers were reminiscent of the Mediterranean. A stretch of the Carquinez Scenic Highway had fallen into the sea but it was still possible to cycle along the edge. The shadow of a hawk glided along beside me. Otherwise the peaceful path was empty. Still in the Mediterranean, I arrived at Antioch, where the costly motel lured me in with the promise of a special cyclist's discount. As I sat in my room over a supper of plastic ham, processed cheese, brown bread and beer from the local deli (an expensive hotel meant a meagre meal), I dreamed of the delicious dinners I had enjoyed on my terrace restaurant in the real Antioch. Next morning, the new shift at reception knew nothing of the promised reduction and charged me the full rate. I was so angry that I left my precious Italian cycling cap behind in distraction. I asked the way out of central Antioch to the Antioch Bridge. Nobody knew. Everyone had just moved there. The great East–West migration was still in progress.

Cypress and poplars along the Sacramento river, then fig trees, orchards of apples and pears, walnuts and almonds, vines growing as bushes, untrained, and fields of maize. Blackbirds with brilliant scarlet shoulders shouted at me from telegraph wires and dive-bombed me as I passed their nests, just as noisy and aggressive as their plain cousins in England. As it was Saturday, every car seemed to be towing a motorboat and the peace of the river was shattered by roaring engines. Some people were quietly fishing but most were just rushing up and down at speed, for the sake of it. Most enjoyment in the West requires so much noise and hardware.

The great 1988 heatwave had begun and the temperature climbed to 100°F. I had to drape a towel over my head and shoulders and struggle on for 70 miles as there was nowhere to stay before Ione. I tried a bed and breakfast and discovered it was not at all the modest sort of place I knew in England. I cycled up the drive to what is known in America as 'a petite Colonial mansion' and was astounded when the door was opened by a Victorian lady in a long black skirt and a lacy white blouse with leg-of-mutton sleeves. She and her sister, similarly attired, were entertaining their weekend guests to homemade lemonade in their Victorian parlour. They had no vacancies, but as the local hotels 'left much to be desired', they arranged for me to stay with friends in their 1856 farmhouse. I was so hot and weary that I was almost beyond food, but Mrs Scully fed me on brown toast, apricot jam, bananas and tea, which was just right. I slept like a log in my huge Victorian bed.

After a breakfast of buckwheat and almond muffins I set out to conquer the Sierra Nevada, my first major challenge in the USA. At Jackson, an old-fashioned mining town straight out of a Western film, I joined Highway 88, on the route of the famous California Trail. In 1848, at Sutter's Mill near Sacramento, an employee named J. W. Marshall found gold flakes as he was digging a sluice. Within a year 90,000 people had poured into California in one of history's great migrations. When the easily recoverable surface gold of California was exhausted, the prospectors fanned out and by 1875 Colorado, Nevada, Arizona, Oregon, Washington, Idaho, Montana and the Black Hills of South Dakota all had their mining communities. The lure of gold and silver achieved in a few years a density of settlement in the mountain regions of the West which might have taken centuries by any other means.

It took me two days to climb the Sierra Nevada. The road rose steeply from sea level and the oaks, beeches, aspen and limes of Jackson soon turned to pine woods. Highway 88 had just won a prize as America's most scenic highway and I had it almost to myself. My first night out of Jackson I found plenty of accommodation and chose the OK Corral. For $29.68 I got a motel room with two double beds and a convertible couch – a bargain for a family, but rather expensive for one. Hotel-users pay a high price for the luxury of solitude. The next day I was really out on my own. At Ham's Station, once a stagecoach stop but now serving petrol and coffee, I was told by a Highway Maintenance man that the season had scarcely begun and there was no accommodation open before Caples Lake, another 34 miles up the mountains.

The scenery was magnificent and, like everything else in America, on a grand scale. I felt like a tiny beetle, crawling up through the desolation of the El Dorado National Forest, 24 miles of steep rocky outcrop and giant pines. Distances were geared to the motor car. Europe had been more populous, with little village inns along the approaches to the Great St Bernard, while much of the East had still moved at the speed of bullocks and camels, four slow feet not four fast wheels, and tea-stalls had been spaced accordingly. On the Sierra Nevada there were no people and no refreshments.

At 7,500 ft I reached the snowline and stopped to put on a T-shirt under my long-sleeved blouse and a scarf over my head. Although the air was chilly, the sun was strong and my hands, scalp and back were burning. I had run out of water and was panting with thirst and altitude. When finally I got clear of the forest and careered down to Silver Lake, I was greeted at the store by a gang of roadworkers. 'You must be the gal who's cycling to New York.' In the afternoon, a van drew up and asked if I was all right for water. I was given free iced tea at Kirkwood, where they always looked after long-distance cyclists. At five o'clock I staggered into the lodge at Caples Lake. 'Hi! You made it! We were waiting for you,' said the two boys in charge, both cyclists themselves. As always in the world's empty places, a benevolent watch had been kept. I had felt alone all day but in fact my progress had been carefully monitored. It had taken me ten hours to cover 40 miles, much of it on foot, as I had climbed from 4,321 ft to 7,953 ft. There was a spectacular view over the brilliant blue lake from my bedroom windows but no food at the lodge, so I had to cruise back down the mountain to Kirkwood and toil up it again after dinner. Though I had started out unwillingly, I soon felt the exhilaration of the mountain air and, without my heavy panniers, I flew like a bird.

The next day was my fifty-fifth birthday. A short climb took me up to 8,573 ft and I stood alone in the early morning at the top of the Kit Carson Pass, surrounded by the grandeur of the snow-covered Sierra Nevada. I had never had a more magnificent gift.

Kit Carson was the trapper who had led Captain John Fremont of the US Army Topographical Corps over the Sierra Nevada in 1844. Through his pass more than 3,000 waggonloads of settlers a year had toiled into California in all climatic conditions, suffering from cold, exposure, sickness and hunger. It was a chastening thought which reduced my own achievement, on a modern ten-speed bicycle after a night in a comfortable lakeside lodge, to its true proportions. There was a

monument to Kit Carson and beside it a less serious one to
Snowshoe Thompson, A True Pioneer. A granite column,
deliberately snapped off near the top, it was 'an emblem of that
life which was worn out apparently without an object' and had
been erected by the Transierra Roisterous Alliance of Senior
Humbugs and other equally comic donors.

It was all too good to last. Into that silent paradise roared a
well-meaning but garrulous couple. They leapt from their car,
asking me all the usual questions about my trip and my bicycle,
enthusing loudly, enquiring about my breakfast and offering to
share their thermos of soup with me. I shot through the pass.
The snowy pines of the Toiyabe National Forest melted into
the budding spring greenery of Hope Valley, where cowboys
were at work in the lush cattle country. Near Genoa I passed a
cemetery, all that was left of an early settlement where the first
white woman to travel West had made her home. Then I
cruised into Carson City, capital of Nevada. I had cleared my
first hurdle.

Carson City's population had doubled every decade since
1950 and its settlers played at The Wild West. Levis, check
shirts and high-heeled Western boots were topped with ten-
gallon hats or baseball caps, which were kept on indoors. Along
Highway 395, the main street, Cactus Jack's Megabuck, The
Carson Nugget, The Horseshoe Club and Sierra Sage offered
bar poker, pool, slots, shuffleboard and keno but behind the
strip of casinos and pawn shops was a different, tranquil world
of elegant wooden houses shaded by mature trees. The State
Capitol had a slim Doric portico, a lantern and a silver dome,
since Nevada was the Silver State. It was a pleasant city for a
short break. I rested through the heat of the day in my motel,
befriended by Loy, the manageress. I was such a 'gutsy lady'
that she charged me only the commercial rate, normally
reserved for truckers, and gave me free passes to dine in the
casinos. I lunched on bananas and cherries, took a siesta,
bought a new cycling cap and had a fine adjustment made to my
back wheel to cut out a bit of friction. My bicycle needed to be
in perfect shape for the Nevada Desert.

The Carson City Tourist Office were worried. 'There's real
serious desert out there.' Postcards showed a human skeleton

half buried in the sand: 'The traveller who didn't make it.' I was told there was *nothing* between Carson City and Fallon, 64 miles away. As I stood in the motel lobby drinking my morning coffee, they begged me not to go. Loy offered to drive me across the desert on her next day off.

I left at 6.45 in the morning chill and sprinted out of town to join Highway 50, which proclaimed itself on all the signs 'The Loneliest Highway in America'. I was prepared for utter desolation but the stretch to Fallon was less empty than I had expected. The occasional farmhouse and a few small settlements rose out of the sagebrush and cheat grass. At Silver Springs, a wretched cross-roads in a waste of grey grit desert where the locals had assured me there was *nothing*, I found two motels and even a saloon advertising 'Live Music. Dancing Weds and Sats.' I wondered who on earth came to such a god-forsaken hole to dance. Perhaps the spirits of the Forty-Niners from all those ghost towns marked on the map?

Cycling was exhilarating. At an altitude of 4,000 ft the air was crisp, the sky was blue and the excellent, empty tarmac unrolled into the far distance. I had left the California Trail at Carson City and was now travelling along the Pony Express route, speeding along like those daring riders who carried the mail between Sacramento and St Joseph, Missouri. 'Young, skinny, wiry fellows not over eighteen. Must be expert riders willing to risk death daily. Orphans preferred. Wages paid $25 a week.' Although the Pony Express operated for only eighteen months, between April 1860 and October 1861, it became one of the West's most romantic and potent legends. It went out of business four days after the completion of the transcontinental telegraph line.

The 114-mile stretch of Nevada Desert between Fallon and Austin really *was* serious – first sagebrush prairie, then salt flats; as most of Nevada lay in the Great Basin, its rivers flowed inwards to form salt sinks. The road climbed and I saw rolling cattle country not unlike the Anatolian Plateau, except that it was spring in Nevada, greener and less dusty. The colours were magnificent. Grey-green sagebrush, the colour of olive leaves, brilliant green grass dotted with yellow flowers like wild lupins and distant, purple mountains against a cloudless, powder-blue sky. The desert was a series of shallow valleys. A long, gradual descent led to an empty basin where the road was visible for miles and miles until it was lost over the next slow incline.

Three small places were marked on the map. After 30 miles I was confident that I should see Frenchman down in the next hollow, but when I got to the top of the long rise there were no buildings to be seen – just a continuation of the empty road leading to the next range of purple hills. I was disappointed, but not dismayed. It was still only ten o'clock and I had plenty of water left.

Middlegate, at a road junction 47 miles from Fallon, did exist: a bar, a filling station and a few mobile homes. I stopped in the bar for a coffee and a delicious ham and egg muffin and the owner told me that Frenchman had been pulled down two years ago. She had written to the authorities in Fallon, suggesting that they put up a notice on the outskirts, warning travellers that the next gas and supplies were 47 miles across the desert, not 30, since a number of people had got themselves into difficulties. They had accused her of trying to get free advertising and had done nothing, so cars were still getting stranded. She confirmed the existence of Cold Springs, fifteen miles further along the highway.

Historic Markers appeared at the roadside from time to time and I always got off to read them. It was easy to pull up on a bicycle; motorists were usually travelling too fast to stop. Just before Cold Springs, a green hollow in the purple hills, I found the stone ruins of a station which the Marker said had been a stagecoach stop on the Wells Fargo Line as well as a Pony Express Station. Cold Springs, the scene of fierce battles with the Pi-Ute Indians, had sheltered Sir Richard Burton in October 1860. 'The station was a wretched place half-built and wholly unroofed,' wrote the great Victorian traveller, but there was 'good water in a rivulet from the neighbouring hills'. More than a century later, Cold Springs was still offering food and drink to the traveller, together with a tank of petrol, the twentieth-century equivalent of a change of horses. There was a Highway Maintenance Post beside the filling station and a cluster of mobile homes. What the station no longer offered was accommodation, but I knew that I had to stay there: the valleys were like ovens in the afternoons and I was incapable of cycling another 50 miles under the burning sun. I ordered a coffee at the bar and enquired innocently about bed and breakfast, knowing quite well that there were no such facilities. Then I asked if I could spend the night on the bar floor. 'We can do better than that,' said Roni, the waitress. 'You can have the spare trailer next to mine. It's awful lonesome out there and I'll be glad of a bit of company.' The trailer was almost derelict, full of junk, empty Coke cans and cigarette ends, but there was a mattress on the floor and, unlike Burton, I had a roof over my head.

At six o'clock I went over to the bar and found it packed with cowboys. It was Saturday night and they were all there for their weekly celebration. I was immediately taken in hand by Cody, who bought me a beer and told me his life-story. He had been a computer software salesman with a wife, a Porsche and a home in Santa Clara, keeping up the pace with the help of cocaine. One day, before it was too late, he had just walked out, leaving the house, the Porsche and the bank balance to his wife and had come back to his roots in Nevada. Now he was working as a cowboy for $400 a month and his keep. He had managed to give up cocaine and was at peace with himself. He said that he recognised a fellow-spirit. As is the way with Americans, Cody had poured out his history and analysed his emotions and now he expected me to reciprocate. I was saved by his boss, who joined us at that point, paid for another round and told me about his 300,000-acre ranch. The cowboys were anxious about my safety and, as always, they mistrusted their neighbours. 'You'll be fine out here in the West. Everybody's real friendly and easy-going and you'll get no interference. But you watch out when you get East! They're not like us over there.' They wanted to buy me whisky with my chicken nuggets and French fries but I resisted. Three beers were enough for a cyclist with serious desert to cross. I slid out to my trailer for a chilly night under the desert moon, leaving Roni to cope with the cowboys and their whisky. Despite her late night, Roni banged on my trailer door just after dawn to tell me she was going to put on the coffee. She insisted on treating me to breakfast, obviously pleased to have someone, and that someone another woman, to talk to. She had come out to Cold Springs three weeks before to help a friend, but was finding it very lonely. She missed her family in Arizona. I gazed out at the grey grit desert and wondered how long a girl of her age would be able to stand it.

The next stage was shorter, though the passes were high. New Pass (6,348 ft) was a narrow, two-mile defile through towering rocks, invisible from the plains below – the perfect spot for an Indian ambush. A strong, chill wind rose up from the south and I knew it was bringing a storm. I pedalled hard up to Austin, a silver-mining town perched in the fold of a mountain, and got there an hour before the snow.

'We're having a real nasty spring,' said the motel owner. When I woke up to a blizzard and eight inches of snow on the ground at the end of May, I thought that was an under-statement. I holed up for two days, writing letters, doing crosswords, watching television and reading my history of India. Austin had one street. I listened to travellers' tales. A woman from San Francisco had cycled round the world, like me. She had phoned home to say that she was only two days away – and no one had seen or heard of her since. Most of the tales were similarly discouraging. The only one that cheered me was the one about the old man who used to walk from Austin to Eureka every week to visit his daughter, stay overnight and then walk back. Eureka was my next stop. If an old man could cover the 71 miles on foot, I could surely get there on a bicycle.

Austin Summit at 7,484 ft was the highest point on the next stage and Austin that week had more snow than any other place in Nevada. After three nights there a slight thaw began, so I decided to set out. If I managed to get over Austin Summit, my way would be clear; if not, it was only three miles back to the haven of the Mountain Motel. I piled on all my layers of clothing and plodded up past the silver and turquoise mines. The summit was deep in snow, but passable, as the snow-plough had cleared the road. I slid down the mountain to the sagebrush desert and the heat came up to meet me. It was a strange day. I went up and down like a yo-yo, piling on the layers for the snow-covered passes, then stripping down to a thin shirt for the hollows between. Eureka lay in a pass through the Diamond Mountains; I could see their peaks from 50 miles away. They produced a weird reflection on the asphalt, so that the hot shimmering road through the desert seemed to be covered in snow. The country was empty except for a few sheep. I survived on four cinnamon buns and my bottle of water. In Eureka, another one-street mining town where the wooden shopfronts had porticos and colonnades, I found the old Western hotel of my fantasies, a period piece, a survival from the great prospecting days. It was 31 May, the anniversary of my departure from London. I had cycled 71 miles over four mountain passes, in extremes of heat and cold, and still felt brisk enough to explore the town. What an improvement on the overweight, underfit creature who had struggled to cycle the 40 flat miles from St Paul's to Gillingham.

The road on to Ely was 78 miles, with four even higher passes, but by now I was confident enough to relish the prospect. Every day was a challenge and every evening a triumph. The spectacular scenery, the crisp mountain air and the solitude bathed and refreshed the spirit. My elation grew with my stamina and I bowled along, singing Tom Lehrer to the startled cattle: 'Mid the sagebrush and the thistles, I'll watch the guided missiles, While the old FBI watches me . . .'

In Ely I had my best meal in America. There was a large Basque community in the area and the Plaza Hotel and Restaurant were run by a splendid old Basque lady in a red and yellow pinafore. 'If anyone has the guts to cycle across the Nevada Desert, the least we can do is give her a good dinner.' And what a dinner it was. Fresh bread and butter, pungent cheese and a litre of red wine appeared first. Then a tureen of delicious vegetable soup, a grilled slice from a leg of lamb with petit pois, bacon, beans and chips and a bowl of salad. I had to pass on dessert and finished off with a morsel of cheese and another glass of wine. The food was subtly seasoned with herbs and I realised how much I was missing European cuisine. I stayed an extra day in Ely, just to eat another delectable dinner.

The next stretch looked unmanageable. It was 155 miles to Delta and, apart from Major's Place, 27 miles from Ely, there was nothing marked on the map. Would I have to break my record after all and hitch a lift? The waiter at the Plaza said he thought he had seen a motel on the Nevada/Utah border. To my delight, the Tourist Office confirmed it and I knew then that I could complete Nevada under my own steam.

It was very hot again so I set off early, before the pale moon had set. Sentimental Western music flooded the café on the outskirts of Ely, washing over the hectically coloured posters of Jesus, Marilyn Monroe, a horned owl, two white kittens in red bows, a stag at bay and a teddy bear in sunglasses, grey jumper and red leggings throwing snowballs. On the window sill beside me were plaster figurines of two horned owls, two Red Indians, a pheasant and Jesus in His crown of thorns. The coffee and pancakes were good. Then I was out in the desert again with the wind whistling through the sagebrush and the cycle spokes, the chirping of unseen birds, crickets and the occasional sonic boom. A bullet-riddled roadsign near four or five scattered mobile homes said 'Congested Area. No Shooting.' I passed a Shoshone Indian Reserve, a scrappy village of trailers and wooden homes no different in appearance from the other small settlements in the area. The ranches here were a far cry from *Dallas*.

The forecast I heard in the Border Motel was a continuation of the unseasonable heat, with temperatures due to rise above 100°F in Utah, and a strong south wind. I considered waiting to see if the weather would improve but the prospect of a whole day in a motel in the middle of the desert was unappealing. I set my alarm for four, got breakfast in the 24-hour restaurant and tucked away as many cans of fruit juice as I could find corners in my baggage. It was 90 miles to Delta and the road was absolutely empty. When I left Nevada at the motel exit and crossed from Pacific to Mountain Time, the sun was still so low that each grain of sand was casting its shadow.

Looking back, I wonder how I got through that day. I travelled east-south-east at first, so that the wind from the south gusted diagonally across me, crashing against my panniers and throwing me off balance; I found it slightly less tiring if I tacked from side to side across the traffic-free road. After a long climb through the Confusion Range, the road turned south and I rode straight into the teeth of the wind. Flying sand cut into my face and I had to cover it with my red silk balaclava and dark glasses.

I looked like Batman. There were mile-posts and between each
pair of posts were twelve road-side markers with reflectors. I
kept myself going by counting each twelve markers and at each
mile-post I would allow myself four sips of liquid and a short
rest. There were ten miles of this slow, agonising toil before the
road turned east again through King Canyon and the Skull
Rock Pass. I learned later that the temperature had risen to
110°.

By early afternoon, I was out of liquid. My only hope was to
flag down a camper, an RV (recreational vehicle), as they are
known in the States. Campers always carry water – and they are
safe: the world's criminals rarely travel in them. They usually
have young families on board or retired couples. I stood in the
burning sun, choosing a small rise from which I could see a long
way in both directions and I waited. Ten minutes went by;
fifteen minutes; and still the road was empty. Then the unmistakable bulk of a large RV lumbered over the horizon. I rushed
into the middle of the road and waved my arms. The RV flashed
its lights and began to slow down. I was in luck. There were two
bicycles hooked to the front. I had chanced on a couple of
fellow-cyclists, returning to California after a holiday in Colorado. Their RV was air-conditioned and I spent a blissful
twenty minutes in its cool interior. I drank a whole jug of water
without pause, then an icy Coca Cola from the fridge. It was
nectar! I filled my water bottle and set out again. The road
turned north-east and soon I was speeding along the last 40
miles to Delta with the power of the wind for once at my back.
When I enquired the rate at the first motel I came to, the
proprietor said, '$18.53 – unless you're a Senior, in which case
it's $15.' I certainly felt like a Senior after 90 miles of desert and
I undoubtedly looked like one, but sadly I was too young to
qualify for the discount.

After the exhilaration of Nevada, the Utah Desert with its
low, barren hills seemed dull, scrubby and stifling. It took me
another two days to struggle across to Salt Lake City and a day's
rest to unwind when I got there. As I took my ease in that green
oasis, I thought cycling could never be quite such an adventure
again. I had conquered the desert, my second major American
hurdle.

17

The Oregon Trail

SALT LAKE CITY – HEBER CITY – VERNAL –
STEAMBOAT SPRINGS – FORT COLLINS – JULESBURG
– NORTH PLATTE – FORT KEARNEY – MARYSVILLE –
ST JOSEPH – FORT MADISON – NAUVOO

And the desert shall rejoice and blossom as the rose.

(Isaiah)

WHEN the Americans moved West in their search for land and religious freedom, they colonised the continent in waves, spreading first from the eastern seaboard to the crest of the Appalachians; then to the eastern Mississippi region; then from the Mississippi to the edge of the Great Plains. There settlement stopped. The arid, treeless, windswept plains with their extremes of climate were as forbidding as the Rockies beyond. And their Indian tribes were the most formidable in America. They had learned the use of the horse from the Spanish Americans and, until the invention of the Colt six-shooter, the settlers were no match for them. Families in search of a new life had only one option – to move in convoy across these dangerous, inhospitable lands to the Pacific and settle beyond them in the rich farming country of Oregon.

That was the start of the Oregon Trail. The first wagon-train crossed the Great Plains in 1830, the first missionary in 1834 and the first women, Narcissa Whitman and Eliza Spalding, in 1836. Between 1840 and 1866, two and a half million settlers hitched their ox-wagons for the 2,000-mile journey. They assembled on the banks of the Missouri at Independence, Kansas City or St Joseph, where major conurbations grew up to meet their requirements. They travelled up the Little Blue river, along the south bank of the North Platte river, up the

Sweetwater river, over the Continental Divide at South Pass, then down the Snake and Columbia rivers to the Oregon seaboard. Forts were set up along the route to provide military protection, safety overnight within the stockades, supplies and services. The California Trail, the Pony Express route, the Mormon Trail and the Overland Stage route followed the Oregon Trail, with variations, as far as the Sweetwater river before branching off to their different destinations.

In Salt Lake City I was at the end of the Mormon Trail. The Mormons were the outcasts among the migrants. Hounded out of their homes in Nauvoo on the Mississippi, they had crossed the Missouri at Omaha, travelled along the north bank of the North Platte river to avoid friction with the other pioneers, and settled on land that no one else wanted, the desert beside the Great Salt Lake. There they followed their beliefs and practised their polygamy without interference. Under the leadership of Brigham Young (who had 26 wives and 56 children), they survived by making friends with the Ute Indians and damming the rivers to provide irrigation. Their desert blossomed into a wealthy, fertile state.

Salt Lake City and its surrounding agricultural land was a miracle of green shade in that blazing summer of 1988. Juab, Jericho, Abraham, the Jordan river, Mount Nebo . . . As the names intended, I thought of the Promised Land. I arrived in time for the Gina Bachauer International Piano Competition, and air-conditioned Mozart added to my pleasure in revisiting what must be the friendliest, cleanest and safest city in the United States.

From Salt Lake City my next hurdle, the Rockies, was all too plainly visible. I cycled out up Emigration Canyon, past the monument overlooking the city on the spot where Brigham Young had declared, 'This is the place.' I was toiling on up the steep hill when a jogger appeared, coasting down towards me with long, easy strides. As our paths crossed, he shouted, 'Ya gonna make it, baby!' I was inordinately cheered. It seemed like a prophecy. From that moment, with 8,500 miles behind me and only about 3,000 left, I began to feel that my goal was in sight, that I really would make it.

I had only one possible route across Utah and the Rockies

and unfortunately it was not the Oregon Trail. As the trail was still the easiest route, following the line of least resistance, it had developed into one of the main roads West, a freeway prohibited to cyclists. I had to take Highway 40, which ran further south. It was a road which climbed up steeply from the Great Salt Lake, soon reaching 8,000 ft at Daniels Pass. Since I retained altitude through the Uinta National Forest and the Colorado Desert, the Rockies were not nearly such hard work as the Sierra Nevada. My highest pass, at 10,276 ft, was at the top of a gradual climb of only a few thousand feet, whereas the Sierra Nevada had risen from sea level to 8,573 ft in two arduous days' cycling.

My problem was the unpredictable wind. America was having freak weather. Meteorological reports showed that the current of air which should have brought wind and rain straight across the central States from the West Coast to the East was, for some reason, dividing into two, one stream curving north and the other south, so that even Arizona and Texas were getting more westerly winds and more rain than the centre: between the two streams there was drought and turbulence. When I should have had the wind behind me all the way, it blew from the east for days on end. If I turned north or south and hoped for a respite, it would veer capriciously to blow into my face again. It was always strong and it always seemed to be against me. Mountains are predictable and inevitable. Wind is unfair and I bitterly resented it. Without my red balaclava, gloves, long sleeves, trousers and long socks to protect my skin, I should have shrivelled to a walnut in its hot, pitiless blast.

Climbs up pretty canyons of oak, lime and silver birch were followed by expanses of high, open grassland, where the wind howled and raged. I had to pedal hard, even downhill. 'You need a lot of mental stamina for a trip like this,' was one apt comment that came my way. After Roosevelt the greenery ended and I was back in desert with red sandstone outcrops and swirling dust. It was here that I got my fifth puncture. A man in a ten-gallon hat and a pick-up truck ran me the five miles into Vernal. As the hard shoulders were rough, I played safe, buying a new inner tube and using my one remaining spare tyre to replace the one which had worn bald. It was only my third rear tyre and fourth inner tube.

I was now in dinosaur land. Tourists were flocking to the Vernal Garden Museum where life-sized models of prehistoric monsters peered through the foliage. The model brontosauri, stegosauri and tyrannosauri reges were much more fun than the skeletons in most museums and I could see why the place was a mecca for children. Dinosaurs were big business: in a town named Dinosaur, you could even dine on brontoburgers. Just over the Colorado border, in the Dinosaur National Park, I visited the Morrison Formation, a rockface where the public watched from an observation platform while palaeontologists excavated fossilised monster bones. It was an enormous fossil graveyard. At the entrance to the park stood the Dinosaur National Monument. It was somehow so pompous that I had a vision of dinosaurs laying down their lives for their country.

When I talked to motorists they complained of the boring, empty desert, but crawling along as I did, I found it full of interest and variety. The prairie dogs stood on their hind legs by their burrows, cheeping loudly to warn neighbours of my approach. The danger signal was passed along the highway from burrow to burrow, like a desert telegraph. It was ironic that they were far more worried about a harmless cyclist than they were about the motorists who mowed them down in their hundreds. The carnage on the road was depressing. Deer, skunks, jack rabbits, racoons and swarms of cannibalistic brown grasshoppers. Living creatures were harder to find and spotting a scampering jack rabbit in the scrub would leave me feeling pleased with myself for hours. Above all, I had chanced on the brief springtime of the desert, those few glorious days when tall yellow desert plumes, purple lupins, the white evening primrose with its yellow centre, and red and yellow cactus flowers carpet the desert floor. My reward for endurance, I thought.

When I reached the Rockies' green trees and rich pastures, where fat cattle and beautiful horses grazed among the wild irises and lupins, I knew I was starting to climb in earnest. In Steamboat Springs, a popular winter ski resort, the Pioneer Museum had a section devoted to the history of the sport.

Women in long skirts and felt hats posed for the camera in rows of sepia prints. Their cheerful determination to ski, despite the inconvenience of their clothing, brought to mind one of the quips at that year's Democratic Party Convention: 'Ginger Rogers could do everything Fred Astaire did – *and* she did it backwards in high heels!'

After a lovely ride up the Yampa valley, through the Routt National Forest, I was amazed to find myself soaring over the Continental Divide almost without effort. I was so used to cycling by now that mountains were scarcely more arduous than the flat: I just changed gear and kept on pedalling. To my considerable satisfaction, I climbed right over the Rockies without once having to get off and push. In fact, the altitude seemed to affect me more when I was not cycling. Walking about in the evenings, my legs felt leaden, I panted, my heartbeat was intrusive and I was always on the verge of a headache. All these symptoms disappeared as soon as I got on my bicycle – or perhaps I just forgot about them. The Rabbit Ears Pass up at 9,426 ft was the place where I crossed the Continental Divide, though even that was not the highest point on my trip. I still had the Cameron Pass to face, at 10,276 ft, more than 2,000 ft higher than the Great St Bernard.

Switching to Highway 14, I spent the night in Walden. There the tiny Michigan river ran down to meet the equally tiny North Platte, the stream which would swell to become the major river on the Oregon Trail. Notices in the town listed the creatures we were permitted to shoot – deer, elk, black bear, mountain sheep and sage grouse. Fishing was also allowed. The restaurant was full of men in cowboy hats and spurs talking about hunting while their wives and children in shorts got on with their dinners. Colorado seemed a holiday paradise for these shooting men, but I wondered how their wives passed their days.

The day I climbed my highest mountain was one of my most idyllic. There was no wind in the morning and I rode for miles in the spring sunshine through meadows of lupins and yellow wallflowers. A stiff ten-mile pull took me up to the top of the Cameron Pass, where a solitary RV was parked. I asked for water and was offered a lunch of chilli dogs and coffee as well.

Just as we were starting our al fresco meal the wind got up, swift clouds scudded across the sky and it began to rain. We retreated into the RV and watched in amazement as the rain turned to snow, then to hailstones the size of marbles. The weather had changed in an instant. Once again, I seemed to be a charmed traveller. Had I not found the Baileys and been invited to lunch, I should have been out in those bouncing hailstones with nowhere to shelter.

My enemy, the wind, was icy at that altitude. When the sky cleared and I began my descent, I needed balaclava, gloves and all my layers to keep frostbite at bay. The first half-hour was alarming, with ice on the road and a steep gradient, but then the descent became more gentle, the sun reappeared and I cruised downhill the whole afternoon, following the Cache La Poudre river as it crashed over rocks through tall, narrow canyons and on through smiling valleys. I freewheeled for 50 glorious miles through the Roosevelt National Park. For once, there were live animals; I saw deer, a chipmunk, prairie dogs and a beaver. As evening fell, I found a small two-roomed cabin overlooking the river and a cheerful restaurant beside it, run by two girls under the supervision of an elegant Siamese cat. I slept easily. I had left my half-headache and thumping heart behind in the high Rockies and had only the sound of rushing water for company. Next day I reached Fort Collins and picked up a splendid pile of letters from American Express. I had cleared my third hurdle.

I was already six days ahead of schedule. Fifty miles between stops had been the very minimum across the magnificent emptiness of my first four states. The way ahead looked flatter, more populous and possibly rather dull. I decided to smarten the pace deliberately, to get even further ahead: an average of 60 miles a day, six days a week, would reduce my crossing from twelve weeks to ten and that would save me money as well as time. America was less expensive than England and northern Europe but it was still hard to keep within my budget. In any case, even if living had been the cheapest in the world, I should still have wanted to cross the continent quickly. The spectacular part was behind me and after more than a year on the road I was beginning to look forward to home.

I made an excellent start next day, achieving my record

mileage for the whole trip – 105 miles across the Pawnee National Grasslands to Sterling. It was easier riding on the Great Plains, though I had to shelter in a café until the afternoon temperature dropped from 98° to 90°. Colorado was one of the few states not suffering from drought and the farmers were rubbing their hands at the prospect of extra profit from their flourishing maize and wheat. At Julesburg on the South Platte river I joined up again with the Pony Express and the Overland Stage route and followed them across Nebraska to the town of North Platte, where I finally met the Oregon Trail. I stopped to read a wayside Historical Marker on the outskirts of town and suddenly felt so faint that I had to crouch with my head between my knees. I learned afterwards that the temperature was 109° at the time.

I was now in the land of legend. From North Platte I visited Scout's Rest, the ranch of William Frederick Cody, 'Buffalo Bill'. At fourteen, Cody started work as a Pony Express rider out of Julesburg. He earned his title when he was employed by the Kansas Pacific Railroad to scout for Indians and provide the railroad crews with meat. He won a $500 bet in 1869 by killing 69 buffalo in eight hours. He invented the rodeo and took his Wild West Show on tour throughout America and Europe, making and losing several fortunes in the process. Scout's Rest was a museum of the Wild West as well as a home. I was delighted to find an old photograph of one of his star attractions, Annie Oakley, reading outside her tent with her famous rifle propped up – against a bicycle. And she *did* get a man with a gun, contrary to the words of the song. Frank Butler, a well-known target-shooter, lost by one pigeon when the fifteen-year-old Annie challenged him at a Thanksgiving Day Match in Cincinnati. A year later they were married and Butler retired from shooting to become Annie's manager.

Cody's invention was still alive and well. The state was celebrating 'Nebraskaland Days' and there was a big rodeo and county fair in North Platte. I watched a cattle-penning competition. A team of three cowboys rounded up a group of calves and drove them into a pen. Then the startled little things were driven out of the pen by a steward, only to be driven back in again by another trio of cowboys. This went on all afternoon, to the beasts' increasing bewilderment.

But for all the noise of the rodeos, 'Nebraska, where Corn is King and Alfalfa Queen' was a worried, sun-stricken state. The corn and alfalfa were shrivelling in the fields, the fish were dying of heat and lack of oxygen in the shallows of the normally strong-flowing Platte and the churches were praying for rain. I burnt my hand quite badly on a motel door-knob and though I managed to keep on cycling, I had no energy to do anything in the afternoons but lie on my bed in a darkened room and watch television. Fortunately, it was Wimbledon, which made a change from that inexplicable American passion, baseball – grown men in Victorian underwear playing rounders.

As the Platte river route was the easiest and most obvious crossing of the Great Plains, it was the line chosen for the railway. The Union Pacific kept me company along Highway 30, and Historical Markers stood on the sites of battles between the construction teams and the Cheyenne Indians. The Indians rightly foresaw that improved communications along 'The Great Medicine Road of the Whites' would bring even more settlers into their lands and they fought bitterly for their prairies and their way of life. But construction went on, despite the battles, the ambushes and the scalpings. In May 1869, the Central Pacific from the west coast joined up with the Union Pacific from Nebraska at Promontory Summit, Utah, and migration west transferred to the train. It was the end of the Oregon Trail.

It was also the beginning of the last major wave of settlement. The railway brought coal to the Great Plains, access to markets for cattle and grain, and speedy transport for the militia to deal with Indian attacks. In a drive to people the last empty spaces, railway and steamship companies advertised in northern Europe, offering land on credit as well as reduced passenger fares and free transport of household goods. Germans, Swedes, Norwegians, Danes and Irish flooded in, giving a northern European stamp to the Last Frontier. Settlements grew up along the railway line, usually twelve or fifteen miles apart. They are still there and they all look alike. The Farmers' Cooperative Association grain silo and the huge rotating drums to dry out the alfalfa stood beside the railway station. There was a gas station opposite, a café or bar and a small cluster of wooden houses and mobile homes. Sometimes there was a church of one of the stricter Protestant sects. Sometimes there was a general store, or even a row of shops, but they were usually boarded up: everyone had a car and drove to the city to shop. The land undulated so slightly that only a cyclist would notice. Grassland alternated with arable, hundreds of miles of dying wheat and corn. As I cycled out of one small town I could see the silo of the next shimmering in the heat ahead of me. Within fifteen minutes the water in my bottle would be hot enough to brew tea and only the thought of the ice-cold Pepsi in the next café kept me going.

I was often the only living creature on that burning Nebraska highway. The drivers on the Union Pacific were as delighted to see me as I was to see them. We broke each other's monotony. As the huge freight trains came into sight, sometimes with as many as 140 cars (I counted them to have something to do), their mournful sirens would wail a greeting and a waving hand would appear from the driver's window. Then all was emptiness again. If the wind was against me or across me, I would work out the number of pedal revolutions to a mile in different gears. Counting and calculating helped me along. On the one magic day when the wind was behind me I added a new cycling tune to my repertoire – a speeded-up version of the Radetsky March.

'I guess you get tired of all these motels.' 'I bet you can't wait to get back home, to get back into your own kitchen.' 'I bet you can't wait to sleep in your own bed again.' How wrong they all were. I had spent the night in almost 400 hotels, rarely sleeping in the same bed for two nights running, and yet I never tired of the life. Each evening I unpacked my pannier in a new bedroom, glad to be there and feeling as if I had come home. And after years of family cooking, eating in restaurants, whatever the standard of the food, was infinitely preferable to shopping, cooking and washing up afterwards. I *was* weary of the heat and the constant effort of travelling. I wanted to be still again. But I could be still just as happily in a motel as in my own home. My journey had taught me to feel safe and easy anywhere. Security had become a state of mind, not a familiar building to hide in. It was interesting that American women always asked, 'Aren't you scared?' while the invariable question from American men was 'Aren't you lonesome?'

I visited Fort Kearney, the oldest fort on the Oregon Trail, a home station for the Pony Express and the base of the Pawnee Scouts. It had been reconstructed to form a State Historical Park, with replicas of the original buildings. I remember little of the site, as my elderly companion took all my attention. He attached himself to me near the entrance and told me he had come to Kearney from Kansas for a high school reunion. He had never been back to his school since the day he left and obviously had very cold feet about the gathering in prospect. Would anyone he knew still be alive? Would he recognise them if they were? Would they recognise him? What on earth would he talk to them about? He was a very modest man, so I tried to bolster him up. I told him I had been a headmistress and knew from experience that old students usually felt nervous when they went back to school for the first time after a long gap but that once they had broken the ice, they had a marvellous time and were glad they had plucked up courage. He followed me round the stockade, the parade ground and the reconstructed stores, talking his problem through and looking for encouragement. I cycled out of Kearney, reflecting that no nation is quite so confiding as the Americans. They have to discuss their problems and any ear will do.

I turned south at Kearney, leaving the North Platte river and crossing a corner of Kansas. Inevitably, the wind was from the south until I turned east at Marysville, when the wind turned too and blew at 25 mph directly against me. The daytime temperature never fell below 100°. If Homer had known about bicycles, he would have devised another punishment for the souls of the damned in Hades – cycling for all eternity under a blazing sun along a straight, treeless road into the teeth of a hot, wild wind. I never doubted that I should make the crossing, but why did it have to be so hard?

Kansas made up for its weather by the warmth of its wonderful people. The owner of my Marysville motel had been based in Suffolk with the USAF during the Second World War. He got out all his photographs to show me and came to my room in the evening with a huge slice of his wife's newly baked angel cake and some special hickory-smoked cheese for me to try. He was a cyclist too; his ambition was to cross Kansas from north to south in three ways – on a bicycle, on a horse (he showed me his English saddle with pride) and jogging. The old lady who seemed to live in the next motel room to mine came to my door with a jug of iced tea as I was unpacking my bicycle, and the cheerful waitress who served my pancakes at 6 a.m. next morning said, 'You enjoy them now!' and smiled at me as if she meant it. A notice behind her counter read, 'Sure, God created man first. But then, you always make a rough model before producing the PERFECT EXAMPLE.'

Sunday in Kansas was dry, as I discovered when I went into a filling station to buy my evening beer. I had dreamed of that chilled beer all through the heat of the day. The proprietor apologised. 'I know it's a dumb law, but I didn't make it.' We were overheard by a young man in regulation Levis and baseball cap who dived out to his truck and returned with two cans of beer from his icebox, which he insisted on giving to me. 'Now ain't that a real nice Kansas boy!' said the proprietor. I was the first person they had ever met from London, England, and they declared they would do anything for my accent. It was always a winner in the States. Even a gang of rip-roaring Hell's Angels displayed the same old-world courtesy. They slouched over in my direction, thumbs stuck in leather jacket pockets. Five were long-haired and the sixth had a shaven skull and I watched their approach with some apprehension. 'You crossin' the States on that bike or sumpin'?' asked Yul Brynner. When they heard about my travels, one of the long hairs said, 'Wow! You really are some great lady. It's a privilege meeting you, ma'am.' And they all queued up to give me a respectful handshake.

Hebron, Seneca, Hiawatha, Troy. I loved the place names. In Troy, Kansas, I amused myself by taking some photographs to place beside my pictures of Troy of the Trojans. It was a typical small town with a row of shops and a neo-Classical town hall. Everyone stopped to talk to me and immediately I entered the café, the owner of *The Kansas Chief*, the oldest newspaper in the state, came rushing along to interview me.

St Joseph was a Victorian Newcastle-under-Lyme which proclaimed 'Jesus is King of Our Town' on a giant hoarding. I crossed 'the wide Missouri'. It was a great moment, though the river had shrunk in the drought to a miserable stream among sandbanks. The only hotel quoted me $47. 'Oh dear!' I said. As there was no choice I was just about to accept, when the receptionist told me he could do it for $27. I took the room gratefully and spent two luxurious nights there.

St Joseph's Robidoux Landing was one of the starting points for the Oregon Trail. It was also the start of the Pony Express route. I visited the main stables and the Patee Hotel, once the Pony Express headquarters. The hotel is now a museum of the great pioneer days and the best one I saw in the States, with everything from early railcars to bawdy house tokens: 'Good for one screw. Madame Ruth Jacobs Prop.' The reconstructed Buffalo Saloon, where I drank my morning Pepsi, carried the warning: 'This is a High Class Place. Please Act Respectable.' But modern St Joseph was a far cry from that bustling, prosperous frontier town. A brightly painted river boat, *The Spirit of St Joseph*, was moored at the Robidoux Landing, but the city itself had lost its spirit and its sense of purpose. The elegantly pedestrianised centre was empty and all the shops boarded up. I passed one sandwich shop but no stores where I could buy my own provisions. The huge Queen of the Apostles Roman Catholic church dominated the city from its hilltop, but when I climbed up there I found it was all façade. Its twin Gothic spires gave height and the impression of grandeur to a modest building, which was only eighteen pews deep. It seemed symbolic of a depressing city.

Missouri, where I crossed from Mountain to Central Time, was my next state and I soon renamed it 'Misery'. It really was my low point in the States. Drivers were unused to cyclists and were aggressive on the road, shouting, jeering and blaspheming at me out of the windows of their broken-down jalopies. The landscape was a close succession of stunted sugarloaf hills, difficult to cycle. The descents were too short to take me up the following climb and if I did manage to gain momentum, there was invariably a rickety bridge down in the dip with such an uneven surface that I should have gone flying over the handlebars had I tried to take it at speed. It was high glacial prairie land with sheep on the hills and miles of wind-torn, treeless desolation. Furthermore, it turned cold and rained, though not enough to break the drought. I opened one eye in the mornings to the grey sky and one ear to the howling wind and was tempted to stay in bed, but the motels offered only *Hog Extra* and *Farm Journal* and the local food was execrable. I pined for fruit and fresh vegetables. There was nothing for it but to grit my teeth and persevere.

To add to my problems, there were dangerous dogs. Unexpectedly, I had more trouble with guard dogs in these parts than anywhere else in the world. Dogs dislike bicycles and I had been really afraid of attack by savage brutes in Anatolia or mangy, rabid strays out East. At a party in Ankara, I had told a Turkish cyclist I was terrified of meeting a sheepdog in eastern Turkey. I knew they wore leather collars with long steel spikes, as they had to protect their flocks from wolves, and they were trained to be very aggressive. He had given me extremely useful advice, based on experience. 'Never try to escape, because they're much faster than you are. They'll grab you by the ankle and pull you down. The only thing to do is face up to them. Get off your bike and put it between yourself and the dog. He won't attack you through the bike, because it's the bike he's afraid of. Speak to him gently. As soon as he sees your two legs, smells you and hears your voice, he'll realise that you're a human being – and he isn't trained to attack humans, unless they're actually interfering with his flock. He has his work to do and he'll soon turn round and go back to his sheep. If he doesn't calm down, it will be only a matter of moments before the shepherd arrives to see what the trouble is and meanwhile you'll be safe behind your bicycle.' It had all sounded so sensible that I had gained confidence immediately. In fact, I had been lucky in the East and had never had to practise the technique. It was in the Midwestern States that I was attacked. Alsatians, Dobermans, Rottweilers, terriers, even snappy little dachshunds, all came tearing out of their farmyards as I cycled past, barking furiously or snarling through great, bared teeth. The farmhouses stood alone on the plains, miles from their neighbours, and I could see that they needed protection, but their protectors were sometimes really ferocious. To my relief, the technique worked and I rendered up thanks to my Turkish friend after every close encounter with a horrible hound.

Over the border into Iowa the sun came out again. I followed the Mormon Trail to the Mississippi, crossing that depleted river at Fort Madison, then following it down the Illinois bank to Nauvoo. For me it was the end of a trail which had started in San Francisco. As I toured the reconstructed Mormon town, I reflected that I had probably come as near as a modern traveller could to those epic journeys of the nineteenth century. The physical effort of cycling 2,300 miles across mountains, deserts and prairies in harsh climatic conditions had given me a real feeling for the enormous achievement of those early pioneers, who had toiled with their creaking ox-wagons or laden hand-carts across the immense landscape, braving Indian attack, natural disasters, cholera, hunger, thirst and exposure to open up the West. Although, by their standards, I had done it in comparative comfort and safety, I had still done it, every mile of it, by my own effort. I had done it the hard way.

18

The Cumberland Pike

NAUVOO – PEORIA – MARION – FORT RECOVERY –
GRANVILLE – ZANESVILLE – BARNESVILLE –
WHEELING – UNIONTOWN – SOMERSET – BEDFORD
– CHAMBERSBURG – GETTYSBURG – YORK –
LANCASTER – KING OF PRUSSIA – LAMBERTSVILLE –
NEW YORK

It's dogged as does it. It ain't thinking about it.
(Anthony Trollope)

ILLINOIS and Indiana were much like Missouri and Iowa.
Though they had been settled earlier, their people came of
the same Teutonic and Nordic stock. Tall, blond and well-
built, they had grown positively huge on America's plenty. You
need to visit the Midwest to know what real obesity is. Giants of
both sexes with giant children shambled through the shopping
malls, munching hot dogs, chips and ice creams and swilling
down litre cartons of diet coke – to help them lose weight. Their
thighs were so fat they could no longer walk with legs parallel,
but had them splayed out in isosceles triangles. Their arms
stuck out semi-horizontally, resting on their rolling hips.

'All you can eat for $3.99.' I ordered the pork chop special
and the waitress brought me two huge chops, a huge baked
potato, three sorts of vegetable, a huge salad and my own
private, personal loaf on its own breadboard, with a bowl of
butter served out in ice-cream scoops. Roast rib of beef was just
that – a thick rib all to myself, a complete family joint. I was
encouraged to finish off with a few bits of fried chicken from the
buffet or a couple of barbecued spare ribs. Then what about the
desserts? Surely I wanted a selection of those? They were meals
fit for an ogress. Even the ice creams defeated me; I could only
manage kiddikones. As I sat before the groaning table, I would
sometimes think of the Guptas' evening meal in Gyanpur and
feel ashamed of such gluttony.

The Fourth of July 1988 was a tense day. The small communities had little to celebrate anyway. The drought was killing their crops and closing stretches of their life-line, the Mississippi, to river traffic. Even the traditional fireworks were banned in many states because of the fire risk. Then, on the eve of Independence Day, came the dreadful news that the American Navy had shot down an Iranian passenger aircraft over the Strait of Hormuz, mistaking it for a fighter. A stillness seemed to fall over the land, compounded of sorrow, guilt and fear. Would the Ayatollah exact some wildly disproportionate revenge? As Independence Day passed without retribution, we all began to breathe a little more freely. I celebrated by watching the city firework display over Peoria Lake. Next day I was laid low with a migraine. My body, which is far more sensible than I am, had had enough of the heat and the strain and decided to keep me supine in bed until supper-time.

I was really pushing myself now, cycling anything from 75 to 90 miles every day. I though I was doing well until I was overtaken by a young architect from New York, who was averaging 150. I was interviewed by the press or local radio in a succession of small towns – 'Grandmother of Seven Cycles Across States!' – 'The Cycling Grandmother' – and I had a recurrence of my Malaysian athlete's foot. Otherwise, my days were uneventful. No challenge, no adrenalin – just more miles to get under the wheels. I knew I had finally left the West behind when I crossed into Ohio and Eastern Time. Men no longer wore their hats indoors.

In Fort Recovery, on the border, there was only one place to stay, an old fashioned bar/restaurant which offered 'sleeping rooms'. Mine had no window but it was air-conditioned and cheap. My neighbours, with whom I shared the bathroom and the television lounge, were two young telephone engineers. Next morning I found them both asleep on the lounge floor, fully dressed and surrounded by empty beer cans. They had not found the energy to go to bed. It was the day a runway at Dayton International Airport buckled in the heat. After dinner in the downstairs restaurant, the speeding waitress found a few moments to join me at my table. 'I just wanted to come and thank you. You've transformed my life,' she announced. As I sat in startled silence, she told me her story. She had just gone through a very bitter divorce. Her ex-husband was unemployed and unable to pay her any maintenance, so she was working weeks in a factory and weekends in the restaurant to support herself and her children. Life was very hard and she had thought everything was over for her. Then she had met me and heard what I was managing to do – at my age and on my own – and had decided that if I could do it, so could she. She was going to start acting positively and planning her future. Her family had originally come from Italy and she had always wanted to go there. In ten years' time, her children would be off her hands. 'If I start saving now, even if it's only a couple of dollars a week, I can go off on a long trip to Italy and visit all my relations.' Her face was alight with happiness and enthusiasm. I gave her a good tip to start off her savings account. Even if she never got to Italy, she had a dream which would help her through the difficult years. I felt amazed at the impact I had made, and very humble. The waitress in Fort Recovery was the most voluble, but there were many others who felt similarly inspired. There was the sprightly old lady who told me she had always wanted to walk the Appalachian Trail but had decided she was past it. Having met me, she had changed her mind: if I could cycle all the way round the world, she could certainly walk a miserable thousand miles or so. Usually, such people were small-town Americans who rarely travelled outside their own state and had never had a conversation with a foreigner before. They asked me questions about the food we ate in Europe, the kind of hotels we had, how much things cost and whether people were friendly. I loved watching their anxieties clear until the moment when they would suddenly decide to take the plunge. They would go to Europe next year! I felt like a cycling gad-fly, stinging them into visions of a wider world.

I had a sociable time in Ohio. In Zanesville I tripped over the edge of a grate in the hotel drive and hurt my knee. In that litigious land my accident struck terror into the hearts of the management. I was offered free medical treatment and free accommodation until my knee improved, so I had a restful couple of days, reclining on my bed, and having long conversations with the friendly receptionist over complimentary coffees in the lobby. In Barnesville, I booked into a Victorian bed and breakfast and soon found myself helping my hostess and her mother prepare for a charity supper and concert in the Memorial Park. Nancy was Chairman of the Friends of a local retirement home and this was their major annual fund-raising event. I loaded cakes and pies into the car, set out tables and chairs by the lake and helped with the serving. It was a lovely, balmy evening, with a gentle breeze drifting over the lake. After the concert by Queen Anne's Lace, I was invited onto the stage to draw the raffle. Everyone was wonderfully welcoming and I felt very much a part of the community. I had come in from the outside, no longer the detached observer. Nancy would take no payment for my room and she arranged for me to spend the next night with her sister Luella and family on the Ohio river: there was a big country and western festival in the hills above Wheeling and she doubted if I should find a hotel room. Across the Ohio lay West Virginia. 'You mind how you go,' said Tommy, Luella's son. 'They're real hillbillies over there, not like us here in Ohio. You watch your bicycle!'

Ohio had been a transition state. One foot was still in the West: cowboy clothes, country and western music and giant Bible Belt churches, quite out of proportion to the size of the towns. But the lakes of yellow waterlilies and the green, wooded hills had signalled the approach of the Appalachians, America's eastern mountain chain. I had joined Highway 40 at Zanesville. On the map it had dots along it, indicating that it was considered 'scenic'. From experience, I knew that really meant 'hilly'.

Highway 40, the National Road or Cumberland Pike, was the oldest federal road in the United States. Originally a buffalo trail used by the Indians, it was widened to a wagon route during the second wave of westward migration, from the crest of the Appalachians to the banks of the Mississippi. The victories of Forbes and Wolfe over the French, leading to the Treaty of Paris in 1763, removed the French barrier to expansion into the Mississippi basin and settlers poured up the Potomac river to Cumberland, then took the old trail west to Wheeling on the Ohio and on to the Mississippi at St Louis. Jefferson had a vision of an all-weather macadamised road to cater for their

needs and Congress began to set funds aside and survey the
route in 1808. By 1815 the road ran from Cumberland to
Wheeling but it took until 1852 to travel through Columbus and
Indianapolis to Vandelia. The State of Illinois finally completed the stretch to St Louis. The road was built of crushed
rock with a gravel surface and sloping sides for drainage. As I
cycled along its modern asphalt, I passed the original
milestones and tollhouses, the bridges, taverns and stables.
They were built of grey stone and were Georgian in style. In an
hour I had cycled out of the Victorian West into the Georgian
East, out of the West Virginian panhandle into the Commonwealth of Pennsylvania.

I climbed the Appalachians. They were hard cycling, especially
as my knee was still painful after my fall. Running from north-
east to south-west, they formed a series of parallel ridges,
beautiful wooded hills, but long and steep. Though the temperature had dropped to the high 80s, it was humid in the thick
vegetation and the wind was capricious. When it rained, it was
like cycling through a sauna. 'How do you manage it?' asked a
man in a garage. I sometimes wondered myself. Near Chambersburg, where I stopped for an iced tea, a man with an ice
cream strolled over and engaged me in conversation. We talked
about my trip. Then he asked, 'Where do you stay at nights?'
    'Usually in motels.'
    'Do you ever stay in people's homes?'
    'Sometimes,' I replied, with caution.
    'Say, do you really? You wouldn't come and stay with us,
would you? It would be a real pleasure for Evelyn and me.'
When I learned that he was the Pastor of the local Church of the
Brethren, I accepted cheerfully. It was the start of a happy few
days.
    Charles and Evelyn lived in a gracious white house standing
back from the road at the end of an avenue of mature trees. In
the intervals between being a pastor's wife and working full-
time in hospital administration, the energetic Evelyn sold
antiques from home, specialising in Victorian oil lamps. They
were a wonderfully kind and enthusiastic pair, with a passion
for chocolate marshmallow ice cream which they dived for in

moments of weariness or celebration, as a drinker dives for his bottle.

Their church was holding a Revival Week, with special services every evening; I went along with them the first night to hear the visiting evangelist. On a spiritual level the service was deeply earnest, though the lack of ritual made it seem almost casual. Charles began by telling the congregation about me and my bicycle ride and how he had met me in the local store. Then he reminded them that he had offered a prize to anyone who managed to bring a stranger to one of the Revival Week services and claimed it for himself. We sang spirited hymns led not by a choir but by a buxom woman with a powerful voice, who stood out at the front with a microphone. When we prayed, we turned our backs to the altar and knelt on our padded pews. In the course of his harangue about the sinful, artificial lives we all lead, the evangelist chastised the women for 'sitting there, all made up, like a bunch of Episcopalians'. When I was thanking the preacher on the way out I confessed to being one of those terrible Episcopalians. The good man was covered with confusion and I regretted my little joke. For followers of such an austere Protestant sect, the people I met after the service seemed extraordinarily cheerful.

My next overnight stop should have been Gettysburg, but it took little to persuade me that the city would be too hot, too crowded with tourists and too expensive. I stayed on with Evelyn and Charles, making daily sightseeing trips. It worked out well. I cycled the seventeen miles to Gettysburg in the mornings, then Evelyn met me in the evenings, immortalised me on cine film at different 'sights' and drove me home for supper. Friends and relations called to meet me and the days passed agreeably. I was excused the service one night when Charles' sister-in-law, Cora, joined us for supper. She had been a missionary nurse in Ethiopia, Somalia, Tanzania and Kenya and we had a good time, swapping travellers' tales.

The black spot emotionally was the Gettysburg battlefield itself. I took a bus tour with a guided commentary and looked in dismay at the row upon row of State and regimental memorials to the fallen. Mounted generals surveyed the scene from the ridges. Those whose horses had one leg raised had been wounded in the battle; those with two legs raised had been killed. The three-day battle in July 1863 had marked a decisive point in the Civil War, the repulse from Northern territory of General Robert E. Lee's invading Confederate Army. But the war had dragged on for another two years after Gettysburg, killing 600,000 out of a total population of only 32 million. Of the three million men who went to war, over one million were casualties. It was a horrible squandering of human life, which a new nation could ill afford. The depression I had felt among the graveyards of northern France swept over me again and it took all Charles' and Evelyn's cheerfulness to get me through the rest of the day.

After my Chambersburg interlude, gloom took an ever firmer hold. I got my sixth puncture in New Oxford and lost three hours getting it repaired. The rain poured down and I cycled through hilly old Townes, full of Kountry Korners, Kopper Kettles, Kobweb Korners and Shoppes. Motel vacancies were hard to find and my evening beer impossible. I was so weary that even friendly overtures seemed intolerable. Newspapers and crossword puzzles were no protection from talkative strangers, all asking the same questions about my travels and usually criticising my choice of route across the States. They always knew a better way to go. They were confident and individualistic with that buoyant, restless, inquisitive character forged in Frontier days. I began to hide in my motel room to escape the endless socialising, feeding on pizzas heated in filling station microwaves. I was sorry Pennsylvania had come at the end of my trip. It was a beautiful state, which had played a key role in American history, yet it was wasted on me. I had had enough of travel.

Michael Dukakis was elected Democratic Presidential Candidate, with Lloyd Bentsen as his running-mate. I rushed to the television every evening to watch the unfolding drama and the razmataz of the convention. British politics were never such fun. Out West, few had mentioned the forthcoming presidential elections. In Pennsylvania they were much more interested in politics and were agonising over their votes. Neither Dukakis nor Bush was an inspiration to them and traditional party supporters had grave reservations about their candidates.

Bush's campaign manager complained of 'an outbreak of apathy', but my impression was that the voters were deeply worried, not apathetic.

It was a fine Sunday when I cycled through York, Lancaster and the Pennsylvania Dutch country, so the local tourists were out in force. The Dutch were not Dutch at all but Germans – 'Deutsch' – and they displayed a Teutonic resignation as the stream of cars full of prying trippers crawled nose-to-tail through their charming villages. Fundamental Protestants who have rejected the modern world for a life of simple self-sufficiency, the Pennsylvania Dutch have windmills to pump their water and generate their electricity. They ride in covered horse-drawn buggies and will not be photographed. The men and boys wear black suits, white shirts and broad black hats, while the women and girls wear long plain dresses with white muslin pinafores and caps. They are excellent farmers. The Mennonites and Moravians, or 'Fancy Dutch', do quite well out of the visitors, taking them on guided tours of typical farms, selling them plants and items of traditional crafts and feeding them on shoofly pie and other Pennsylvania Dutch specialities. There is even a Dutch Wonderland theme park. The Amish, the strictest sub-sect, generally refuse even to talk to strangers.

My bicycle distinguished me from the hordes. Buggies trotted by and families gave me friendly waves. A girl carrying a basket of eggs on her arm surprised me by shouting 'Hi!' It was the normal teenage greeting but it seemed somehow incongruous coming from a girl in a seventeenth-century mob cap and a long grey dress. My chain came off when I changed gear clumsily at a corner. It happened beside a farmyard where twenty buggies were parked and all their owners were having a big family reunion. As I stopped to deal with the chain, an Amish man came out with two little boys, dressed in black like miniature adults, to see if I needed any help. Again, it seemed somehow odd that such an antique figure should ask the same questions, in the same style of speech, as the men in baseball caps. 'You must be very brave people over in London – coming here on a bicycle and cycling all the way to New York on your lonesome. I couldn't see myself getting on a bike and riding across London.' I smiled to myself at the vision of the Amish in his black suit, long beard and flat black hat cycling round Hyde Park Corner. We agreed that horse-drawn vehicles and bicycles were the only civilised forms of transport. Bird-in-Hand, Paradise, Intercourse, Christiana, Honey Brook, Brandywine Manor – I enjoyed my journey through the Pennsylvania Dutch country much more than my gloom had led me to expect. My bicycle had once more been my passport.

At King of Prussia, a mail-drop I had chosen simply because of its irresistible name, I walked into the American Express office. 'Let us guess who you are,' they said. 'You're Mrs Mustoe and we've had to make a whole new rack for your mail!' It was a picturesque exaggeration, of course, but I did get a very nice stack of letters, which cheered me immensely. I also got my flight ticket from New York to Dublin, booked, printed out and invoiced at the prod of a few computer keys – unlike Malacca, where a similar purchase had taken three days.

Norty Stewart's brilliant route took me near to the major cities yet I rode down leafy lanes, through villages and quiet suburban estates. Bucks County was so like 'beechy Bucks' that I wondered if Penn's Quakers had felt at home there or if the resemblance to that familiar landscape had left them feeling homesick. I began to feel rather homesick myself as I cycled through Wells, Warminster, Bridgeport, North Wales, Street and New Britain. The countryside and architecture were similar; only the endless, steaming, sultry heat was different.

In the late afternoon I reached the Washington Crossing, where George Washington crossed the Delaware river on Christmas Day 1776, on his way to defeat the British at Trenton. Over the river was New Jersey. I cycled upstream to New Hope and Lambertsville, twin towns on opposite banks of the Delaware, and found pretentious little resorts, full of antique shops, gifte shoppes and expensive restaurants. They were so crammed with tourists that I decided to press on to Somerville. Five miles out of Lambertsville, on a high plateau, I was caught by a sudden storm. Thunder and lightning ripped the sky and I was terrified on that exposed height on a metal bicycle. I sheltered in a car repair shop until it closed at 5.30 and I had to move on. There was a farmyard with an open garage and I crept inside. Two small faces appeared at an upstairs window and I could guess what was happening inside: 'Mummy, there's somebody in our garage.' A few moments later, a slightly nervous young woman came out onto the porch. 'Can I help you?' 'Do you mind if I just shelter here until the storm passes over?' 'No. Please do,' was the polite reply. With that she disappeared indoors, obviously paused for reflection, then reappeared to invite me inside. It was the start of a lovely evening.

Cindy and Randy lived in an old stone-built farmhouse which they were gradually doing up; in fact, Randy's business was the restoration of Georgian properties. They put me up in the most elegant guest apartment which they had built at the top of a converted chicken house, above Randy's office. I played with the children, Elizabeth and Sam, watched by their fat elderly spaniel, Fred, and variegated Casey, the cat. Chicken casserole and white wine made a wonderful change from the inevitable restaurant steaks, and conversation flowed. We talked into the early hours and they begged me to stay another day or two, but exactly because I was so happy and comfortable there I was afraid to linger. I had to keep up the momentum. Before I left, Cindy got me to speak to her father on the phone in Manhattan, so that I should know someone there, in case of difficulties.

Norty's one and only mistake occurred on the approach to New York. He had routed me through Elizabeth and over the Goethals Bridge to Staten Island, but the regulations had changed and bicycles were no longer allowed on the bridge. I visited the police station and the town hall to plead my case, but without success. As there was no ferry either, I had to pay a grumpy taxi-driver $24 just to carry my bicycle and me over the short span of the Goethals Bridge.

I cycled across Staten Island to the Manhattan Ferry terminal, where there were no signs directing cyclists and no officials in sight. The policeman I asked was sour and unhelpful. Cindy was right; she had warned me that New Yorkers were abrasive, if not downright rude, and you had to be feeling buoyant to cope with them. I was not feeling buoyant but I finally got myself onto the ferry and photographed the Statue of Liberty looming through the heat haze. Then my spirits began to rise. The view of Manhattan from the approaching ferry was spectacular. It was my first visit to New York and I began to feel very pleased with myself for having made it on a bicycle. The ferry docked and I pedalled proudly up West Broadway, past the Wall Street canyon, across Washington Square and up Sixth Avenue, the Avenue of the Americas. Fifth Avenue might perhaps have had a more dashing ring but unfortunately it was one-way, in the wrong direction. To my surprise, there were cycle paths full of swooping, helmeted youngsters on bicycles and roller skates. There was even a negro on a penny farthing. New York was noisy, brash, cheerful, dirty, casual, multi-racial and eccentric. I was going to like it.

I checked in at the legendary Chelsea Hotel, New York home of Dylan Thomas, Brendan Behan, Henry Miller, Thomas Wolfe and O. Henry. A life-sized papier-mâché fat woman swung from the vestibule ceiling on a swing, the window was full of giant puppets, and abstract paintings and geometric sculptures provided wall-to-wall and floor-to-ceiling cover. An opera singer and a pianist on my floor practised all day and the lift doors would open to reveal a pop group or a black model in a leotard with two Afghans on leads. It was just the right kind of zany hotel for a rather zany city.

It had taken me exactly ten weeks to the day to cross the 3,539.3 miles of the United States of America. I was so worn out by the terrain and the heat, and so relieved to have reached New York, that I lapsed almost into unconsciousness. Although I had a large double bed I somehow managed to fall out of it in the night, crashing the back of my head on the corner of the bedside chest. Blood poured down. At three o'clock in the morning I sat on my own in my hotel room, my head swathed in a cold, wet bath towel, panicking at the blood which was streaming over my neck and shoulders and trying to decide whether to ask reception for an ambulance. I had never felt so alone in my life. Two crimson bath towels later the bleeding stopped and I was able to sleep again, propped up with pillows in a sitting position. It was a dramatic end to my journey.

I nursed my sore head in the hotel for the next three days, sad about my missed opportunity. The Big Apple would have to wait for my next visit. I felt weak and wobbly from shock and the loss of blood; I had a throat infection; my knee ached; and my athlete's foot had turned into ringworm. Lacking the strength to follow up introductions, or even to walk beyond the corner delicatessen, I dozed on my bed, ploughed through the daily mountains of *The New York Times* (the first paper I had seen for months with serious international coverage) and watched some excellent television. Then I cycled out to John F. Kennedy International Airport and got my seventh puncture on the rutted, glass-strewn Queensboro Bridge. As always, Providence cared for me. A helpful negro fellow-cyclist took me through the back streets under the bridge and there I found a new inner tube and a Vietnamese immigrant to fix it for me. I got to the airport on time.

Watling Street Again

> 'Oh Ratty!' he cried. 'I've been through such times
> since I saw you last, you can't think! Such trials,
> such sufferings, and all so nobly borne!'
>
> *(Kenneth Grahame)*

I felt very nervous when I landed in Dublin. Newspapers
carried headlines of a fresh IRA killing and the English
accent, which in America had been 'real neat', was now a cause
for anxiety. But I relaxed when I found that I was 'luv' like
everyone else in the airport coffee shop.

After all those weeks of heat and drought, Ireland was
unbelievably green and beautiful. The dawn broke over an
amazing silver sea and I saw the silver estuary of the Shannon
glinting through a patchwork of dark green fields. There was a
soft grey light over the dreaming hills and the clouds shaded
from palest dove grey to deep charcoal. The air was crisp, cool
and clear to breathe, and a little gentle drizzle between spells of
weak sunshine gave the final touch of perfection. I bowled along
in easy comfort past the Dublin Customs House, over the
Liffey, through Georgian Merrion Square, past the first day of
the Dublin Horse Show to the ferry at Dun Laoghaire. There
were many cyclists in the city but they were clerks and workmen
riding out of necessity, unlike the students and environmen-
talists of New York, or the likes of me.

I had chosen to fly to Dublin rather than to Heathrow
because I wanted to end my journey, as I had begun it, on

Watling Street. The northern arm of the road ran from the Roman ford at Westminster to Marble Arch, then up the present A5 to Wroxeter in Shropshire, where a network of other Roman roads connected it with Wales and the north-west. I could follow the Romans nearly all the way home from Holyhead, calling in at Chester on the way to stay with John and Irma.

My two spare tyres had been a gift from the manufacturer, who was hoping that I should be able to cycle round the world on a set of four. The front tyre and inner tube had held out remarkably well, without a single puncture, but the rear tyre was the last of the spares and it was bald. I gave up the losing battle to get back to London on it when I got another puncture seven miles out of Holyhead – my third in eight days' cycling. Fortunately, it happened opposite a lay-by with a hamburger stall. I treated myself to a hot bacon sandwich and a mug of tea while I waited for the transport I knew would appear. My luck could never run out so near to home. Sure enough, a driver soon pulled up with an empty lorry. He not only drove me back to Holyhead but found me a cycle shop too. I stayed in Holyhead overnight while the new tyre was fitted.

Anglesey was once a stronghold of the Druids, who caused so much trouble to the Romans. Tacitus recounts a spectacular battle on the Menai Straits when Nero's Governor of Britain, Suetonius, tried to subdue the island. He was opposed by black-robed women brandishing torches, their hair dishevelled like the locks of the Furies, and mobs of Druids screaming curses, as well as by more conventional troops. It still felt like a Druid land, old, bleak and mysterious. I thought of Stevenson's 'Hills of sheep and the homes of the silent, vanished races And winds austere and pure', as I cycled across the island under the grey skies with their swift, scudding clouds. After the static weather of the continents I had crossed, I was newly amazed at the speed of change in our wind-swept heavens.

The Romans crossed the Menai Straits at Caernarfon (Segontium), the destination of the main military road from London. There was obviously an overland road from Caernarfon to Chester (Deva), but its path through the mountains of Wales had been lost as far as Caerhun (Canovium) in the Vale of Conwy. From there it could be seen crossing the Conwy river at Tyn-y-groes, then proceeding in a series of minor roads through broken, hilly country to St Asaph, there to merge with the A55 and follow it, with variations, into Chester.

I had to cross the Menai Bridge to Bangor, then cycle along beside a wild grey sea to Conwy. Holiday-makers along the coast were resolutely sporting shorts and sundresses; locals were recognisable by their anoraks and thick winter jerseys. After a night in Conwy, I left its magnificent battlements behind and followed the west bank of the river up to Tyn-y-groes where I crossed the bridge near the site of the old ferry and the Roman ford, and set out to find Betws-yn-Rhos. The lanes were short of signposts and hideously steep. As I pushed my bicycle up their almost perpendicular slopes, I decided that the Romans must have used the road only for mounted mess-engers: an army with its impedimenta could never have man-aged the hills. I stopped at a village pub for a sandwich and my first half of English bitter and got into conversation with a telephone engineer. When I checked the route to Chester, only 30 miles away, he was amazed that I was planning to get there that afternoon. 'I hope you've got a good pair of legs on you!' he said. The marvellous quirkiness of the English language! That superfluous 'on you' somehow gave the statement tremendous vigour. An easier afternoon took me past St Asaph's tiny cathe-dral, through Holywell and past the border castles of Ewloe and Mr Gladstone's Hawarden into beautiful Chester, glowing deep pink in the evening sun. I took photographs of the Roman street grid while I waited impatiently for John and Irma and our family reunion.

The ride to London from Chester was plain sailing. I left the city through Bridge Gate, the Roman exit for London, and cycled across the River Dee. After a detour to avoid the grounds of Eaton Hall, I returned to the Roman road through Tilston, Malpas, Whitchurch and Wem to Shrewsbury. The day was sunny but not too hot, and my route took me along B roads and quiet country lanes. I looked at the English landscape with fresh pleasure, noting how the trees dotted the countryside and grew haphazardly in the hedgerows, creating pools of dense, random shade where other countries had rigid avenues of trees.

Even when I joined the A5 at Shrewsbury, the land was still peaceful and unspoilt. Motorways syphoned off the traffic and no one would ever have guessed that Wolverhampton, Birmingham and Coventry lay just a few miles off my road.

Wroxeter (Viroconium) was an important cross-roads city, where Watling Street from London met another Roman road, also called Watling Street in mediaeval times, running north to south and connecting the two fortress cities of Chester and Caerleon, near Cardiff. Wroxeter's ruins consisted of one high fragment of bath wall and a few stone foundations – the kind of site which puts the uninitiated off archaeology for life. I hastened by.

Wellington, Oakengates, Crackleybank, Weston under Lizard, Gailey Hill, Cannock Chase, Brownhill Common. I had forgotten that cycling could be such a pleasure. The Roman road, the A5, skirted in an easy rural sweep round the Black Country towns. It was noticeable that the motorway took a higher, more difficult route over the Wrekin. Roman surveyors aligned their sighting marks from one high point to another, which meant that important cross-roads and changes of direction often occurred on high ground, far from the major conurbations. High Cross (Venonae) was a perfect example of this. It was on an empty plateau, with nothing in sight but one farmhouse, yet it was the point at which Watling Street met the Fosse Way, one of the most important junctions in Britain's Roman road network. I scrabbled in the bushes along the grass verge and found the monument, set up by the Earl of Denbigh in 1713, to mark the spot. Four Doric pilasters facing the four roads were said to have been topped by a sundial and a gilded globe and cross, but unfortunately lightning had struck and only a poor brick ruin with a little stone facing remained.

The grey stone and golden lichen of Northamptonshire replaced the brick of Shropshire, Staffordshire and south Leicestershire. The sun shone and a gentle breeze from the west helped my bicycle along. England was at its best and I wondered why I had ever gone away. I crossed the Chilterns and spent my last night on the road in St Albans (Verulamium) in an old inn with oak beams and uneven mediaeval floors.

Watling Street was cleverly routed into London, avoiding the low ground and streams to the east. As a Londoner, I was now entering familiar territory and I felt wonderfully elated as I cycled through Radlett and Elstree to Edgware and saw my first red London bus. The Roman road ran straight as an arrow down Cricklewood Broadway and the Edgware Road to Marble Arch. Within sight of the arch, a car made an illegal U-turn and I had to tumble onto the pavement to save myself. It would have been the final irony had I been mown down by a car within a hundred yards of journey's end.

My send-off had been so exhausting that I was determined to slip back into London quietly, without fuss. I negotiated the hair-raising traffic to reach the Marble Arch island where Priscilla was waiting with her bicycle to photograph my return. Then we cycled off together to her house for tea. I had circled the globe not in 40 minutes, like Puck, but in 439 days. I had cycled 11,552.1 miles through fourteen countries and three continents. I had spent £4,896 on food, accommodation and sundries and £1,127 on fares. I had sent 283 postcards and 101 letters. I had lost 23 lb in weight. I was glad to be home.